F. SCOTT FITZGERALD:
THE PRINCETON YEARS

Selected Writings, 1914 – 1920

Edited and with an Introduction by Chip Deffaa

CYPRESS HOUSE PRESS

F. SCOTT FITZGERALD: The Princeton Years
Edited and with an Introduction by Chip Deffaa

Cypress House Press
155 Cypress Street
Fort Bragg, CA 95437
1 (800) 773-7782
email: qedpress@mcn.org

Publisher's Cataloging in Publication

Fitzgerald, F. Scott (Francis Scott), 1896–1940.
  [Short stories. Selections]
  F. Scott Fitzgerald : The Princeton Years / edited and with an
introduction by Chip Deffaa.
  p. cm.
  Includes biographical references.
  LCCN: 96-85280
  ISBN: 1-879384-29-9

  1. Manners and customs — Fiction.   I. Deffaa, Chip, 1951 –
II. Title.

PS3511.I9A6 1996   813'.52
                                                   QB196-40065

Published in cooperation with The Princeton Tiger, Inc.

Cover design by Jonathan Bumas

First Edition
10 9 8 7 6 5 4 3 2 1

Printed in Canada by Hignell Printing Limited

DEDICATION

For Henry Martin (still roarin')
and the late Scottie Fitzgerald Smith
with gratitude

THE PRINCETON TIGER ~

The Billet Doux

CONTENTS

Introduction 3

Fitzgerald's *Tiger* and *Nassau Lit* Work, Sequenced Chronologically

1914
1. "There Was Once," *The Tiger* 25

1915
2. "Shadow Laurels," *The Nassau Lit* 27
3. "May Small Talk," *The Tiger* 32
4. "The Ordeal," *The Nassau Lit* 33
5. "How They Head the Chapters," *The Tiger* 37
6. "A Cheer for Princeton" *(miscellaneous)* 38
7. "The Conquest of America," *The Tiger* 40
8. "Three Days at Yale," *The Tiger** 42

1916
9. "Our Society Column," *The Tiger** 46
10. "What Happened to Susie," *The Tiger** 49
11. "The Awful Optic," *The Tiger** 51
12. "Yais," *The Tiger* 53
13. "To My Unused Greek Book," *The Nassau Lit* 55
14. "Our Next Issue," *The Nassau Lit* 57
15. "Jemina, A Story of the Blue Ridge Mountains, by John Phlox Jr.," *The Nassau Lit* 58
16. "The Usual Thing, by Robert W. Shameless," *The Nassau Lit* 61
17. "Little Minnie McCloskey," *The Tiger* 65

18. "One from Penn's Neck," *The Tiger* 66

19. "A Litany of Slang," *The Tiger* 68

20. "Triangle Scenery by Bakst," *The Tiger* 68

21. "Futuristic Impressions of the Editorial Boards," *The Tiger* 69

22. "A Glass of Beer Kills Him," *The Tiger* 70

23. "Oui, le Backfield Est from Paris," *The Tiger* 70

24. "When You Find a Man," *The Tiger* 71

25. "Things That Never Change! Number 3333," *The Tiger* 71

26. "The Lost Lover," *The Tiger** 72

27. "The Old Frontiersman," *The Tiger* 73

28. "Bohemia," *The Tiger** 74

1917

29. "The Debutante," *The Nassau Lit* 77

30. "Book Talk: *Penrod and Sam*," *The Nassau Lit* 83

31. "Boy Kills Self Rather Than Pet," *The Tiger* 85

32. "Things that Never Change. No. 3982," *The Tiger* 85

33. "Precaution Primarily," *The Tiger* 86

34. "The Spire and the Gargoyle," *The Nassau Lit* 89

35. "Why Boys Leave College," *The Tiger*** 95

36. "Rain Before Dawn," *The Nassau Lit* 97

37. "Book Talk: David Blaize," *The Nassau Lit* 98

38. "A Few Well-Known Club Types and Their Futures," *The Tiger* 99

39. "McCauley Mission - Water Street," *The Tiger* 100

40. "Popular Parodies - No. 1," *The Tiger* 100

41. "The Diary of a Sophomore," *The Tiger* 101

42. "True Democracy," *The Tiger* 102

43. "Undulations of an Undergraduate," *The Tiger* 104

44. "Kenilworth Socialism," *The Tiger* 105

45. "Tarquin of Cheepside," *The Nassau Lit* 106

46. "The Prince of Pests," *The Tiger* 110

47. "These Rifles," *The Tiger* 111

48. "It is Assumed," *The Tiger* 112

49. "Ethel Had Her Shot of Brandy," *The Tiger* 112

50. "Yale's Swimming Team," *The Tiger* 112

51. "Babes in the Woods," *The Nassau Lit* 114

52. "Princeton - The Last Day," *The Nassau Lit* 119

53. "Book Talk: *The Celt and the World*," *The Nassau Lit* 120

54. "Sentiment — And the Use of Rouge," *The Nassau Lit* 122

55. "On a Play Twice Seen," *The Nassau Lit* 131

56. "Book Talk: *Verses in Peace and War*," *The Nassau Lit* 132

57. "Book Talk: *God, The Invisible King*," *The Nassau Lit* 133

58. "The Call," *The Tiger*** 134

59. "Ennui" *and* "The Caws of War," *The Tiger*** 136

60. "Somewhere in France," *The Tiger* 137

61. "The Dream and the Awakening," *The Tiger* 138

62. "The Cameo Frame," *The Nassau Lit* 140

63. "The Pierian Springs and the Last Straw," *The Nassau Lit* 142

64. "The Staying Up All Night," *The Tiger* 148

65. "Intercollegiate Petting-Cues," *The Tiger* 150

66. "The Petting Party," *The Tiger*** 151

67. "Our American Poets," *The Tiger* 152

68. "Aviators Going to Breakfast," *The Tiger*** 153

69. "Cedric the Stoker," *The Tiger* 154

1918

70. "City Dusk," *The Nassau Lit* 156

1919

71. "My First Love," *The Nassau Lit* 158

72. "Marching Streets," *The Nassau Lit* 159

73. "The Pope at Confession," *The Nassau Lit* 160

1920

74. "Sleep of a University," *The Nassau Lit* 161

Acknowledgments 164

About the Editor 166

Credits 167

Questionable attribution.

**Not by Fitzgerald but included for context-setting purposes.*

F. SCOTT FITZGERALD

THE PRINCETON YEARS

INTRODUCTION

"It was always the becoming he dreamed of, never the being...."
— F. Scott Fitzgerald, *This Side of Paradise*

Collections of the early works of famous writers can be dreary affairs, of interest only to scholars. But since F. Scott Fitzgerald served such a short apprenticeship — he was barely out of Princeton University when he wrote his first novel — his early writings are of unusual interest. Shortcomings may be in evidence — we are, after all, catching Fitzgerald in the process of becoming a professional writer — but so, already, are a surprising number of strengths. We can witness, as we read his undergraduate writings, the development of his style. This collection assembles Fitzgerald's known contributions to two Princeton publications, *The Tiger* and *The Nassau Literary Magazine*. This is the first time that all of these materials have been gathered in one book; they have been sequenced chronologically, with annotations, so that readers may observe Fitzgerald's progress. But before we get to Fitzgerald's collegiate writings themselves, a bit of background and context-setting seems appropriate.

An examination of the Fitzgerald papers at Princeton's Firestone Library establishes that Fitzgerald's zeal for writing emerged early. An entry in his "Ledger" for January 1907 — he was just 10 — records the fact that he'd ambitiously begun "a history of the U.S. and also a detective story about a necklace that was hidden in a trap-door under the carpet. Wrote celebrated essay on George Washington & St. Ignatius." He did not, alas, save copies of those earliest works — not even his "celebrated" essay on George Washington. But from the age of 13, he did begin preserving some of his work. One can read the action-filled, if often rather conventional, stories that Fitzgerald wrote as a boy in his native St. Paul, Minnesota, and as a youth of 15 and 16 at the Newman School in Hackensack, New Jersey, to which his parents sent him in 1911. (Those very early writings are not included in the present collection.)

In the first story that Fitzgerald saved, "The Mystery of the Raymond Mortgage" (1909), it's certainly easy to tell who's the good guy because he has laudable "erectness of posture" and "his chin showed him to be of strong character." The writing is so melodramatic it can, at times, be unintentionally amusing ("we stood there aghast in the presence of death"). The plot is not always easy to follow — the tale appears to have been set down in haste — but there's a certain energy that carries the reader along. One fellow boards a train from Ithaca to Princeton. Hoping to overtake him, a pursuer then boards an even faster train from Ithaca to Princeton! That no trains, in real life, actually ran from Ithaca to Princeton did not get in the way of Fitzgerald the story teller. (Such minor discrepancies would periodically crop up in his professional writings, too.)

Fitzgerald at age 15

It's interesting, though, that even at age 13, Fitzgerald seems to have had Princeton in mind as a destination.

Within a few years, Fitzgerald was producing stories that were notably smoother flowing. In the inventive "A Luckless Santa Claus" (1912), a woman scoffs at her beau's tightfisted way with money: "Why, I don't think you could give away twenty-five dollars in the right way to save your life." Anxious for her approval — Fitzgerald would forever be writing of men willing to do seemingly anything for the women they adored — he attempts valiantly to give away money to strangers in New York; he gets rebuffed and finally roughed-up. *That's* what comes from listening to a woman, Fitzgerald seems to be suggesting.

Fitzgerald learned that through writing he could win acclamation, which was important to him since he was not athletic enough to ever become a champion on the playing fields — something he admitted often fantasizing about. The Christmas 1912 edition of *The Newman News* included Fitzgerald's first published poem, titled simply "Football," with such lines as: "Crash! they're down; he threw him nicely, — / Classy tackle, hard and low" and "What is this? A new formation. / Look! their end acts like an ass. / See, he's beckoning for assistance, / Maybe it's a forward pass." As juvenile as this poem may be, Fitzgerald later noted that writing it "made me as big a hit with my father as if I had become a football hero....It was in my mind that if you weren't able to function in action you might at least be able to tell about it, because you felt the same intensity — it was a back door way out of facing reality."

In the voluminous outpouring of poems, play scripts, song lyrics (and even one football cheer), parodies, jokes, ideas for cartoons that others drew, and increasingly complex and subtle short stories that Fitzgerald went on to produce while a student at Princeton, one can trace his dramatic growth towards a major artist. In later years, Fitzgerald said that he considered his first mature writing to be "The Spire and the Gargoyle," a story that was published in the *Nassau Literary Magazine* in February 1917. You can read that Fitzgerald story, and all those that preceded and followed it at Princeton, here.

Actually, Fitzgerald's student and professional literary careers overlapped: Fitzgerald's first novel, *This Side of Paradise* (1920), and his first two books of short stories, *Flappers and Philosophers* (1920) and *Tales of the Jazz Age* (1922), incorporated material Fitzgerald had produced while at Princeton. In fact, one Princeton wag, exaggerating a bit, suggested that *This Side of Paradise* was not so much a novel as "the collected works of Scott Fitzgerald."

When Fitzgerald entered Princeton University in September of 1913, his two chief goals were to make the Triangle Club, which produced highly professional original musical comedies that went on national tours, and to be published in *The Tiger*, the Princeton humor magazine. (He was following in the footsteps of author Booth Tarkington, then one of Princeton's most famous living alumni, who was closely associated with both organizations.) Fitzgerald's song lyrics were accepted for three successive Triangle shows; they represented a significant part of his undergraduate creative output. His lyrics, at their best, had a dashing spirit that still comes across, eight decades later. Consider this chorus from "Safety First": "For the men who thrill you / May be clerks by day, / So wed a man who's prosperous tho' meek / Or else you'll take in washing by the week; / Though he's most entrancing / And he knows new steps, / And calls himself a Duke or Count / Or Baron at the worst, / Just ask to see his bank account, / For Safety First!" Incidentally, the John Church Company of New York, Cincinnati, and London published the scores of all three Triangle shows for which Fitzgerald supplied lyrics: *Fie! Fie! Fifi!* (17 song lyrics), 1914; *The Evil Eye* (17 song lyrics), 1915; and *Safety First* (21 song lyrics), 1916 — Fitzgerald's first profes-

sionally published words. The 55 Triangle show songs for which Fitzgerald wrote lyrics (which are not gathered in the present collection) would make a small book of their own.

Fitzgerald was committed to contribute more than just lyrics to Triangle productions. He wrote the script for the Triangle musical comedy *Fie! Fie! Fifi!*, which was initially accepted but then revised by an older student who in the end refused to give Fitzgerald credit as a co-author (although he allowed as how Fitzgerald had conceived the "plot"). It is impossible to discern how much of Fitzgerald's writing survived in the final version of the show. Fitzgerald subsequently wrote another Triangle script, but to his dismay it was rejected outright. (Fitzgerald was simply not as talented at writing scripts as he was at writing narrative fiction. As a mature writer, he made one attempt to write a play for Broadway, *The Vegetable*, but it flopped out of town. In later years, Fitzgerald also labored mightily — but rather unproductively — on film scripts.)

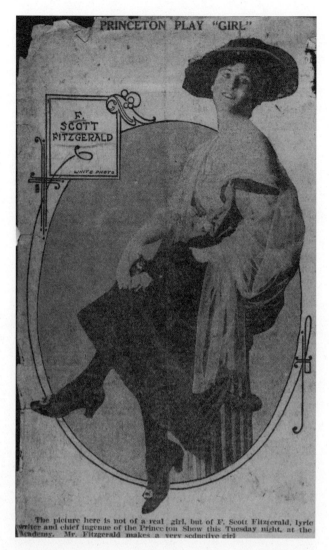

PRINCETON PLAY "GIRL"

The picture here is not of a real girl, but of F. Scott Fitzgerald, lyric writer and chief ingenue of the Princeton Show this Tuesday night, at the Academy. Mr. Fitzgerald makes a very seductive girl

Fitzgerald felt that Triangle was a rather tough nut to crack. He was pleased, though, that *The New York Times* and other papers ran a publicity photograph of him — as one of the members of the all-male show who appeared in drag — saying he was "considered the most beautiful 'show girl'" in the new Triangle Club production, *The Evil Eye*. Incidentally, that photo (reproduced here) brought him several admiring letters from men, plus an offer from an agent to get him work as a female impersonator.

The Tiger proved to be more receptive to Fitzgerald's offerings than the Triangle Club. According to biographer Andrew Turnball (*Scott Fitzgerald*, Scribners, 1962), once Fitzgerald got his first unsigned piece in *The Tiger* at the start of his freshman year, he "bombarded that magazine with poems of the moon-croon-June variety, he-and-she jokes and pseudo-comic sketches. He lay in wait for the editor outside his classes and slipped manuscripts into his hand on Nassau Street. As the editor was about to retire, he gave in from sheer weariness and printed a second squib by Fitzgerald."

Fitzgerald's work continued to appear in the magazine through the issue of November 10, 1917. The full extent of Fitzgerald's contributions to *The Tiger* seems to be unknowable. Fitzgerald biographer Matthew Bruccoli (*Some Sort of Epic Grandeur: The Life of F. Scott Fitzgerald*, Harcourt Brace Jovanovich, 1981) notes that few of Fitzgerald's *Tiger* pieces — the earliest published in February of 1917 — were actually credited to him in the magazine; in those days *The Tiger* simply did not credit most items. (The magazine's senior-most contributors might be credited by their initials for their longer works.) A number of additional pieces — the earliest published in December of 1914 — can be confirmed to be Fitzgerald's since he clipped them and preserved them in the scrapbook where he kept copies of his work. However, it appears he did not bother (or remember) to clip and save each and every last contribution to *The Tiger*. For example, one does not find in his scrapbook a three-line bit of humorous verse which ran in the June 1916 *Tiger*: "Wouldn't it be nais / to sit on a dais / with Thais." But John McMaster '19, an editor of *The Tiger*, was quite certain Fitzgerald wrote that piece; he distinctly remembered adding the title ("Yais") himself. Fitzgerald also did not save in his scrapbook "The Conquest of America," which ran in the Thanksgiving 1915 issue of *The Tiger*; however, the magazine's whimsical attribution of authorship to one "Mr. Fitzcheescake" seems a rather transparent way of crediting Fitzgerald. In addition, it's written in the style he employed for humorous material in that period. Those pieces, along with the ones preserved in Fitzgerald's scrapbook and/or credited to him by his initials in the magazine itself, are included in this collection. (We have also included — as *possible* Fitzgerald works — five pieces of more

doubtful provenance, originally published in *The Tiger* without a byline and not found in Fitzgerald's scrapbook, that McMaster suggested to Bruccoli may have been by Fitzgerald: "Our Society Column," "What Happened to Susie," "The Awful Optic," "The Lost Lover," and "Bohemia," as well as one piece which Landon T. Raymond '17 informed Bruccoli *Tiger* cartoonist Alan Jackman '17 had recalled as having been conceived by Fitzgerald, "Three Days at Yale.") Fitzgerald may well have written other pieces, or prompted with casual remarks drawings that were executed by *Tiger* illustrators, which we have no way of identifying. For an item-by-item listing of *Tiger* and *Nassau Lit* writings attributed to Fitzgerald, see Bruccoli's *F. Scott Fitzgerald, a Descriptive Bibliography, Revised Edition*, University of Pittsburgh Press, 1987, which draws upon earlier research by Fitzgerald scholar Henry Dan Piper. Bruccoli is the foremost living Fitzgerald authority, and all who write about Fitzgerald are in his debt.

Edmund Wilson

While an undergraduate, Fitzgerald startled his friend Edmund Wilson '16 — eventually to become America's most influential literary critic — by asserting that he aspired to be one of the greatest writers who ever lived. Wilson, who looked down on Fitzgerald back then and who would, even in later years, be slow to accept Fitzgerald as a major writer, hardly thought *The Tiger* was the place for any man with serious literary aspirations to publish; *The Tiger*, Wilson noted with disdain, was popular. He certainly never wrote for it. Fitzgerald, along with many other talented Princeton students down through the years, never saw anything wrong with popularity.

Wilson thought much more highly of *The Nassau Literary Magazine* (or *Nassau Lit*, as many students informally called it) than *The Tiger*. *The Lit*, founded in 1842 (40 years before *The Tiger*), was generally recognized as *the* undergraduate publication for Princeton students who took their writing seriously.

The Tiger, after all, even printed such trivialities as snappy come-backs to current newspaper headlines (of which Fitzgerald contributed his share). They also reprinted occasional gags from other leading college humor magazines such as *The Yale Record, The Harvard Lampoon*, and the Cornell *Widow* (all three of which Fitzgerald personally felt were generally superior in quality to *The Tiger*), along with the original stories and cartoons for which they were best known. Although *The Lit* occasionally did publish humorous material — including some of Fitzgerald's, as we shall see — it strove for a considerably more refined tone, overall, than did *The Tiger*. *The Lit* acknowledged the arrival of *The Tiger* in 1882 with faintly patronizing praise, observing that the new magazine appeared to have been modeled on *The Harvard Lampoon* (which had been founded in 1876), adding: "None of the articles are excruciatingly funny but a vein of light humor runs through the whole thing that renders it very pleasant reading."

Wilson, whom Fitzgerald would later describe as his longtime "literary conscience," headed *The Nassau Lit* for 1915-16. Another *Lit* mainstay was Fitzgerald's rather academic, aesthetic friend, "class poet" John Peale Bishop '17 (the model for the character Thomas Parke D'Invilliers in *This Side of Paradise*), from whom Fitzgerald said he learned more than most of his English professors. Both Bishop and Wilson, who were certainly better-read than Fitzgerald was, helped shape his literary tastes. (Other important contributors to *The Lit* during Fitzgerald's stay at Princeton included his friends Townsend Martin and Alexander McKaig, who in

John Peale Bishop

later years would enjoy success as a playwright and a producer, respectively.) As time went on, Fitzgerald, encouraged by Wilson and Peale, did focus increasing energies on *The Lit*, but he still continued to write for *The Tiger*. He was establishing a pattern he would maintain throughout his life, of writing some pieces aimed at a presumably discerning literary audience, and others aimed directly at a much more general audience. (Those who know Fitzgerald only from his novels and finest, oft-reprinted short stories may be surprised by just how slight many of his popular magazines stories could be; they also may be disheartened to learn how much more financially remunerative it often was for him to write such potboilers than his best-remembered works.)

Beginning in 1915, Fitzgerald's more ambitious pieces — the short stories, plays, and poems in which he invested the most effort and which generally elicited the strongest emotional response from readers — went to *The Nassau Lit*. He continued contributing to *The Lit* until 1920. The best of his *Lit* pieces provided, as he would later observe, the foundation for his subsequent literary career. But it's also worth noting that his *Nassau Lit* work was not *always* better than his *Tiger* work. Some of his *Nassau Lit* lines of verse have the stiff, affected feel of a college undergraduate laboring hard to be "literary," without any genuine feeling (lines like "Golden, golden is the air / Golden is the air..."). His *Nassau Lit*

poems do not always have the freshness, honesty, or insight of such simpler but more charming *Tiger* contributions as "The Staying Up All Night" or "The Dream and the Awakening." *The Tiger* provided an outlet for his exuberant side.

Fitzgerald had considerable affection for *The Tiger* and *The Lit*. He was justifi-

ably proud to be a key contributor to both of them. In Fitzgerald's December 1927 *College Humor* article, "Princeton," he wrote that *The Lit* "is the oldest college publication in America. In its files you can find the original Craig Kennedy story, as well as prose or poetry by Woodrow Wilson, John Grier Hibben, Henry van Dyke, David Graham Phillips, Stephen French Whitman, Booth Tarkington, Struthers Burt, Jesse Lynch Williams — almost every Princeton writer save Eugene O'Neill."

And student magazines, it's worth bearing in mind, were generally much stronger and more important in Fitzgerald's day than in ours. Colleges had fewer extra-curricular options for creative students then than they have today. Now, college students can choose to spend spare hours, if they wish, working on campus radio stations, or making recordings, films or videos. At Princeton back then, creative-types found their outlets in the theater — the Triangle Club — and the publications, including *The Nassau Literary Magazine*, *The Tiger*, *The Princeton Pictorial Magazine* (or *Pic* — no longer in existence), and *The Daily Princetonian* (the student newspaper). Such student publications were independent, self-supporting entities; they were not subsidized by the university. Advertisers eager to reach well-heeled Princeton students were plentiful. (And maybe some old grads in the business world were opting to place ads in Princeton student publications simply to help the students out; Princeton alumni have always been notoriously loyal.) In Fitzgerald's time, one found ads in *The Tiger* not just for Princeton businesses, but for the Vanderbilt Hotel in New York ("An hotel designed to appeal to the conservative," declared a December 1915 ad. "The honor of the patronage of Princeton men requested"). One found ads in *The Tiger*, too, for Virginia's Hot Springs, Kiam's Houston clothing store ("the South's greatest store for men and boys"), European cruises, and Al Jolson's latest smash hit at Broadway's Winter Garden Theatre, *Robinson Crusoe Jr.* Ads for the likes of Lydia E. Pinkham's Vegetable Compound were aimed at *Tiger* subscribers at Seven Sisters schools and other young ladies who at-

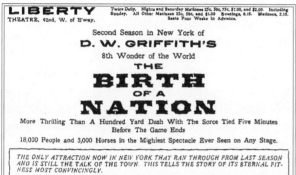
promoted itself vigorously to such prep school students, encouraging them to join it as soon as they got to Princeton, so as to make valuable connections with upper-classmen who would be useful business contacts in later life. *The Tiger* also boasted it was better known outside of Princeton than any of the other campus publications, with copies available for purchase "at all Union News Company stands." And during his tenure at Princeton, Fitzgerald noted, *The Lit* also made "a successful bid for popular attention"; a lot of people suddenly seemed to be reading — and commenting upon — what was being printed within its pages. (He gave Bishop a lot of the credit for that.) Whatever status Fitzgerald would acquire at Princeton he knew would be due to the quality and quantity of his writing; he had no other way of becoming a Big Man on Campus. While an undergraduate, Fitzgerald was glad to get favorable (if sometimes cautiously voiced) notices of his writing in publications ranging from

tended proms and house-parties at Princeton, which was of course all male. The student magazines were nearing their peak years while Fitzgerald was at Princeton. They would reach their all-time peak strength in the next decade, when *The Tiger* (conceivably exaggerating somewhat — its circulation figures were not audited) would claim to have a circulation of 10,000 copies per issue with subscribers in "both hemispheres." The magazine would be profitable enough to give the University $1,000 towards the cost of building the new chapel, and also to run contests awarding readers such prizes as a new Dodge Six Cabriolet and a trip to Europe. Editors could participate in the magazine's profits.

Fitzgerald knew that what he wrote for *The Tiger* and *The Nassau Lit* was reaching many fellow students at Princeton, some alumni, as well as some students at other colleges and even the leading prep schools that were considered "feeder schools" for Princeton. *The Tiger*, in keeping with the robust capitalist spirit of the age,

THE TIGER

INTERCOLLEGIATE · NO

The Daily Princetonian to *The Williams Literary Review*.

Fitzgerald's unusually prolific undergraduate literary output was achieved at a price, though; his grades suffered as he focused his energies on his extra-curricular writing rather than course work. When one instructor cautioned Fitzgerald that his habitual tardiness in getting to class was jeopardizing his academic standing, he responded buoyantly: "Sir — it's absurd to expect me to be on time. I'm a genius!"

In December of his junior year, Fitzgerald was forced to withdraw from Princeton "for scholastic deficiencies," according to the official record. Fitzgerald was profoundly embarrassed by the turn of events. Having contracted a case of malaria earlier that year, he maintained he was leaving Princeton simply because of his health problems, a face-saving fiction that his friends easily saw through. His grades at Princeton were often in the fifth group (or D- range). He had not been a great student at the far-less-demanding Newman School, either, averaging only about a C – there. As Jeffrey Meyers noted in his biography *Scott Fitzgerald* (HarperCollins, 1994), Wilson and Bishop mocked Fitzgerald with a poem they published in 1916, in which they had him concluding: "No doubt by senior year / I would have been on every committee in college, / But I made one slip: / I flunked out in the middle of junior year."

For Fitzgerald, the pain of flunking out of Princeton was deeply felt; "failure" was becoming a part of his self-definition. Increasingly in his fiction from that point afterwards, one finds his male heroes failing in some significant way or another; the disillusioned hero of "The Spire and the Gargoyle," who is "unprepared" for an important examination because, he feels, he's misused his time, is a forerunner of the classic Fitzgerald male heroes of later years who seem doomed to fail in essential ways. Sometimes Fitzgerald addressed the matter of failure rather lightly. (His own favorite scene in *This Side of Paradise* was the one in which the leading character holds an envelope that he knows contains either a pink slip telling him he can continue at Princeton or a blue slip telling him he must leave. As his friends look on, he opens the envelope and nonchalantly announces: "blue as the sky, gentlemen.") But failure, however addressed, would be a primary concern of Fitzgerald the writer.

In the fall of 1916, Fitzgerald returned to Princeton for another attempt at his junior year — again with some horrendous results as far as grades were concerned. One can't blame him for wanting to devote more of his time to *The Tiger* and *The Lit* than to studying, say, chemistry and history (both of which he failed that term, although he did well in English Renaissance poetry and French romantic literature). Writing would be his life's work; he had been blessed with a rare gift for it, and he was eager to devote himself to developing that gift. One cannot assume he would have been using his time more wisely had he spent more time on assigned course-work than on his writing, as the University wanted him to.

But he felt humiliated when, one afternoon in March of 1917, he was informed that his continuing academic difficulties made him ineligible for consideration as president of Triangle or editor of *The Tiger*, the two positions he most dearly coveted. Success in such activities as Triangle and *The Tiger* — and the prestige that followed — certainly meant more to him than success in the classroom. Years later, he recalled his feelings clearly: "To me college would never be the same. There were to be no badges of pride, no medals after all." Losing any chances to head *The Tiger* and the Triangle Club was a huge blow. He observed: "It seemed on one March afternoon [in 1917] that I had lost every single thing I wanted...." In subsequent years, that acutely painful sense of having lost all that really mattered to him would be re-created, in different guises, in one work of fiction after another, from "Babylon Revisited" to *Tender is the Night*.

In September 1917, Fitzgerald gamely started his senior year, aware that — the way his academic career had gone to date — flunking out of Princeton for good was a real possibility. He roomed in Campbell Hall with John Biggs Jr. '18, later to become a distinguished judge, a not-so-

Tiger board members, 1917 – 18. Fitzgerald, back row center, stands behind John Biggs, Jr.

distinguished novelist, one of very few friends who would attend Fitzgerald's funeral, and finally Fitzgerald's literary executor. In the fall of 1917, Biggs was serving as editor of both *The Tiger* and *The Nassau Lit.* In his 1927 article "Princeton," Fitzgerald recalled happily that when *The Tiger* "was late to press, John Biggs and I used to write whole issues in the interval between darkness and dawn." But that situation was not to last for long.

By the fall of 1917, of course, America was involved in the Great War. Princeton's enrollment stood at just 60 percent of what it had been a year earlier, and five students a week were leaving to go off to the war. *The Tiger* editor's position changed three times within a year as a result. Military courses replaced academic ones. Sentries patrolled some walks at night. Along trenches dug by students, near Palmer Stadium, the use of the Browning gun was demonstrated by Princeton President John Grier Hibben '82. Undergraduates were proud of the fact that with the exceptions of Annapolis and West Point, Princeton was giving a larger portion of its students to military service than any other institution. (Fitzgerald wrote his friend Wilson, already in the service, keeping him abreast of what was happening in *The Lit* — or "*Litt*," as Fitzgerald rather idiosyncratically abbreviated it.) The military fervor of the times was reflected in the pages of Princeton's undergraduate publications. Fitzgerald's growing interest in the war can easily be inferred from some of his later *Tiger* and *Nassau Lit* contributions. His early references were all lighthearted, but that mood could not be sustained indefinitely.

Tiger readers were told they could affix a penny postage stamp to the magazine's cover, drop it off at any post office, and send it to our boys overseas to help boost their morale. A *Tiger* writer complained in jest that one could not walk across the campus without hearing someone trying to sing, hum, or plunk on a mandolin the strains of George M. Cohan's "Over There." It was easier, of course, to make mock complaints about a popular war song than to speak of the mounting casualty tolls. Fitzgerald, noting that 21 of his classmates were killed in the war, later wrote, "Everything around us seemed to be breaking up." He had little interest in international affairs and did not consider himself as particularly patriotic, but going into the military seemed the natural thing to do at this time, as natural as going to Princeton had seemed when he was a student at Newman.

Fitzgerald received a commission as a second lieutenant in the infantry, October 26, 1917, ordered smartly tailored uniforms for himself from Brooks Brothers, and reported to Fort Leavenworth, Kansas, November 20th. One of his last *Nassau Lit* poems, "City Dusk," proudly bore the byline: "F. Scott Fitzgerald, Lieutenant 45th Infantry." While on leave from the service, Fitzgerald returned to Princeton, staying at Cottage Club and working on the manuscript of an autobiographical novel that he was then calling *The Romantic Egotist*; it would eventually evolve into *This Side of Paradise*. He was glad to be back, for a while, among familiar faces and surroundings. He deeply loved Princeton. But his academic career was over; he never graduated from

Princeton. The armistice came soon enough to save him from having to go overseas where he expected, not unreasonably, to perish in battle, as so many young lieutenants did. In September 1919, Scribners accepted his manuscript of *This Side of Paradise*; the book was published the following March. Its tumultuous public reception — the initial printing sold out within just three days — established Fitzgerald as not just a professional writer, but as a spokesman for his generation, a role he would continue to play for the remainder of the decade.

Fitzgerald's contributions to *The Tiger* are a mixed lot. Much of what he produced is extremely lightweight, though lively; it sounds exactly as if he had thought of it while staying up all night to get an issue out. And yet there is, at times, something quite recognizably Fitzgeraldian in the rhythms of the writing, as well as in the choice of subject matter.

Fitzgerald achieved his renown as a chronicler of the 1920s, capturing the spirit of its youth, his own generation. And he was certainly observing, and writing about, that generation while at Princeton, which makes his early work far more relevant than that of most writers. Fitzgerald once recalled that a *Tiger* contribution of his that drew great attention on campus was a single line that he had printed as an "intercollegiate petting cue" in 1917: "You really don't look comfortable there." It wasn't a line that he had created; it was merely one that he had heard a fellow use as a come-on to a girl, had taken note of, and recorded. Fitzgerald had a good ear. And he was particularly observant of the social maneuverings, snobbery, and calculated strivings to gain advantages that he saw at Princeton.

In *This Side of Paradise*, Fitzgerald reflected: "None of the Victorian mothers — and most of the mothers were Victorian — had any idea how casually their daughters were accustomed to being kissed." In his writings throughout the '20s, Fitzgerald gave them some idea. The females of his short stories were not perched on pedestals. They drank, they honed their "lines" with as much skill and cynicism as the men did, and at times they could even be downright dangerous. The teenage girls Fitzgerald described in "Little Minnie McCloskey," a Fitzgerald *Tiger* offering of 1916, would evolve into the flappers of his famed *Saturday Evening Post* stories within just a few years. If Fitzgerald's early female leads often seemed to resemble one another, it may be because they shared the same model: Ginevra King, a wealthy, self-absorbed, and extremely popular young woman from Lake Forest, Illinois, for whom he fell hard. Though Fitzgerald's wife, Zelda, would subsequently serve as a model for a number of other female characters, King was, by Fitzgerald's admission, the first love of his life. Their romance began in January of 1915; it was over for good in January of 1917. In the months right after their break-up, he was more prolific than usual, as if desperate to find an outlet for the emotional turmoil he'd been through. King was the inspiration for such characters as Helen Halcyon in "The Debutante" (a play published

Ginevra King

in the January 1917 *Nassau Lit* and reprinted in this collection), Isabelle in *This Side of Paradise* (1920), Judy Jones in "Winter Dreams" (1922), Daisy Buchanan in *The Great Gatsby* (1925), and Josephine in the various "Basil and Josephine" short stories (1930-31). (King, incidentally, later acknowledged recognizing in some of Fitzgerald's work a very accurate portrayal of her young self.) As Helen Halcyon remarked with satisfaction, concerning the fellows she encountered (in "The Debutante"): "I like the feeling of going after them.... Then I like the way they begin to follow you with their eyes. They're interested. Good!" But the painful point for Fitzgerald was that she was much more interested in luring fellows than she was interested in them. Fitzgerald, incidentally, saved for the rest of his life all of the letters King had ever sent to him; he even had typed copies of them bound. In 1917, King casually threw out all of the letters that he had sent to her. Being dumped by King was — along with his academic failures — one of the most deeply affecting experiences of Fitzgerald's Princeton years. Even near the end of his life, he would be jotting in his notebook how very hard he'd taken things in his youth, especially rejection by King. But she helped provide a model (as would Zelda, whom he met in 1918) for one of his most important recurring literary creations, the seductive female who thwarts, demoralizes, and to one degree or another weakens the male who falls in love with her.

For *The Tiger*, Fitzgerald noted breezily that the most important lessons he learned in college had not been learned in the classroom ("Undulations of an Undergraduate"). He sought also to record the flavor of "The Staying Up All Night." He took jabs at the Princeton's exclusive eating clubs with both "The Diary of a Sophomore" (who deserts his old friends when he has a chance to climb socially by joining a prestigious club) and the incisive "A Few Well-Known Club Types and Their Futures" (drawn by Lawrence Boardman '18; that the concept was Fitzgerald's is evident from the fact that he placed this cartoon in the scrapbook where he saved published material he had written). But he also spoofed the leaders of the anti-club revolt which captured the imagination of a number of conscientious Princetonians in the spring of 1917. Although Fitzgerald was quite friendly with — and had considerable respect for — one leading member of the anti-club movement, Henry Strater (the model for idealistic Burne Holiday in *This Side of Paradise*), Fitzgerald did not really identify with the movement's egalitarian spirit. Fitzgerald was, after all, a proud member of one of the most prestigious and exclusive of Princeton's eating clubs, Cottage. Fitzgerald had Alan Jackman '17 draw a cartoon entitled "Kenilworth Socialism — An eighth member measuring the mashed potatoes," which was intended to poke fun at the anti-club types. The cartoon, Jackman recalled for *Tiger* graduate board members, showed seven clearly recognizable Princetonians — from left to right, Jack Nicholas (*Daily Princetonian* chairman), Lewis N. Lukens (who would later serve as a class president), George Perkins (who would also serve as a class president), Alexander McKaig (*Daily Princetonian* editor), Robert Schmertz (active in many student organizations), Arthur Savage (who was to die in battle in World War One), and Charles Highley (a prominent football team member) — who had opted to eat at the Kenilworth Inn restaurant on Nassau Street, rather than be members of any snobbish, undemocratic, private eating club. They were each being given equal portions of mashed potatoes by a black waiter, the putative "eighth member" of their group. (In reprinting period cartoons such as this one, in which blacks are depicted in stereotypical fashion, we do not wish to cause anyone offense today; we simply want to open a window onto the world in which Fitzgerald grew up. The values expressed in such works reflect those of their creators at the time, not of the present collection's editor or publishers.)

In June of 1917, Fitzgerald offered *Tiger* readers a youth dreaming of becoming the next Rupert Brooke. Was he merely dealing with a common-enough collegiate dream of the time — or, as I suspect, more specifically one of his own dreams? Of course he loved Brooke's poetry; even the title of *This Side of Paradise* was borrowed from a Brooke poem. Fitzgerald had a romanticized view of military service, of heroically giving one's life in the prime of youth, as the handsome young Brooke had. The comic strip, which you'll find reproduced in this collection, was definitely conceived and written by Fitzgerald. Illustrator Alan Jackman '17 confirmed, in a letter to *Tiger* trustee Henry Martin, July 22, 1980, that he had printed the initials "F.S.S. '18," instead of "F.S.F. '18," by mistake. The cover of the June 1917 "War Number" of *The Tiger*, showing a startled American nurse in France discovering that the bandaged soldier on the bed before her is the man with whom she once walked along Princeton's Lake Carnegie, was conceived by Fitzgerald. It takes on added poignancy when one realizes that the artist, John V. Newlin '19, who left Princeton

THE TIGER

JANUARY

Vol. 26.   No. 7.

lished in *The Nassau Literary Magazine* in 1915
— provided the genesis for the short story "Benediction," published in H. L. Mencken's respected
magazine, *The Smart Set*, in 1920 and also included in *Flappers and Philosophers* that same
year. (It was among the stories Fitzgerald particularly liked in that collection, even as he cor-
rectly dismissed some of the other stories in the
collection as "trash.") "The Debutante," initially
published in *The Nassau Lit* in 1917, was revised
for publication in *The Smart Set* in 1919; ultimately, it became part of *This Side of Paradise*
(Amory's meeting with Rosalind). "Babes in the
Wood," which Fitzgerald wrote as a kind of fol-
low-up to "The Debutante" for *The Lit*, likewise
found its way into *The Smart Set* and eventually
This Side of Paradise (where it became Amory's
first meeting with Isabelle). "Jemina, A Story of
the Blue Ridge Mountains," Fitzgerald's rather
obvious parody of the work of then-popular writer
John Fox Jr., originally published in *The Nassau
Lit* in 1916, subsequently wound up in *Vanity*

Fitzgerald, age 20

for wartime ambulance corps duty, died on a
battlefield in France about a month after the cover
appeared. For his sacrifice, *The Tiger* announced
in the next issue, he was awarded the Croix de
Guerre. In collaboration with Biggs, Fitzgerald
wrote the story "Cedric the Stoker" shortly before he himself left the campus for service.

Fitzgerald's *Tiger* contributions, of course, lack
the maturity and polish of his later works. These
are the quickly-turned-out offerings of a very
young man. He crafted his *Nassau Lit* contributions more deliberately; some pieces he was subsequently able to re-use. "The Ordeal," about the
second thoughts of a Jesuit novice — written
while Fitzgerald himself was in the process of
questioning his Catholicism, and initially pub-

Fair, and then in *Tales of the Jazz Age*. Another of Fitzgerald's *Nassau Lit* pieces, "Tarquin of Cheepside," was expanded and included in *Tales of the Jazz Age*, where it was titled, with the spelling of the last word corrected, "Tarquin of Cheapside." (Although not a great story in either version, it was definitely improved when Fitzgerald revised it; students of Fitzgerald should enjoy comparing the two versions.) The poem "Princeton — The Last Day" (with its unforgettable closing reference to "the splendor and the sadness of the world" — Fitzgerald would spend the rest of his life documenting "the splendor and the sadness of the world") wound up, in prose format, in *This Side of Paradise*. Fitzgerald also mined "The Spire and the Gargoyle" and "Sentiment — And the Use of Rouge" for nuggets he was able to use in *This Side of Paradise*.

Fitzgerald was between 17 and 20 years old when he created most of the pieces collected in this book; he still had much to learn about his craft. You certainly won't find short fiction in this collection that is in the league of "The Diamond as Big as the Ritz" or "The Rich Boy," two of his more celebrated later short stories. The seams show all too clearly in an early effort such as "Shadow Laurels" from 1915 (a young man seeking to find out what his father had been like — to better understand, no doubt, who he is himself — finds with improbable swiftness the people who can tell him just what a fascinating failure his father had been). In the better-constructed "The Pierian Springs and the Last Straw" from 1917 — how much Fitzgerald had learned in just a couple of years! — he demonstrates a keen grasp of how to create a mood. The story's overall atmosphere reminds me of *The Great Gatsby* which would come eight years later. And Fitzgerald knows how to keep a reader interested. No one could read that story's opening sentence without wanting to read more: "My Uncle George assumed, during my childhood, almost legendary proportions." The character of the uncle, like Gatsby, is most intriguing if elusive. (And, in characteristically Fitzgeraldian fashion, he is ruined by a self-centered woman.) Fitzgerald also makes good use of the device of telling his story through

an observing, reflective character (as he would in both *The Great Gatsby* and *The Last Tycoon*), creating a heightened feeling of believability. Fitzgerald was already an effective story teller.

But in the years between "The Pierian Springs" and *The Great Gatsby*, Fitzgerald would learn invaluable lessons in how to build tension slowly and carefully, so that the ultimate emotional release for the reader would be far greater. In none of the stories in this collection does Fitzgerald emotionally devastate the reader, something he would grow breathtakingly proficient at in later years. (If you need an example of what I'm talking about, read "Babylon Revisited," from 1931.)

But if these early stories are not nearly as satisfying as the best stories Fitzgerald would produce in later years, a few of them — despite their flaws — are nonetheless more absorbing, intense, and meaningful than many of the polished but superficial commercial stories he would hack out

JUNE, 1922   35 Cents

The SMART SET

Edited by
George Jean Nathan
and
H.L. Mencken.

"The Diamond as Big as the Ritz"
By F. Scott Fitzgerald

in later years when in need of cash. In this collection's best stories, whether Fitzgerald is dealing with the wrestlings of conscience ("The Ordeal"), the sparrings of courtship ("Babes in the Woods"), or the suffering a woman can cause a man ("Sentiment — And the Use of Rouge"), the reader can appreciate his seriousness of purpose, his psychological awareness, and his already impressive crisp prose style. Although he is still a rather green writer, he is trying his hardest. I would much rather read these sincere early efforts than some of his later slick magazine stories, which, although written with admirable facility, read as though he didn't really care about what his characters were doing. Or what he was doing.

Fitzgerald proclaimed in April of 1920: "An author ought to write for the youth of his own generation, the critics of the next, and the schoolmasters of ever afterward." Embraced by his contemporaries as a voice of their generation, he enjoyed popularity throughout the high times of the 1920s. His earnings were substantial. (He eventually became, he believed, the highest paid short story writer in the world.) He lived lavishly. But he was widely rejected in the grimmer '30s, written off as a symbol of the discredited "Lost Generation," a specialist in tales of irrelevant, self-indulgent rich people. (Some critics, such as the ever-perceptive Gilbert Seldes, did continue to champion him but they exerted limited influence.) To pay huge bills for treatment of Zelda's mental illness, Fitzgerald had to spend much of the 1930s laboring on magazine stories (for which he was paid declining fees) and film scripts in which he himself often did not believe and which did nothing to enhance his standing. His letters in his last decade, as alcoholism and an array of other problems took their toll on him, make for heartbreaking reading.

A total of only 40 copies of Fitzgerald books were sold during the last year of his life. Embittered by failures, he wrote his daughter Scottie in October of 1940: "Life is essentially a cheat and its conditions are those of defeat." On December 21, 1940, while he was reading a Princeton Alumni Weekly article about football, he suffered a fatal heart attack. *The Chicago Daily News* observed: "When he died at 44, F. Scott Fitzgerald, hailed in 1922 as the protagonist and exponent of the Flapper Age, was almost as remote from contemporary interest as the authors of the blue-chip stock certificates of 1929."

Fitzgerald may have died believing he'd been defeated. But since his death, the restoration of his reputation as one of our finest writers has been both profound and enduring. Edmund Wilson contributed to the restoration: first by editing Fitzgerald's unfinished novel, *The Last Tycoon* (1941) (even in fragmentary form, its integrity and beauty were undeniable); second by editing an assemblage of clear and insightful writings by Fitzgerald, *The Crack-Up* (1945), which further forced critics to acknowledge Fitzgerald's stature. The biographies and critical studies of Fitzgerald's work which followed, paced by Arthur Mizener's powerful *The Far Side of Paradise* (Houghton Mifflin, 1951), fueled growing interest in him.

If I may be permitted to conclude this introduction with some personal reminiscences, I would like to tell how it is that I've come to be editing this collection. By my generation — I reached adolescence in the early '60s — Fitzgerald had become one of the standard authors, one of the recognized masters of American literature being taught in secondary schools and colleges everywhere. And as an adolescent, I simply responded to the vitality of Fitzgerald's prose as I did to that of few other writers. James Thurber expressed how I felt when he wrote: "Fitzgerald's perfection of style and form, as in *The Great Gatsby*, has a way of making something that lies between your stomach and your heart quiver a little." Even the teacher who joylessly dissected *The Great Gatsby*, day after day in one of my English classes, was unable to dampen my ardor. She treated the book as a series of symbols, quizzing us on such things as the meaning of the eyes of Dr. Eckleburg. That wasn't the way I was dealing with the book at all. I was helplessly succumbing to the romanticism of Gatsby (gazing at the green light at the end of his unattainable — and undeserving — beloved's dock), savoring the sweet sadness of Fitzgerald's carefully shaped prose (there isn't an extraneous word in the book), involuntarily committing to permanent memory lines like: "And so we beat on, boats against the current, borne back ceaselessly into the past." Whoever else, I asked myself, wrote such lines?

If *This Side of Paradise* lacked the power, cohesiveness, and moral seriousness of *The Great Gatsby*, it struck me as a more vibrant book, its more youthful spirit then even more in tune with my own; I relished it. Those two books were enough to confirm Fitzgerald as my favorite fiction writer. (The audacious, ebullient author-adventurer Richard Halliburton, whom I'd found a boundless source of inspiration since discovering him at age 13, was then my favorite non-fiction writer.) And as I went on to read Fitzgerald's taut short stories — "Absolution," "May Day," "Winter Dreams," "Crazy Sunday," "Family in the Wind," "The Long Way Out," "The Freshest Boy," and more — I became an admirer for life. Even then I understood enough about writing to sense the hard work behind such impeccably phrased — and fundamentally honest — texts.

Being a completist by nature — once I'd discovered Halliburton, I scoured second-hand shops to soon acquire every book he'd written, augmenting those my family already had, and I was just as dogged about acquiring records of vintage jazz musicians I liked — I tried to collect copies of everything Fitzgerald had ever written and everything written about him. That proved to be surprisingly difficult. For one thing, some of his books, like *Taps at Reveille*, had sold quite poorly upon initial release; used hardbound copies were much harder to find than Halliburton's books. In addition, I soon realized that Fitzgerald had been more prolific than my high school teachers had suggested, with something like 160 short stories to his credit, plus assorted essays, besides the five well-known novels. And there was still a continuing flow of new material being produced about him.

Despite diminishing returns, I struggled to find the more obscure writings. In a dedicatory poem that prefaced *The Crack-Up*, Edmund Wilson offered a recollection of the Fitzgerald he knew as a Princeton undergraduate, standing before a mirror squeezing out a pimple. For a reader who was just in his teens, that was a humanizing image: a Fitzgerald so young he was still bothered by pimples. Wilson went on in his poem to note that he was once again editing Fitzgerald's work, just as he had first done in the spring of 1915 when Fitzgerald left the manuscript of "Shadow Laurels" at his door. Wilson recalled a bit of "Shadow Laurels," too — just enough to make me curious about it and other pieces Fitzgerald had created as a Princeton student.

When I first became aware of Fitzgerald, in the early '60s, it was impossible to find his undergraduate work; none had ever been reprinted. Then, in 1965, some of his prep school and college writings were collected in *The Apprentice Fiction of F. Scott Fitzgerald, 1909-1917*, edited by John Kuehl (Rutgers University Press). Six years would pass before additional collegiate writings were reprinted in *F. Scott Fitzgerald in His Own Time: A Miscellany*, edited by Matthew J. Bruccoli and Jackson R. Bryer (Kent State University Press). Those two important and valuable books — which gathered most, but not quite all, of the undergraduate pieces attributed to Fitzgerald — have long been unavailable, necessitating this volume.

I got to see Fitzgerald's undergraduate writings — and in their original contexts, which made them even more meaningful for me — when I matriculated at Princeton in 1969. I didn't pick Princeton because it was associated in my mind with Fitzgerald (and Halliburton!), though that of course didn't hurt. Fitzgerald wrote in *This Side of Paradise* that he thought of Princeton as being "lazy and good-looking and aristocratic — you know, like a spring day. Harvard seems sort of indoors." That had a certain resonance for me. I'd loved Princeton — the beauty of the gothic architecture got to me — since my first boyhood visits, long before my brother Art enrolled there as a student in 1966, long before I learned that we happened to be descendants of a past

Princeton president, Samuel Stanhope Smith. Princeton was the only college for which I even bothered filling out an application.

As an undergraduate, it meant something to me that Fitzgerald had once been part of Princeton, even living for a while in one of the same dorms I lived in, Campbell. When I'd visit my friend Mark Pugliese in 185 Little Hall, we both got a kick out of knowing that his very room had once been Fitzgerald's.

In the offices of *The Tiger* (for which I eventually became an art director) and also at the Princeton library, I enjoyed looking through back issues, taking inspiration from the youthful work of *Tiger* contributors who had gone on to attain success as writers, cartoonists, or what have you: Booth Tarkington, Whitney Darrow Jr., Jimmy Stewart, Bill Brown, Henry Martin, John McPhee, Robert A. Caro, Frank Deford, Michael Witte, and above all Fitzgerald. I remember the thrill I got, the first time I spotted the initials "F. S. F." under one of his poems, "The Staying Up All Night"

(which, for some reason, has stayed with me since I first read it).

I must confess, though, I was also a bit disappointed by some of Fitzgerald's early material. Coming from an unusually diverse extended family, with relatives and ancestors of considerably varied religious, racial, and economic backgrounds, I was put off by Fitzgerald's occasional expressions of elitism and narrow-mindedness; I had to remind myself that he was a product of his times and look past such things.

But, even if social attitudes and tastes in humor do change over the years, human nature doesn't seem to change that much. Many observations in Fitzgerald's work remained right on target. And the Princeton that Fitzgerald described was also, in many ways, quite recognizable — despite all the talk, when I was a student, about the welcome emergence of a new, more fair-minded, socially conscious, and egalitarian Princeton.

Reading Fitzgerald's early work, flawed though it may have been in various ways, fascinated me. At times the voice was so obviously his, as we'd all come to know it from his mature writings — perhaps sounding a bit more effervescent and sure of himself, perhaps a bit more awkward about making transitions from one point to the next, but readily recognizable nonetheless. If some of his earliest work seemed rather clumsy or inconsequential, that only served to give me added inspiration. That such a youth could mature into so sublime a prose stylist seemed enough to give any aspiring writer — as I fancied myself — some hope.

I don't want to overstate, though, how much thought I gave to Fitzgerald back then. For I was at least as curious and enthusiastic about other subjects, ranging from jazz to theater to Halliburton. And I'd periodically meet students who were more "into" Fitzgerald than I was. After all, I hadn't been named for Fitzgerald, as I understood dazzling Triangle Club star A. Scott Berg '71, had been. Berg not only had Fitzgerald's books, he even had some dust-jacketed original editions, which I thought was fantastic. At Princeton, Berg was already writing about

Fitzgerald's editor Max Perkins, which he later expanded into a definitive biography. At the Princeton library's theatre collection, where I worked as a student assistant, curator Mary Ann Jensen mentioned to me that not one day— *not a single day* — went by without at least one person making use of the Fitzgerald papers at the Princeton library. So I knew there was a lot of interest in Fitzgerald. At any given moment, it seemed to me, some student somewhere was getting hooked on Fitzgerald.

I might also mention that because I was at Princeton during such heady, politically active times — my friends and I were striking against the war in Vietnam, and urging the University to open itself up more to the world at large, and passionately debating everything from the morality of stock-ownership in companies that did business with South Africa to aspects of gay rights — thoughts of Fitzgerald were often crowded out by current issues. Most of the time, the latest deeds of Richard Nixon and his cronies seemed much more relevant.

But Princeton had a way of periodically reminding me of Fitzgerald, helping keep alive my interest in him. At Princeton, for me, the past and the present always seemed to co-exist in some curious and agreeable way. Here's one small example. I can remember walking up University Place towards the office of *The Tiger* one afternoon, when I heard a quaint, melodious recording — two vaudeville-era voices harmonizing sweetly on "Turn Off Your Light, Mister Moon Man" — coming out a dorm window opening on to the street. I stood there, transfixed by the vintage music, until the fellow who was playing the recording spotted me and said hello. "Who's that singing?" I asked him. "It's Nora Bayes and Jack Norworth. On an album I just got called *Originals of Musical Comedy, 1909-1935*. It's very good." It sounded good indeed. I headed to the U-Store and bought a copy. But not before introducing myself to the fellow who was playing the album. He turned out to be a member of my class by the name of Charles Scribner III. If you don't immediately recognize the name, his great-grandfather had been the original publisher of

Fitzgerald himself (who, I might add, had also listened to Nora Bayes and Jack Norworth in his youth, even noting that fact in a journal entry). This Scribner's father and grandfather had been publishers of Fitzgerald's books, too. Whether he would even remember that trivial, chance encounter we had today, I don't know; but whenever I play that album, or open up my copy of the latest edition of *The Short Stories of F. Scott Fitzgerald* (Scribners, 1989), which happens to have a foreword by that very same Charles Scribner III — I'm reminded of it.

When I graduated in 1973, my most burning desires were to travel to some of the foreign lands Halliburton had described and to write about him. After that, I was unsure. To my surprise, I eventually wound up writing about the performing arts in general — and jazz in particular — for *The New York Post*. I've been their jazz critic for more than a decade now and have also written seven music-related books. The title of one of those seven books, incidentally — *Voices of the Jazz Age* (University of Illinois Press, 1990) —

Zelda and F. Scott Fitzgerald with their daughter, Scottie

was chosen to echo Fitzgerald, who coined and popularized the term "the Jazz Age." For about 15 years, I've been a trustee of *The Tiger*, too.

Around 1980, *Tiger* trustees José Pincay-Delgado and Allen Scheuch asked me to be one of the co-editors of *Roaring at One Hundred*, a book collecting the best of *The Tiger*, to be released in celebration of the magazine's centennial in 1982. I would be responsible for the section covering the magazine's boom years, 1915-1931. I enjoyed reading the nearly 10,000 pages of *The Tiger* that were published in those years, before making selections for the book and writing an introductory essay. (Earle Coleman, archivist of Princeton's Seeley G. Mudd Library, and his assistants were of invaluable help, since the library had copies of issues that *The Tiger* itself seemed to have lost. They have my gratitude.) Despite unfortunate expressions of prejudices of one sort or another that occasionally cropped up in old issues of *The Tiger*, most of the material I went through held up rather well. Reading all of those back issues got me thinking about Fitzgerald again.

I carefully re-examined all of Fitzgerald's early *Tiger* work — and then his *Nassau Lit* work as well. I was particularly happy to be able to choose for inclusion in *Roaring at One Hundred* a couple of Fitzgerald's *Tiger* contributions, "The Dream and the Awakening" and the cover to the war number, which had never before been reprinted. (Those who might be interested in purchasing *Roaring at One Hundred* may write *The Tiger*, 48 University Place, Princeton, NJ 08540.)

I contacted Fitzgerald's daughter, Scottie (by then Mrs. C. Grove Smith of Washington, D. C.), suggesting that — if it was all right with her — I eventually hoped to be able to reprint some of her father's old *Tiger* pieces not just in *Roaring at One Hundred* but perhaps in *The Princeton Alumni Weekly* or a commercial magazine or book. She was extraordinarily generous and supportive, giving me carte blanche permission to reprint any or all of them, wherever I wished. The matter of permissions is of course now moot, since all of F. Scott Fitzgerald's *Tiger* and *Nassau Lit* writings, having been published more than 75 years ago, are in public domain; but they were not in public domain when she so freely gave me permission to do with them whatever I chose, and her unusual act of kindness deserves to be remembered. I only regret that I was not able to fulfill within her lifetime my vow to complete this project. Scottie Fitzgerald Smith died of cancer of the esophagus in 1986.

In the 1980s, I was unfortunately unable to find any magazine that wanted to reprint collegiate writings of F. Scott Fitzgerald — and this despite the fact that by 1980, Scribners had sold more than 12 million copies of Fitzgerald's various books, and sales of *The Great Gatsby* alone were running around 300,000 copies a year. Even *The Princeton Alumni Weekly* hesitated. Though I've periodically contributed to the magazine, enjoying warm relations with a succession of conscientious editors — Lanny Jones, Chuck Creesy, Andrew Mytelka, Jim Merritt — the magazine seemed in no hurry to run another Fitzgerald-related piece, noting they'd done quite a bit on him over the years. I wondered if an underlying reason may have been that Princeton has long seemed ambivalent about Fitzgerald. Even though Fitzgerald is, along with Woodrow Wilson and James Madison, one of Princeton's most famous alumni, there's been resentment in some quarters that he helped promulgate an image of Princeton as "the pleasantest country club in America," in the words of an oft-quoted line from *This Side of Paradise*. That image, it should be noted, pre-dated Fitzgerald; in fact, it was actually Francis L. Patton, whose tenure as Princeton's president ended 11 years before Fitzgerald even matriculated, who first likened Princeton to a country club, but the association of the image with Fitzgerald has prevailed. The university will periodically celebrate Fitzgerald, but it also understandably likes to emphasize that in various ways today's Princeton is, happily, different from the one Fitzgerald described.

Public interest in Fitzgerald, the writer and the man, has continued to grow with the passage of time. Nowadays more copies of his books are actually sold each year than were sold in total in all the years of his life. And every time it seemed

I'd almost forgotten about Fitzgerald, I'd hear from some member of the Princeton community who'd turned up a Fitzgerald-related item he or she figured I'd appreciate — a clipping, or xerox, or photo, or book — and find my curiosity about him revived. (The same thing has happened with Halliburton for me.) And the one-hundredth anniversary of Fitzgerald's birth — he was born in St. Paul, Minnesota, on September 24, 1896 — has further heightened public interest in him.

I am pleased to have an opportunity now to introduce and annotate this collection, which is being published by Cypress House (with the cooperation of The Princeton Tiger, Inc.) in time for the celebration of Fitzgerald's centennial. Most of these pieces have been out of print for years. And this is the first time that many of these pieces have been reproduced with samplings of artwork that originally accompanied them. Seeing the lively period artwork — even if sometimes scaled down a bit to fit this book's slightly smaller page size — should help give a feel for how these pieces were originally published, and enable us to better understand Fitzgerald's world. Most of the drawings that adorn this book have been culled from issues of *The Tiger* published between 1914 and 1917; only a few drawings have been culled from *The Nassau Lit* of that era, since *The Lit* very rarely used artwork back then. (Fitzgerald, of course, did not draw any illustrations himself. In a handful of cases, clearly indicated, he is known to have provided concepts or captions to artists who then executed his ideas. The remaining period drawings by his contemporaries have simply been chosen to help put Fitzgerald's work in context.) Spelling errors and inconsistencies found in Fitzgerald's work, as originally published in *The Tiger* and *The Lit,* have been retained in this anthology.

I'd like to think this collection may be of value to Fitzgerald scholars and enthusiasts, young and

F. SCOTT FITZGERALD
Study by Gordon Bryant

old, who — having admired his mature work — may simply be curious, as I once was, about how he got started. As we proceed through these disparate stories, poems, jokes, and sketches, created just prior to his rise to national renown with the publication of *This Side of Paradise*, we can almost hear Fitzgerald find his own unique voice.

These early works — by turns impudent and high-spirited, reflective and regretful — help bring us close to an unforgettable writer...still very much in the process of becoming.

Opening ~ Numbers

PRINCETON TIGER

THERE WAS ONCE . . .

There was once a second group student who lived in Holder. He thought that solitude would give him a first group. So he moved to Patton, where he lent an unwilling ear to the following:

1:30 – 2:30 p.m.	Shrill soprano shrieks of the soccer team.
2:30 – 3:30 " "	Session of the gun club.
3:30 – 4:30 " "	Interclass baseball game on Brokaw. (Continuous cheering.)
4:30 – 5:30 " "	Engines puffing up and down for their afternoon exercise.
7:00 – 8:00 " "	Mandolin or banjo in Brokaw.
8:00 – 9:00 " "	Triangle practice in Casino.

The next day the student moved back to Holder.

———

1. "There was once..." *The Princeton Tiger*, XXV (December 1914), p. 5. Unsigned. Known to be by Fitzgerald because he preserved a clipping in the scrapbook where he kept his published juvenilia, now part of the Fitzgerald Papers at the Princeton University Library. This rather slight piece, from the winter of Fitzgerald's sophomore year, is the earliest *Tiger* piece that we can identify as being his, although he contributed to the magazine during his freshman year as well. Considering his academic difficulties, it seems fitting that the earliest known Fitzgerald *Tiger* contribution involves a student vainly trying to improve his grades.

(At Princeton, first group meant highest standing; second group, high standing; third group, satisfactory; fourth group, below average; fifth group, poor; sixth group, unsatisfactory; seventh group, very unsatisfactory.) Seeking quieter surroundings, the student in this piece switches dorms, moving from Holder, which was at the northern end of the campus and had a reputation for rowdiness, to Patton, which was then the southernmost of all dorms, and was by athletic practice fields. At the time he wrote this piece, incidentally, Fitzgerald was himself residing in Patton (room 107) — presumably writing from personal experience.

CONTENTS FOR APRIL 1915

"Shadow Laurels"...................*F. Scott Fitzgerald*   1

The Prelude (Verse)...............*Edmund Wilson, Jr.*   11

The Heritage...........................*W. S. Dell*   12

Francis Thompson (Verse)...........*John Peale Bishop*   32

Stendhal.........................*Edmund Wilson, Jr*   33

Rose-Dust (Verse)..................*John Peale Bishop*   39

The Joys of Sciolism.....................*Allan Hunter*   40

Editorial   43

Gossip   48

Book Talk   53

The Nassau Literary Magazine is published every month from November to June inclusive by the students of Princeton University. Its purpose is to express undergraduate views of life and literature. Contributions of short stories, literary essays, and poetry are solicited from all students, and thoughtful discussions of college questions are particularly acceptable.

The terms of subscription are $2.00 a year, payable in advance. Single copies are on sale at the University Store, Sinclair's, and Van Marter's, 25 cents. Subscribers who fail to receive any issue should notify the Business Manager.

(*Entered as second class matter in the Post Office at Princeton, N. J.*)

The Turmoil of the Office.

The Nassau Literary Magazine

Volume LXXI   **April 1915**   **No. 1**

"SHADOW LAURELS"

(*The scene is the interior of a wine shop in Paris. The walls are lined on all sides by kegs, piled like logs. The ceiling is low and covered with cobwebs. The midafternoon sun filters dejectedly through the one-barred window at the back. Doors are on both sides; one, heavy and powerful, opens outside; the other, on the left, leads to some inner chamber. A large table stands in the middle of the room backed by smaller ones set around the walls. A ship's lamp hangs above the main table.*

As the curtain rises there is knocking at the outside door—rather impatient knocking—and almost immediately Pitou, the wine dealer, enters from the other room and shuffles toward the door. He is an old man with unkempt beard and dirty corduroys.)

Pitou—Coming, coming—Hold tight! (*The knocking stops. Pitou unlatches the door and it swings open. A man in a top hat and opera cloak enters. Jaques Chandelle is perhaps thirty-seven, tall and well groomed. His eyes are clear and penetrating, his chin, clean shaven, is sharp and decisive. His manner is that of a man accustomed only to success but ready and willing to work hard in any emergency. He speaks French with an odd accent as of one who knew the language well in early years but whose accent had grown toneless through long years away from France.*)

Pitou—Good afternoon, Monsieur.

Chandelle—(*looking about him curiously*) Are you perhaps Monsieur Pitou?

Pitou—Yes, Monsieur.

SHADOW LAURELS

(The scene is the interior of a wine shop in Paris. The walls are lined on all sides by kegs, piled like logs. The ceiling is low and covered with cobwebs. The midafternoon sun filters dejectedly through the one-barred window at the back. Doors are on both sides; one, heavy and powerful, opens outside; the other, on the left, leads to some inner chamber. A large table stands in the middle of the room backed by smaller ones set around the walls. A ship's lamp hangs above the main table.

As the curtain rises there is a knocking at the outside door — rather impatient knocking — and almost immediately Pitou, the wine dealer, enters from the other room and shuffles toward the door. He is an old man with an unkempt beard and dirty corduroys.)

Pitou — Coming, coming — Hold tight! (*The knocking stops. Pitou unlatches the door and it swings open. A man in a top hat and opera cloak enters. Jaques Chandelle is perhaps thirty-seven, tall and well groomed. His eyes are clear and penetrating, his chin, clean shaven, is sharp and decisive. His manner is that of a man accustomed only to success but ready and willing to work hard in any emergency. He speaks French with an odd accent as of one who knew the language well in early years but whose accent had grown toneless through long years away from France.)*

Pitou — Good afternoon, Monsieur.

Chandelle — (*looking about him curiously*) Are you perhaps Monsieur Pitou?

Pitou — Yes, Monsieur.

Chandelle — Ah! I was told that one would always find you in at this hour. (*He takes off his overcoat and lays it carefully on the chair*) I was told also that you could help me.

Pitou — (*puzzled*) I could help you?

Chandelle — (*Sitting down wearily on a wooden chair near the table*) Yes, I'm a — a stranger in the city — now. I'm trying to trace someone — someone who has been dead many years. I'm informed that you're the oldest inhabitant (*he smiles faintly.*)

Pitou — (*rather pleased*) Perhaps — and yet there are older than I, ah yes, older than I. (*He sits down across the table from Chandelle.*)

Chandelle — And so I came for you. (*He bends earnestly over the table toward Pitou.*) Monsieur Pitou, I am trying to trace my father.

Pitou — Yes.

Chandelle — He died in this district about twenty years ago.

Pitou — Monsieur's father was murdered?

Chandelle — Good God, no! What makes you think that?

Pitou — I thought perhaps in this district twenty years ago, an aristocrat —

Chandelle — My father was no aristocrat. As I remember, his last position was that of waiter in some forgotten café. (*Pitou glances at Chandelle's clothes and looks mystified.*) Here I'll explain. I left France twenty-eight years ago to go to the states with my uncle. We went over in an immigrant ship, if you know what that is.

Pitou — Yes: I know.

Chandelle — My parents remained in France. The last I remember of my father was that he was a little man with a black beard, terribly lazy — the only good I ever remember his doing was to teach me to read and write. Where he picked up that accomplishment I don't know. Five years after we reached America we ran across some newly landed French from this part of the city, who said both my parents were dead. Soon after that my uncle died and I was far too busy to worry over parents whom I had half forgotten anyway. (*He pauses.*) Well to cut it short I prospered and—

Pitou — (*deferentially*) Monsieur is rich — 'tis strange — 'tis very strange.

Chandelle — Pitou, it probably appears strange to you that I should burst in on you now at this time of life, looking for traces of a father who went completely out of my life over twenty years ago.

Pitou — Oh — I understood you to say he was dead.

Chandelle — Yes, he's dead, but (*hesitates*) Pitou, I wonder if you can understand if I tell you why I am here.

Pitou — Yes, perhaps.

Chandelle — (*very earnestly*) Monsieur Pitou, in America the men I see now, the women I know all had fathers, fathers to be ashamed of, fathers to be proud of, fathers in gilt frames, and fathers in the family closet, Civil War fathers, and Ellis Island fathers. Some even had grandfathers.

Pitou — I had a grandfather. I remember.

Chandelle — (*interrupting*) I want to see people who knew him, who talked with him. I want to find out his intelligence, his life, his record. (*Impetuously*) I want to sense him — I want to know him —

Pitou — (*interrupting*) What was his name?

Chandelle — Chandelle, Jean Chandelle.

Pitou — (*quietly*) I knew him.

Chandelle — You knew him?

Pitou — He came here often to drink — that was long ago when this place was the rendezvous of half the district.

Chandelle — (*excitedly*) Here? He used to come here? To this room? Good Lord, the very house he lived in was torn down ten years ago. In two days' search you are the first soul I've found who knew him. Tell me of him — everything — be frank.

Pitou — Many come and go in forty years. (*Shakes his head.*) There are many names and many faces — Jean Chandelle — ah, of course, Jean Chandelle. Yes, yes; the chief fact I can remember about your father was that he was a— a—

Chandelle — Yes.

Pitou — A terrible drunkard.

Chandelle — A drunkard — I expected as much. (*He looks a trifle downcast, but makes a half-hearted attempt not to show it.*)

Pitou — (*Rambling on through a sea of reminiscence*) I remember one Sunday night in July — hot night — baking — your father — let's see — your father tried to knife Pierre Courru for drinking his mug of sherry.

Chandelle — Ah!

Pitou — And then — ah, yes, (*excitedly standing up*) I see it again. Your father is playing *vingt-et-un* and they say he is cheating so he breaks Clavine's shin with a chair and throws a bottle at someone and Lafouquet sticks a knife into his lung. He never got over that. That was — was two years before he died.

Chandelle — So he cheated and was murdered. My God, I've crossed over the ocean to discover that.

Pitou — No — no — I never believed he cheated. They were laying for him —

Chandelle — (*burying his face in his hands*) Is that all (*he shrugs his shoulders; his voice is a trifle broken*) I scarcely expected a — saint but — well: so he was a rotler.

Pitou — (*Laying his hand on Chandelle's shoulder*) There Monsieur, I have talked too much. Those were rough days. Knives were drawn at anything. Your father — but hold — do you

28

want to meet three friends of his, his best friends. They can tell you much more than I.

Chandelle — (*gloomily*) His friends?

Pitou — (*reminiscent again*) There were four of them. Three come here yet — will be here this afternoon — your father was the fourth and they would sit at this table and talk and drink. They talked nonsense — everyone said; the wine room poked fun at them — called them "les Académicians Riducules." Night after night would they sit there. They would slouch in at eight and stagger out at twelve —

(*The door swings open and three men enter. The first, Lamarque, is a tall man, lean and with a thin straggly beard. The second, Destage, is short and fat, white bearded and bald. The third, Francois Meridien is slender, with black hair streaked with grey and a small moustache. His face is pitifully weak, his eyes small, his chin sloping. He is very nervous. They all glance with dumb curiosity at Chandelle.*)

Pitou — (*including all three with a sweep of his arm*) Here they are, Monsieur; they can tell you more than I. (*Turning to the others*) Messieurs, this gentleman desires to know about—

Chandelle — (*rising hastily and interrupting Pitou*) About a friend of my father's. Pitou tells me you knew him. I believe his name was — Chandelle.

(*The three men start and Francois begins to laugh nervously.*)

Lamarque — (*after a pause*) Chandelle?

Francois — Jean Chandelle? So he had another friend besides us?

Destage — You will pardon me, Monsieur: that name — no one but us had mentioned it for twenty-two years.

Lamarque — (*trying to be dignified, but looking a trifle ridiculous*) And with us it is mentioned with reverence and awe.

Destage — Lamarque exaggerates a little perhaps. (*Very seriously*) He was very dear to us. (*Again Francois laughs nervously.*)

Lamarque — But what is it that Monsieur wishes to know? (*Chandelle motions them to sit down. They take places at the big table and Destage produces a pipe and begins to fill it.*)

Francois — Why, we're four again!

Lamarque — Idiot!

Chandelle — Here, Pitou! Wine for everyone. (*Pitou nods and shuffles out*) Now, Messieurs, tell me of Chandelle. Tell me of his personality.

(*Lamarque looks blankly at Destage.*)

Destage — Well, he was — was attractive—

Lamarque — Not to everyone.

Destage — But to us. Some thought him a sneak. (*Chandelle winces*) He was a wonderful talker — when he wished, he could amuse the whole wine room. But he preferred to talk to us. (*Pitou enters with a bottle and glasses. He pours and leaves the bottle on the table. Then he goes out.*)

Lamarque — He was educated. God knows how.

Francois — (*draining his glass and pouring out more.*) He knew everything, he could tell anything — he used to tell me poetry. Oh, what poetry! And I would listen and dream—

Destage — And he could make verses and sing them with his guitar.

Lamarque — And he would tell us about men and women of history — about Charlotte Corday and Fouquet and Moliére and St. Louis and Mamine, the strangler, and Charlemagne and Mme. Dubarry and Machiavelli and John Law and Francois Villon—

Destage — Villon! (*enthusiastically*) He loved Villon. He would talk for hours of him.

Francois — (*Pouring more wine*) And then he would get very drunk and say "Let us fight" and he would stand on the table and say that everyone in the wine shop was a pig and a son of pigs. La! He would grab a chair or a table and Sacré Vie Dieu! but those were hard nights for us.

Lamarque — Then he would take his hat and guitar and go into the streets to sing. He would sing about the moon.

Francois — And the roses and the ivory towers of Babylon and about the ancient ladies of the court and about "the silent chords that flow from the ocean to the moon."

Destage — That's why he made no money. He was bright and clever — when we worked, he worked feverishly hard, but he was always drunk, night and day.

29

Lamarque — Often he lived on liquor alone for weeks at a time.

Destage — He was much in jail toward the end.

Chandelle — (*calling*) Pitou! More wine!

Francois — (*excitedly*) And me! He used to like me best. He used to say that I was a child and he would train me. He died before he began. (*Pitou enters with another bottle of wine; Francois seizes it eagerly and pours himself a glass.*)

Destage — And then that cursed Lafouquet — struck him with a knife.

Francois — But I fixed Lafouquet. He stood on the Seine bridge drunk and—

Lamarque — Shut up, you fool you—

Francois — I pushed him and he sank — down — down — and that night Chandelle came in a dream and thanked me.

Chandelle — (*shuddering*) How long — for how many years did you come here?

Destage — Six or seven. (*Gloomily*) Had to end — had to end.

Chandelle — And he's forgotten. He left nothing. He'll never be thought of again.

Destage — Remembered! Bah! Posterity is as much a charlatan as the most prejudiced tragic critic that ever boot-licked an actor. (*He turns his glass nervously round and round*) You don't realize — I'm afraid — how we feel about Jean Chandelle, Francois and Lamarque and I — he was more than a genius to be admired—

Francois — (*hoarsely*) Don't you see, he stood for us as well as for himself.

Lamarque — (*rising excitedly and walking up and down.*) There we were — four men — three of us poor dreamers — artistically educated, practically illiterate (*he turns savagely to Chandelle and speaks almost menacingly*) Do you realize that I can neither read nor write? Do you realize that back of Francois there, despite his fine phrases, there is a character weak as water, a mind as shallow as—

(*Francois starts up angrily.*)

Lemarque — Sit down (*Francois sits down muttering.*)

Francois — (*after a pause*) But, Monsieur, you must know — I leave the gift of — of — (*helplessly*) I can't name it — appreciation, artistic, aesthetic sense — call it what you will. Weak — yes, why not? Here I am, with no chance, the world against me. I lie — I steal perhaps — I am drunk — I—

(*Destage fills up Francois glass with wine*)

Destage — Here! Drink that and shut up! You are boring the gentleman. There is his weak side — poor infant.

(*Chandelle, who has listened to the last, keenly turns his chair toward Destage.*)

Chandelle — But you say my father was more to you than a personal friend; in what way?

Lamarque — Can't you see?

Francois — I — I — he helped — (*Destage pours out more wine and gives it to him.*)

Destage — You see he — how shall I say it? he expressed us. If you can imagine a mind like mine, potently lyrical, sensitive without being cultivated. If you can imagine what a balm, what a medicine, what an all in all was summed up for me in my conversations with him. It was everything to me. I would struggle pathetically for a phrase to express a million yearnings and he would say it in a word.

Lamarque — Monsieur is bored? (*Chandelle shakes his head and opening his case selects a cigarette and lights it.*)

Lamarque — Here, sir, are three rats, the product of a sewer — destined by nature to live and die in the filthy ruts where they were born. But these three rats in one thing are not of the sewer — they have eyes. Nothing to keep them from remaining in the sewer but their eyes, nothing to help them if they go out but their eyes — and now here comes the light. And it came and passed and left us rats again — vile rats — and one, when he lost the light, went blind.

Francois — (*muttering to himself*)—

Blind! Blind! Blind!
Then he ran alone, when the light had passed;
The sun had set and the night fell fast;
The rat lay down in the sewer at last,
Blind!

(*A beam of sunset has come to rest on the glass of wine that Francois holds in his hand. The wine glitters and sparkles. Francois looks at it, starts, and drops the glass. The wine runs over the table.*)

Destage — (*animatedly*) Fifteen — twenty years ago he sat where you sat, small, heavy-bearded, black eyed — always sleepy looking.

Francois — (*his eyes closed — his voice trailing off*) Always sleepy, sleepy, slee—

Chandelle — (*dreamily*) He was a poet unsinging, crowned with wreaths of ashes. (*His voice rings with just a shade of triumph.*)

Francois — (*talking in his sleep*) Ah, well Chandelle, are you witty to-night, or melancholy or stupid or drunk.

Chandelle — Messieurs — it grows late. I must be off. Drink, all of you (*enthusiastically*) Drink until you cannot talk or walk or see. (*He throws a bill on the table.*)

Destage — Young Monsieur?

(*Chandelle dons his coat and hat. Pitou enters with more wine. He fills the glasses.*)

Lamarque — Drink with us, Monsieur.

Francois — (*asleep*) Toast, Chandelle, toast.

Chandelle — (*taking a glass and raising it aloft.*) Toast (*his face is a little red and his hand unsteady. He appears infinitely more gallic than when he entered the wine shop.*)

Chandelle — I drink to one who might have been

all, who was nothing — who might have sung; who only listened — who might have seen the sun; who but watched a dying ember — who drank of gall and wore a wreath of shadow laurels—

(*The others have risen, even Francois, who totters wildly forward.*)

Francois — Jean, Jean, don't go — don't — till I, Francois — you can't leave me — I'll be all alone — alone — alone (*his voice rises higher and higher*) My God, man, can't you see, you have no right to die — You are my soul. (*He stands for a moment, then sprawls across the table. Far away in the twilight a violin sighs plaintively. The last beam of the sun rests on Francois' head. Chandelle opens the door and goes out.*)

Destage — The old days go by, and the old loves and the old spirit. "Ou sont les neiges d'antan?" I guess. (*Pauses unsteadily and then continues.*) I've gone far enough without him.

Lamarque — (*dreamily*) Far enough.

Destage — Your hand Jaques! (*They clasp hands.*)

Francois — (*wildly*) Here — I, too — you won't leave me (*feebly*) I want — just one more glass — one more—

(*The light fades and disappears.*)

(CURTAIN.)

— F. Scott Fitzgerald

---

2. "Shadow Laurels," *The Nassau Literary Magazine*, LXXI (April 1915), pp. 1-10. Fitzgerald is credited by name in the magazine. This play was Fitzgerald's first contribution to *The Lit*, of which Edmund Wilson (known to friends as "Bunny") was then the managing editor. In a favorable, if strangely irrelevant, review of "Shadow Laurels" in *The Daily Princetonian* (April 17, 1915), one L. Wardlaw Miles suggested Fitzgerald "succeeds well for the most part in conveying the intended atmosphere of sordid and suffocating despair, an atmosphere so different from the 'lies, sunlight, and salvation' of our sturdy Anglo-Saxon civilization. The implied contrast — if we read aright — between a French world of ideas plus impotence and an American world of sterile thought plus success is very suggestive."

In writing this play — in which the protagonist learns that his father had been a failure in many ways but loved by friends for the color he added to their lives — Fitzgerald seems to have been dealing with his feelings about his own father, a repeated failure in business undertakings. The father in this tale is remembered as having drunk quite a bit of liquor. While little is known about the drinking habits of Fitzgerald's own father, Fitzgerald recorded in his Ledger, August of 1905, his impression that his father "used to drink too much." Weak fathers would frequently re-occur in Fitzgerald's fiction.

May Small Talk

To get a reputation for ability to chatter
You must learn this little system for your common campus patter.
First you ask about exams and how your victim thinks he's doing,
Speak of war and shake your head and say you think there's trouble brewing.
A word about your bills, and on the chapel question, too,
Then "Gee, but it was mighty tough — you know about the crew."
"Yes, Charlie Chaplin's at the show — a mighty funny thing;"
"Going over Campus now, to hear the Seniors sing?"
"I s'pose since you're a parlor snake you'll bring the girl in June?"
"Oh! eat your soup, for the movie show is starting pretty soon."
"Well, these are busy days for me" — "You've always been a bummer,"
"Yes, meet me here at Morey's School," and "What's the dope this summer?"
You must always ask the heeler, "How he's coming with the Prince,"
And "Coming back here early?" makes the guards and centers wince:
For this is always easier and better far for mine,
Than a continental trancendental consequential line!

---

3. "May Small Talk," *The Princeton Tiger*, XXVI (June 1915), p. 10. Unsigned. Known to be by Fitzgerald because he preserved a clipping in his scrapbook. Here Fitzgerald has taken note of, and recorded, everyday talk he'd heard among fellow students—something he would subsequently do to telling effect in *This Side of Paradise*.

THE ORDEAL

The hot four o'clock sun beat down familiarly upon the wide stretch of Maryland country, burning up the long valleys, powdering the winding road into fine dust and glaring on the ugly slated roof of the monastery. Into the gardens it poured hot, dry, lazy, bringing with it, perhaps, some quiet feeling of content, unromantic and cheerful. The walls, the trees, the sanded walks, seemed to radiate back into the fair cloudless sky the sweltering late summer heat and yet they laughed and baked happily. The hour brought some odd sensation of comfort to the farmer in a nearby field, drying his brow for a moment by his thirsty horse, and to the lay-brother opening boxes behind the monastery kitchen.

The man walked up and down on the bank above the creek. He had been walking for half an hour. The lay-brother looked at him quizzically as he passed and murmured an invocation. It was always hard, this hour before taking first vows. Eighteen years before one, the world just behind. The lay-brother had seen many in this same situation, some white and nervous, some grim and determined, some despairing. Then, when the bell tolled five, there were the vows and usually the novice felt better. It was this hour in the country when the world seemed gloriously apparent and the monastery vaguely impotent. The lay-brother shook his head in sympathy and passed on.

The man's eyes were bent upon his prayer-book. He was very young, twenty at the most, and his dark hair in disorder gave him an even more boyish expression. A light flush lay on his calm face and his lips moved incessantly. He was not nervous. It seemed to him as if he had always

known he was to become a priest. Two years before, he had felt the vague stirring, the transcendent sense of seeing heaven in everything, that warned him softly, kindly that the spring of his life was coming. He had given himself every opportunity to resist. He had gone a year to college, four months abroad, and both experiences only increased within him the knowledge of his destiny. There was little hesitation. He had at first feared self-committal with a thousand nameless terrors. He thought he loved the world. Panicky, he struggled, but surer and surer he felt that the last word had been said. He had his vocation — and then, because he was no coward, he decided to become a priest.

Through the long month of his probation he alternated between deep, almost delirious, joy and the same vague terror at his own love of life and his realization of all he sacrificed. As a favorite child he had been reared in pride and confidence in his ability, in faith in his destiny. Careers were open to him, pleasure, travel, the law, the diplomatic service. When, three months before, he had walked into the library at home and told his father that he was going to become a Jesuit priest, there was a family scene and letters on all sides from friends and relatives. They told him he was ruining a promising young life because of a sentimental notion of self sacrifice, a boyish dream. For a month he listened to the bitter melodrama of the commonplace, finding his only rest in prayer, knowing his salvation and trusting in it. After all, his worst battle had been with himself. He grieved at his father's disappointment and his mother's tears, but he knew that time would set them right.

And now in half an hour he would take the vows which pledged him forever to a life of service. Eighteen years of study — eighteen years where his every thought, every idea would be dictated to him, where his individuality, his physical ego would be effaced and he would come forth strong and firm to work and work and work. He felt strangely calm, happier in fact than he had been for days and months. Something in the fierce, pulsing heat of the sun likened itself to his own heart, strong in its decision, virile and doing its own share in the work, the greatest work. He was elated that he had been chosen, he from so many unquestionably singled out, unceasingly called for. And he had answered.

The words of the prayers seemed to run like a stream into his thoughts, lifting him up peacefully, serenely; and a smile lingered around his eyes. Everything seemed so easy; surely all life was a prayer. Up and down he walked. Then of a sudden something happened. Afterwards he could never describe it except by saying that some undercurrent had crept into his prayer, something unsought, alien. He read on for a moment and then it seemed to take the form of music. He raised his eyes with a start — far down the dusty road a group of negro hands were walking along singing, and the song was an old song that he knew:

"We hope ter meet you in heaven whar we'll
    Part no mo',
Whar we'll part no mo'.
Gawd a'moughty bless you twel we
Me-et agin."

Something flashed into his mind that had not been there before. He felt a sort of resentment toward those who had burst in upon him at this time, not because they were simple and primitive, but because they had vaguely disturbed him. That song was old in his life. His nurse had hummed it through the dreamy days of his childhood. Often in the hot summer afternoons he had played it softly on his banjo. It reminded him of so many things: months at the seashore on the hot beach with the gloomy ocean rolling around him, playing with sand castles with his cousin;

summer evenings on the big lawn at home when he chased fireflies and the breeze carried the tune over the night to him from the negro-quarters. Later, with new words, it had served as a serenade — and now — well, he had done with that part of life, and yet he seemed to see a girl with kind eyes, old in a great sorrow, waiting, ever waiting. He seemed to hear voices calling, children's voices. Then around him swirled the city, busy with the hum of men; and there was a family that would never be, beckoning him.

Other music ran now as undercurrent to his thoughts: wild, incoherent, music, illusive and wailing, like the shriek of a hundred violins, yet clear and chord-like. Art, beauty, love and life passed in a panorama before him, exotic with the hot perfumes of world-passion. He saw struggles and wars, banners waving somewhere, voices giving hail to a king — and looking at him through it all were the sweet sad eyes of the girl who was now a woman.

Again the music changed; the air was low and sad. He seemed to front a howling crowd who accused him. The smoke rose again around the body of John Wycliffe, a monk knelt at the priedieu and laughed because the poor had not bread, Alexander VI pressed once more the poisoned ring into his brother's hand, and the black robed figures of the inquisition scowled and whispered. Three great men said there was no God, a million voices seemed to cry, "Why! Why! must we believe?" Then as in a chrystal he seemed to hear Huxley, Nietzsche, Zola, Kant cry, "I will not" — He saw Voltaire and Shaw wild with cold passion. The voices pleaded "Why?" and the girl's sad eyes gazed at him with infinite longing.

He was in a void above the world — the ensemble, everything called him now. He could not pray. Over and over again he said senselessly, meaninglessly, "God have mercy, God have mercy." For a minute, an eternity, he trembled in the void and then — something snapped. They were still there, but the girl's eyes were all wrong, the lines around her mouth were cold and chiselled and her passion seemed dead and earthy.

He prayed, and gradually the cloud grew

clearer, the images appeared vague and shadowy. His heart seemed to stop for an instant and then — he was standing by the bank and a bell was tolling five. The reverend superior came down the steps and toward him.

"It is time to go in." The man turned instantly. "Yes, Father, I am coming."

II.

The novices filed silently into the chapel and knelt in prayer. The blessed Sacrament in the gleaming monstrance was exposed among the flaming candles on the altar. The air was rich and heavy with incense. The man knelt with the others. A first chord of the magnificat, sung by the concealed choir above, startled him; he looked up. The late afternoon sun shone through the stained glass window of St. Francis Xavier on his left and fell in red tracery on the cassock of the man in front of him. Three ordained priests knelt on the altar. Above them a huge candle burned. He watched it abstractedly. To the right of him a novice was telling his beads with trembling fingers. The man looked at him. He was about twenty-six with fair hair and green-grey eyes that darted nervously about the chapel. They caught each other's eye and the elder glanced quickly at the altar candle as if to draw attention to it. The man followed his eye and as he looked he felt his scalp creep and tingle. The same unsummoned instinct filled him that had frightened him half an hour ago on the bank. His breath came quicker. How hot the chapel was. It was too hot; and the candle was wrong — wrong — everything suddenly blurred. The man on his left caught him.

"Hold up," he whispered, "they'll postpone you. Are you better? Can you go through with it?"

He nodded vaguely and turned to the candle. Yes, there was no mistake. Something was there, something played in the tiny flame, curled in the minute wreath of smoke. Some evil presence was in the chapel, on the very altar of God. He felt a chill creeping over him, though he knew the room was warm. His soul seemed paralyzed, but he kept his eyes riveted on the candle. He knew that he must watch it. There was no one else to do it. He must not take his eyes from it. The lines of novices rose and he mechanically reached his feet.

"Per omnia saecula, saeculorum. Amen."

Then he felt suddenly that something corporeal was missing — his last earthly support. He realized what it was. The man on his left had gone out overwrought and shaken. Then it began. Something before had attacked the roots of his faith; had matched his world-sense against his God-sense, had brought, he had thought, every power to bear against him; but this was different. Nothing was denied, nothing was offered. It could best be described by saying that a great weight seemed to press down upon his innermost soul, a weight that had no essence, mental or physical. A whole spiritual realm evil in its every expression engulfed him. He could not think, he could not pray. As in a dream he heard the voices of the men beside him singing, but they were far away, farther away from him than anything had ever been before. He existed on a plane where there was no prayer, no grace; where he realized only that the forces around him were of hell and where the single candle contained the essence of evil. He felt himself alone pitted against an infinity of temptation. He could bring no parallel to it in his own experience or any other. One fact he knew: one man had succumbed to this weight and he must not — must not. He must look at the candle and look and look until the power that filled it and forced him into this plane died forever for him. It was now or not at all.

He seemed to have no body and even what he had thought was his innermost self was dead. It was something deeper that was he, something that he had never felt before. Then the forces gathered for one final attack. The way that the other novice had taken was open to him. He drew his breath quickly and waited and then the shock came. The eternity and infinity of all good seemed crushed, washed away in an eternity and infinity of evil. He seemed carried helplessly along, tossed this way and that — as in a black limitless ocean where there is no light and the waves grow larger and larger and the sky darker and darker. The waves were dashing him toward a chasm, a maelstrom everlastingly evil, and blindly, unseeingly, desperately he looked at the candle, looked at the flame which seemed like the one black star in the sky of despair. Then suddenly he became aware of a new presence. It seemed to come from the left, seemed consummated and expressed in warm, red tracery somewhere. Then he knew. It was the stained window of St. Francis Xavier. He gripped at it spiritually, clung to it and with aching heart called silently for God.

*"Tantum ergo Sacramentum
Veneremur cernui."*

The words of the hymn gathered strength like a triumphant paean of glory, the incense filled his brain, his very soul, a gate clanged somewhere and the candle on the altar went out.

"Ego vos absolvo a peccatis tuis in nomine patris, filii, spiritus sancti. Amen."

The file of novices started toward the altar. The stained lights from the windows mingled with the candle glow and the eucharist in its golden halo seemed to the man very mystical and sweet. It was very calm. The subdeacon held the book for him. He placed his right hand on it.

"In the name of the Father and the Son and of the Holy Ghost — "

---

4. "The Ordeal," *The Nassau Literary Magazine*, LXXI (June 1915), pp. 153-159. Fitzgerald is credited by name in the magazine. Reviewer Cortlandt Van Winkle conceded in *The Daily Princetonian* (June 9, 1915) that "the interior conflict of the novice is well portrayed" but suggested that Fitzgerald "devote more care to the niceties of speech...." The novice's wavering commitment to his religion is a projection of Fitzgerald's own wavering commitment. In his late teens, encouraged by two prominent Roman Catholics whom he greatly admired—Monsignor Cyril Sigorney Webster Fay, the model for Monsignor Darcy in *This Side of Paradise*, and writer Shane Leslie, whom he'd met through Fay — Fitzgerald sometimes spoke of joining the priesthood, with the goal of eventually becoming a priest-novelist. By the end of "The Ordeal," the novice has successfully fought off the temptations he's faced and committed himself fully to the Church. For this work of fiction, Fitzgerald has provided the outcome he presumably then believed to be right. In real life, however, his own interior conflict would be resolved differently. He would record 1917 as the year that he lost his faith.

Material from "The Ordeal" would be reworked and reused for the short story "Benediction," published by *The Smart Set* in 1920, and collected in *Flappers and Philosophers* later that same year. "Benediction" is listed on the Scribners advertisement for *Flappers and Philosophers*.

5

How They Head the Chapters

A. Detective Story.

Chapter I. The Affair at Brownwill.

Chap. II. In The Dark.

Chap. III. The Hound Hits The Trail.

Chap. IV. A Ray Of Light.

Chap. V. Fresh Developments.

Chap. VI. Gone!

Chap. VII. Caught!

Chap. VIII. Old Jacques Speaks.

Chap. IX. Solved!

B. Chobert Rambers Story.

Chap. I. Auction Bridge.

Chap. II. At Seabreeze

Chap. III. The Shooting Party.

Chap. IV. A Kiss in the Dark.

Chap. V. A Gentleman's Gentleman.

Chap. VI. Rector's.

Chap. VII. Champagne.

Chap. VIII. Arms And The Man.

C. Any Best Seller.

Chap. I. Third Avenue.

Chap. II. Fifth Avenue.

Chap. III. The Big Man With The Lame Head And The Little Girl With The Lame Back.

Chap. IV. A New Start.

Chap. V. Contentment.

Chap. VI. The Operation.

Chap. VII. "Guardian, I Can Walk."

Chap. VIII. The Little Girl And The Big House.

Chap. IX. "The Greatest Of These Is Charity."

---

5. "How They Head the Chapters," *The Princeton Tiger*, XXVI (September 1915), p. 10. Unsigned. Known to be by Fitzgerald because he preserved a clipping in his scrapbook. Fitzgerald offers mock chapter-headings for three types of books (the second — "A Chobert Rambers Story" — refers to author Robert Chambers, whose writing Fitzgerald would parody in the December 1916 *Nassau Lit*; see item number 16).

Fitzgerald may not have done well in most of his academic courses, but he did read a lot while a student at Princeton and took careful note of what he read as a way of teaching himself his craft as a writer. Books were of enormous importance to him — even if, as his friend John Peale Bishop would later recall, he liked to give the impression of having read much more than he actually had. Within the pages of *This Side of Paradise*, Fitzgerald manages to mention no fewer than 64 different books and 98 writers! Plenty of college students with far better academic records than Fitzgerald's would be hard-pressed to name so many books and writers.

6

A Cheer for Princeton

Glory, Glory to the Black and Orange,
It's the Tiger's turn to-day.
Glory, glory, it's the same old story
Soon as Princeton starts to play.
Eli, Eli, all your hopes are dead
For the Tiger's growling in his lair.
Don't you hear him?
You'll learn to fear him,
Try to face him if you dare.

Chorus:
Princeton, cheer for Princeton,
Raise your voices, loud and free
Strong and steady
Ever ready
For defeat or victory.
Princeton, cheer for Princeton,
Always sure to win renown,
So we'll raise our praise to Nassau
To the pride of the Tiger town.

6. "A Cheer for Princeton." Although this piece was not written for either *The Tiger* or *The Nassau Lit*, it has been included to give an idea of Fitzgerald's versatility. Fitzgerald's lyric, "A Cheer for Princeton," won a contest for best new football song. A front-page story in *The Daily Princetonian* (October 28, 1915), headlined "Mass Meeting To-Night to Practice New Song," advised students to bring their copies of the new song (available at *The Daily Princetonian* office) to a gathering at Alexander Hall where they would practice that song, along with established campus favorites like "Going Back to Nassau Hall." The suggestion in lines four and five of the chorus that students be ready for the team's "defeat or victory" is realistic enough, but also a bit unusual; cheers do not traditionally admit the possibility of defeat.

A more prominent story on that same *The Daily Princetonian* front page, incidentally, announced that the book for the new Triangle Show, *The Evil Eye*, had been written by Edmund Wilson Jr. and all of the lyrics had been composed by Fitzgerald, "who was responsible for many of the catchy lyrics in *Fie! Fie! Fi-Fi!*, last year's Triangle Club presentation." That Fitzgerald, a mere sophomore, was beating out upperclassmen in writing competitions, whether for a new football song or a whole Triangle show score, says a lot about his abilities.

We've reproduced, on the facing page, a portion of that October 28, 1915 *Daily Princetonian*.

H · Dei · Sub · Numine · Viget · 1876

THE·DAILY·PRINCETONIAN

VOL. XXXVIII. NO. 294 PRINCETON, N. J. THURSDAY, OCTOBER 28, 1915 PRICE THREE CENTS

SENIOR COUNCIL UNITES SCHOOLS COMMITTEES

Jndergraduate Schools and Publicity Committees Made One Consisting of 12 Men.

COMPETITION FOR JUNIORS WILL COMMENCE TO-MORROW

Dr. Finney and Mr. Pyne Elected to Succeed Themselves as Alumni Trustee Members of Council.

The Senior Council last night ratified a constitution which shall govern he activities of a committee created y combining the present Undergradu te Schools and Publicity Committees. The new committee is known as the Jndergraduate Schools Committee and as charge of all the publicity work one by the undergraduates for Princeton. This committee is divided nto two sub-committees one of which as charge of sending out all publications and literature to the schools, the other forming an entertainment ommittee to look after schoolboys while they are in Princeton at scholastic meets, etc. The former of these ub-committees consists of two Senors and one Junior, the entertainment sub-committee of five Seniors nd four Juniors, making the whole ommittee number twelve men.

Members of the publications subommittee are elected as a result of wo competitions, one held in the fall f each year for Juniors and the other the spring for Sophomores. As a esult of the Junior competition, one nan is taken on in February, and as a esult of the Sophomore competition ne man in May. Thus two men from ach class will be elected during their rst two years in college, and at the nd of their Junior year one of these hall be elected by the whole committee as Chairman for his Senior year. The Junior competition for the Class f 1917 will begin to-morrow, candiates being requested to report to J. . Stockton 1916 in Room 10, Nassau Hall at 7 to-night. On the entertainent sub-committee, four men are ected in the spring of Sophomore ear by the outgoing entertainment ub-committee, to take the place of e four graduating Seniors. A Sectary of the whole committee is elect- l from this sub-committee.

The Council also elected Dr. John . T. Finney '84 and Moses Taylor yne '77 to succeed themselves as lumni Trustee members of the Coun- l.

ARVARD VARSITY DEFEATS SCRUB 18-0 IN SCRIMMAGE

(Special to the PRINCETONIAN)

Cambridge, Mass., Oct. 27.—The cond day of the week's hard driving the University football team consted of a long strenuous scrimmage th the Scrub, resulting in an 18 to 0 ctory for the Varsity. The long nsational end running of Rollins, e powerful line plunging of Horeen and Enwright, the remarkable

PHILOSOPHICAL LECTURE BY PRES. HIBBEN TO-DAY

President Hibben will deliver this afternoon before the members of the Graduate School the fourth of his series of lectures on "Types of Philosophical Theory." To-day his subject will be, "Augustine, the Father of Christian Dogmatics." Under this head President Hibben will discuss the evolution of belief in St. Augustine's experience; his conception of God; his doctrine of personality; the relation of the will to reason; the freedom of the will and divine sovereignty. These lectures are given at 5 o'clock on Thursday afternoons in McCosh 46 and are open to the public.

MASS MEETING TO-NIGHT TO PRACTICE NEW SONG

"A Cheer for Princeton" Will Be Tried for First Time—P-rade Forms at 7.45.

A mass meeting to practice songs and cheers will be held in Alexander Hall to-night at 8 o'clock. A p-rade will form at the Cannon at 7.45. The new song, "A Cheer for Princeton," will be practiced and all men are expected to bring with them copies of this, "Going Back to Nassau Hall," and the list of Princeton songs, now being distributed in the PRINCETONIAN Office.

The words of the new song are:

"Glory, Glory to the Black and Orange,
It's the Tiger's turn to-day.
Glory, glory, it's the same old story
Soon as Princeton starts to play.
Eli, Eli, all your hopes are dead
For the Tiger's growling in his lair.
Don't you hear him?
You'll learn to fear him,
Try to face him if you dare.

CHORUS:

Princeton, cheer for Princeton,
Raise your voices, loud and free
Strong and steady
Ever ready
For defeat or victory.
Princeton, cheer for Princeton.
Always sure to win renown,
So we'll raise our praise to Nassau
To the pride of the Tiger town.

The first verse and chorus of "Going Back to Nassau Hall" are:

When the sons of Princeton gather
anywhere,
There's a place they think of, longing
to be there.
It's the one and only university, situated and celebrated in New Jersey.

CHORUS:

Going back, going back, going back
to Nassau Hall,
Going back, going back to the best
old place of all,
Going back, going back, from all
this earthly ball,
We'll clear the track as we go back,
Going back to Nassau Hall.

TRIANGLE CLUB WILL OFFER 'THE EVIL EYE'

This Year's Book Written by Edmund Wilson, Jr. 1916—Comedy In Two Acts.

TRIP THIS YEAR LONGEST EVER ARRANGED FOR CLUB

List of Bookings Announced Later—Music by Dickey 1917 and Guilbert 1919.

The Triangle Club announces that it will present this year a musical comedy in two acts, entitled "The Evil Eye." The trip to be taken this year is the longest ever arranged for the club. The list of bookings is now being completed and will be announced in a few days.

The book to be used this year was written by Edmund Wilson, Jr. 1916, and is full of clever dialogue. The lyrics have been composed by F. Scott Fitzgerald 1917, who was responsible for many of the catchy lyrics in "Fie! Fie! Fi-Fi!," last year's Triangle Club presentation. The music is by P. B. Dickey 1917 and F. Warburton Guilbert 1919.

Plot of "The Evil Eye."

The scene is laid in the little fishing village of Niaiserie, on the coast of Normandy. At the opening of the first act a shipwreck has just taken place. A girl is the lone survivor. When she recovers it is apparent that she is suffering from aphasia. The shock of the wreck has caused her to lose her memory completely. She has been rescued by Jacques Lonche, who besides being the richest and strongest man in the town, is the possessor of the worst reputation. The peasants believe that he has "the evil eye," for his glance is supposed to bring a curse. He is considered as a sort of superman, who is shunned by all men and who is lonely in his consciousness of superiority.

When the girl whom he has rescued falls in love with him, he believes that at last he is to be blessed with happiness. But this path is blocked by the schemes of the unscrupulous and the superstitions of the vulgar. The Mayor of Niaiserie, whom we may consider the most corrupt official in France, has determined that his daughter, Dulcinea, shall marry Jacques and thus bring into the possession of one family all the local wealth. However, Dulcinea is in love with Claude, an honest villager, who returns her affection. The Mayor then forms a plot with Count La Rochefoucauld Boileau, a disreputable travelling salesman, who peddles perfumery. Boileau agrees to pretend that

(Continued on Fourth Page)

GUN CLUB HOLDS ANNUAL HANDICAP SHOOT TO-DAY

Silver Cup Awarded Winner—Only Club Members May Enter—List of Handicaps.

The annual handicap gun shoot will take place this afternoon over the

FURTHER APPOINTMENTS FOR 1916 HERALD PICTURES

The following Seniors are scheduled to report at White's Studio to-day and make appointments to have their pictures taken for the Nassau Herald: Muirhead, Murdock, Nebeker, Neely, Neuberg, Nichols, Nietzky, Niles, O'Brien-Moore, Ohliger, O'Kane, Osborn, Osmun, Otis, Payne, Payson, Peacock, Pemberton, Perlman, Phelps, Phraner, Pitcairn, Potts, Raymond, Reed, Reynolds, Rhoads, Richardson, Riedel, Ritchey, Ritter, Roberts, Robinson, H. R., Robinson, J. N., Robinson, S. S., Rockey, Rukeyser, Russell, Schwabacher, Scudder, M., Scudder, N. W., Selby, Sellers, Seymour, Shanley, Sharp, Sheets, Shepherd, Shipman.

SECOND VARSITY HAS EASY TIME WITH FRESHMAN TEAM

Georgi and Lamarche Most Reliable Men for 1919, Making Good Interference—Freshman Play Ragged.

The Freshmen were lined up against the Second Varsity for about half an hour's scrimmage in the Stadium yesterday, and, except in a few instances their play was very ragged. Their best exhibition was on the offensive several first downs being made by straight rushing. Lamarche showed considerable ability at open field running, getting away once for twenty yards on a fake formation. Georgi was the most reliable line plunger, and also made some good interference, a lost art to the other men.

Walton, who had been playing a good game at quarter, was injured early in the scrimmage, and had to withdraw from the game. He may not be in shape to play Exeter Saturday, which will be a loss to the team.

The Second Varsity when given the ball tore through the Freshman line for long gains, Law finally carrying it over for a touchdown. Later, after another steady advance they scored again. Thomas figured prominently in many of the long gains.

Later the Second Varsity was allowed to try drop kicks and forward passes with the ball on the Freshmen's 20-yard line. Several touchdowns were scored in this manner. When the Freshmen were given the ball in a like position they also scored.

1919—Winn, le; Saville, lt; Finney, lg; Funk, c; Proudfit, rg; Kirkland, rt; Moore, re; Walton, qb; Lamarche, lhb; Cleveland, fb; Georgi, rhb.

Second Varsity—Moore, le; Love, lt; Heyniger, lg; Gowen, c; Parisette, rg; Kauffmann, rt; Wilson, re; Ames, qb; Thomas, lhb; Law, fb; Haas, rhb.

SECRET PRACTICE UNTIL LATE FOR WILLIAMS SQUAD

(Special to the PRINCETONIAN)

Williamstown, Mass., Oct. 27.—In preparation for the Princeton game on Saturday the Williams football squad put in one of the hardest day's work of the season this afternoon. Practice was held behind barred gates, not

VARSITY SHOWS FIRST REAL OFFENSIVE POWER

Charge of Line And Backs More Closely Unified—Still Room For Improvement.

LAMBERTON GIVEN TRIAL AT END ON FIRST TEAM

Thomas Taken on Training Table—Secret Practice After Scrimmage By Starlight.

Practice to-day will start at 3 at the University Field, and will be secret until the men go over to the Stadium at 4 or a little after. There will be scrimmage at 4.30.

It looked as if the Varsity had begun to solve the mystery of a running attack yesterday, when, after a long preliminary signal drill, consistent gains were made through the Scrub in a short scrimmage. Not only did the line open up better holes, but the backs took advantage of them, and there was considerable more smoothness in the charge. The team for the first time began to act as a unit, the men getting under way more nearly at the same time. There were occasional slumps, but at least there was evidence of the germ of a concerted offense. If this start does not lose impetus, but continues to increase, by the time the Harvard game has arrived Princeton may be able to put on the field a real scoring machine. That ideal is still far distant, however.

Lamberton Better at End.

Lamberton was moved to his old position at end yesterday and given a tryout on the Varsity. He seemed more at home there, and was particularly aggressive on the defensive, getting into nearly every play. He has always been about the fiercest tackler on the squad, and it seems likely that he will push Brown to hold his position for the remainder of the season. He is not quite as fast as Brown in covering punts, and this may count heavily against him.

McLean was the only regular not in the scrimmage. Both he and Eddy were dressed, however, and were given light work. Semmens ran through signals with the Second Varsity and appears to be getting into fair shape. In the scrimmage between the Second Varsity and the Freshmen, Thomas showed up so well that Coach Rush has decided to take him on the training table. If he continues to play the way he has, he will probably be given a chance in Saturday's game.

Excels In Line-Plunging.

Only at the beginning of this week when he was moved from the line to the backfield, did the coaches realize that they had made something of a "find." His strong point is line-plunging, he being apparently endowed with unusual powers of equilibrium, for when he gets started, it always takes a number of men to drag him to earth. He gets away fast, hits the

THE CONQUEST OF AMERICA

(AS SOME WRITERS WOULD HAVE IT)

(MR. Fitzcheesecake, who has written this article, needs no introduction. He has held numerous official positions: he was on three different beats in Trenton, and was for one year Deputy Garbage Man of Bordentown; and we feel that what he writes will be authoritative.) — The Editors.

The American Atlantic fleet has been sunk. The Germans were coming in three thousand transports and were about to land in New York. Admiral Von Noseitch was swimming across with the fleet. Pandemonium reigned in the great city, women and tenors were running frantically up and down their rooms, the men having all left; the police force also, fearing to be called to the colors, had been in Canada for two months. Who was to raise and equip a vast army? The New York Baseball Team had finished in the second division, so Mgr. McGraw gave up all hope and volunteered; the new army, for secrecy, used a subway car to drill in. No help could be had from Boston, for they had won the pennant, and there was nothing on the front pages of the papers to warn the people of the imminent danger. General McGraw intrenched himself in the middle of Brooklyn for, so he thought, not even a German would go there. He was right, but three stray cannon balls came his way and he struck out. The Statute of Liberty had been invested, New York's six million people were all captured; the Germans were upon them before preparation could be ac-

complished. Generals Von Limburger, Munchener, and Frankfurter held a consultation in Busty's the first night: General Von Limburger was going to attack General Bryan and his army of the Raritan in New Jersey; General Frankfurter was going to take a Day-Line boat to Albany and thence to Canada, where three-fourths of the citizens of the U.S. capable of bearing arms had fled for a much-needed rest; while General Munchener with thirty picked men would hold New York. Gen. Von Limburger took the 7 p.m. train to Princeton, near which place Bryan was reported to have fled. Meanwhile all the United States had been captured, save this section of New Jersey. The Pacific Squadron, however, was intact; they had been taken for fishing boats and had escaped without any injury. The besieging army was fast approaching the city; preceptors could be seen running madly to and fro, mostly fro. Bryan drew up his army in the "*Tiger*" Office; they voted five votes to one not to let a German live.

It was February. Glory Be! And meant all fortune to the United States! The Germans advanced. They were held up at Rocky Hill. They readvance; they column right around the old mill; they pass the Prep; they leave the outskirts far behind. They cluster round the Chem. Lab. and then — Bei Reichstag, was ist? The Polar's Recess and the poisonous gases of the Lab hit that vast army at one fell swoop! Long had it been since they had heard the sound of guns and the shock of Polar's Recess made them sore afraid. Some fled to the Nass. It was closed. Some rushed to Joe's. The promise of a small check cashed was too much for them. Some dove toward the Jigger Shop where a raspberry marshmallow nut marangue laid a hundred more beside their graves. Some sank upon the benches on Nassau Street. Both collapsed, each under the strain of seeing the other. Some tried to p-rade around the Cannon, but the prestige of Whig and Clio drove them off to Penn's Neck. And the one man left cried out, "I'm Gish — I touched the Cannon." Bryan's army rushed out of *The Tiger* Office and struck him with the point of a joke — a joke preserved for these many years. America was saved, saved, SAVED, yes — saved by the point of a joke. YE GODS!

7. "The Conquest of America," *The Princeton Tiger*, XXVI (Thanksgiving 1915), p. 6. Unsigned. Fitzgerald did not preserve a clipping in his scrapbook, but the article's whimsical statement that it had been written by one "Mr. Fitzcheescake" would seem to point to Fitzgerald as having been its author. And the style appears consistent with that of other pieces from this period that are known to be his. Incidentally, the word "p-rade," which appears in the final paragraph, is not a typo; it is a Princeton-related term for parade.

Three Days at Yale

(Here follows the appendix of "Ten Days at Princeton," as published
in the Princeton game number of the Yale Record.)

Being an account of the period surrounding the game of November 13th, 1915.

Fred was a Princeton Student. He was a Typical Type and strange to New Haven. He was a gentleman through and through and wanted to See the World. It was his fourth year at Princeton and he inkled that he had a Little Dope on College Life. Still, he wanted to see Yale.

He was big and strong. Six feet and 189 lbs. He had Seen Life, having been brought up amid the Sawdust of the Circus Tent. Nevertheless he had Made Good and overcome the infirmities of his Youth. He was a perfect man to send to gather dope at New Haven.

He left Princeton amid the cheers of the College and the Well-Wishes of even the Qualifying Seminoles. He stopped at New York and Looked the Boys Over at the Martineque, and asked at the Information Bureau at the Grand Central where the Train for New Haven was. They shipped him northwards with a Suit-Case and a package of Seven Point Gum.

THURSDAY — THE FIRST DAY

He arrived at New Haven on the Thursday before the Princeton game. It cost him $6.81 to ask a taxi driver how to get to The Bowl. He decided to walk. The fifth Moving Picture House in succession was Too Much for him; so he flipped a dime to a Newsy for a pass to the Show. A passing Eli took the dime from the kid — the latter didn't care — he was Used to It. He would sell the Eli a New Haven paper for a Quarter instead of Fifteen Cents.

Fred walked on and at the Yale Station introduced himself to a Distinguished-Looking Man. "Professor," said he, "how do you get to Know the Boys here?" "Sir," said the D.L.M., "You insult me! I am the Janitor of Vanderbilt Hall! Professor! As if I'd chew a *pencil*!" whereupon he spat tobacco juice through five gold front teeth. Fred looked on in Awe. He crossed the street and under a Portcullis Effect. Before him was the Yale Fence. He recognized it was a fence by its similarity to the picture in his childhood Mother Goose. He Eased Over and sat down. A Senior, Capless and of frost-bitten ear, but still Capless, hastened by with a look of Chagrin on his face. A second student whispered that no one ever sat on any Part of the Fence except on the Part which was at Pach's Studio. Fred apologized, and said that he hadn't realized before that his informer was a Sophomore. But he said he Did Appreciate the Advice and would Bear it in Mind for the Future. He Wiled Away the Afternoon between Savin Rock, the Dental School and the Hyp. — also between two and five. The Yale Students had started for the Big Bowl, to cheer the Big Team. Tom Shevlin had Told Them to Be There, and Nothing Else Mattered. Several hundred, however, never got past the Taft, for there was a Tea Dance there in honor of the Leading Vaudeville Actress of the Evening. Fred passed within a mile of the Bowl and heard three swear words and a cuss. He knew the boys were being Coached in Practice. He left, blushing to think that his mother's waitress was to see the Game on Saturday.

Thursday evening he began to Look Up the Boys to try to lay a Small Wager on the Game. He found a Big, Hulking, Brute-Faced Youth standing on the corner of Church and Chapel Streets watching a bewhiskered individual switch car tracks. "Sir," said he, "how about a Bet on the Game?" The Eli Looked Him Over, spotted his stick pin, and nodded "Come On." They adjourned to the Heublein. The Tender rushed up — "Dark," said the Visitor. "Give me," tenored the Eli, "a cup of warm bouillon and a Nabisco." "Hell," gurgled Fred, "You must be a Shef Man," whereupon friendship was restored and the Bet Question began.

"What's the Dope on the Game, doc?" Our Hero said. "Well, let's see," chirped the Eli, drawing out a wallet stuffed to bursting with Green and Yellow Backed Bills. He Fingered them Over carelessly, and then drawing out one, said, "I'm a Sport — I'll bet you a Dollar to your Ten." "What!" gurgled Our Hero. "You bet 1 to 10? How so?" "Yes, of course. You see our chances are twice as good as Princeton's so Princeton must give us 10 to 1 odds. Simple?" "Um-m-m, I suppose so. But still, Logically Deep, you Must Admit." "I'll Admit Nothing — not even that our Head Coach has lost even his head itself!" muttered the Eli. "If you won't bet at my odds, you-you-you *Princetonian*, you can go hungry — That's all!" and he gormandized his Nabisco in his Fury.

Fred couldn't Stand It so he sank behind a table and spent the night amid the Sawdust of his Youth. Fond Memories! The only Homelike thing he'd found during his First Day at New Haven.

FRIDAY — THE SECOND DAY

Friday morning he Eased to the University Offices. He wanted to see the Cut System. Instead he found the Office in a Turmoil. One of Yale's Most Famous Athletes had been found to be Ineligible, and a Big Event was to come that afternoon. Something had to be done and Done

Quickly. The Committee was meeting to Discuss the Question. Fred introduced himself, said he was from Princeton and they Invited him to Attend the Meeting. "Just stand in this corner, disguise yourself as a thermometer and keep cool," was his welcome to the gathering.

"Ready Gentlemen?" asked the Spokesman. "Officer, introduce Mr. Ton."

"Ah, Mr. Ton, Pray Come In — Have a Cigar? And may I Light It? We understand that your presence on the Team is Necessary to Win this Event. The Advertising Value of the College will suffer by your absence and Yale's defeat. Consequently we Deem it Necessary that you be Made Eligible. You will listen to the following Cross Examination and any point that does Not Meet with your Approval, you will Call to my Attention. Officer! Call the Janitor of Mr. Ton's Suite."

"You are Mr. Ton's Janitor?" "Yes, Sir."

"You enter his room daily?" "Yes, Sir."

"He has in it a study-Desk?" "Yes, Sir."

"Books on the desk?" "Yes, Sir."

"Also Pencils," interrupts Mr. Ton, "Quite write, sir, quite write." (Continuing to Janitor) "He has been in before 1 a.m. at least 3 times this month?"

"Certainly, Sir! 3 Times! Certainly, Sir! He was Indisposed at least 3 times, Sir."

"You often find papers in his Waste Basket?" "Yes indeed, Sir."

"Well, Gentlemen, it Seems To Me conclusive in the Face of this Scholastic Evidence that we Owe Mr. Ton an Apology for even thinking him Ineligible. You are excused, sir, and we Expect you to Win — Should you not win, you may at once be Declared Ineligible. Good Day, Sir."

Fred's Mercury, as a thermometer, sank 50 points and he fell through the fire escape. "Good Lord and Shades of our Charlie! What would Bill Koons say!"

That Knock-out Drop Laid him Cold for the remainder of the day. He rested against the Old Flag Pole but for some reason or other could not sleep. Toward evening the Strains of Music reminded him that he had a ticket to the Concert. A Taxi Driver charged him $1.50 to get to Woolsey Hall. He dozed through the strains of Banjo

Twanging and Mandolin-ing, until he awoke to the Key-note of Old Nassau. He Jumped to his Feet and the sight that greeted him nearly killed his Lovéd Life. Not an Eli rose as his Song was sung. The Sea of Heads remained beneath him. The few Princetonians present waved their salute to their Alma Mater. They remained on their feet through two songs, but it was not until the Latter Event that the Audience Rose. Fred was cut. Some Things he could Expect, but Such a Sight — Ah, Me! He turned to his Eli Neighbor, "How comes it, Sir, that you do not Politely Honor Us?" "Sir, I do not Understand!" "Why Princeton, Harvard, Dartmouth and Every Other College always rise to the tune of the other's Alma Mater Song. And Yale?"

"Oh, My Dear Man — Yale is like a Cigarette — Distinctly Individual, you know. How can you ask Such a Question? Why we Take It For Granted that All the World knows of Eli's Methods!"

Fred Gurgled Good-Bye and 'phoned for a bed at the Taft.

SATURDAY — THE THIRD DAY

He awoke on Saturday. His Third Day at New Haven. How he longed for home! Still to-day he would see his friends at least. He slept 'til 7 o'clock. He Spent the Morning with the Old Gang. About one, they Eased to the Bowl. Along the road came three Big Grey Automobiles. "Oh, Our Team," called the Princeton Gang. But, No! Un-

familiar faces all, except for having been Seen in the Papers. "Our boys must follow. No. Not a sight on the Street but two Slatted Beer Wagons." "Where are they?" called Fred. "What? What seest we? Ye Gods, there's Nassau's Team inside on benches, while Eli's rose in Steam Heated Autos." He grabbed a Student, "How come it is that we ride in slatted beer wagons in this cold weather?"

"Ah, Sir, Princeton Athletes are Strong and Husky. Air is Good for Them and Springless Wagons jounce away their Nervousness. We have given you what we thought you'd like best of what remained when we were settled. Can you ask for More?" Fred said nothing, but they threw their Informer across a pile of discarded Yale Arm Bands.

"Enter Gate A" — "Quite so, But what is this? A seat for Visitors before the Sun? Why Nassau and John Harvard give the Shady side to Visitors, but Yale? Oh, that's it! You let us have the Sun to Warm Our Bodies! No need to show interest in the Game — quite right, sir, quite right. The Newspapers will give us the Story of it later."

The Game? Well, Princeton's Hopes were Shattered and Yale came out On Top. But Fred expected Nothing after his two previous days. He Left for Home a Saddened and Embittered Student, in full realization of the Truth of the Saying, "For God, for Country, and *for* Yale."

---

8. "Three Days at Yale," *The Princeton Tiger*, XXVI (December 1915), pp. 8-10. Unsigned. Fitzgerald did not preserve a clipping in his scrapbook, but Landon T. Raymond '17 wrote Matthew Bruccoli that Alan Jackman '17, who illustrated this piece, had told him it was "conceived" by Fitzgerald.

Fitzgerald always maintained a considerable fondness for Yale as well as for Princeton. Many of Fitzgerald's literary characters, through the years, were educated at Yale (or "New Haven," as he often referred to it, using the parlance of the time). In a letter Fitzgerald wrote to Princeton's president, John Grier Hibben (June

3, 1920), he proclaimed that he loved Princeton "better than any place on earth," adding curiously: "The men — the undergraduates of Yale and Princeton — are cleaner, healthier, better-looking, better dressed, wealthier, and more attractive than any undergraduate body in the country." In his December 1927 *College Humor* article, "Princeton," Fitzgerald left no doubt about his primary attachment to his alma mater, but observed: "There was a gloss upon Yale that Princeton lacked; Princeton's flannels hadn't been pressed for a week, its hair always blew a little in the wind. Nothing was ever carried through at Princeton with the same perfection as the Yale Junior Prom or the elections to their senior societies." He added that Princetonians tended to have a "scoffing and mildly ironic attitude toward Yale." Harvard barely seemed to figure in Fitzgerald's consciousness.

Academic difficulties forced Fitzgerald to drop out of Princeton in December of 1915, the month that this piece was published; he did not return until the start of the next school year, in September of 1916. Being out of Princeton apparently did not stop him from writing for *The Tiger* and *The Nassau Lit*, though.

Our Society Column

Delightful Debut.

In the magnificent home of Mrs. C. Brussels Sprouts a delightful coming out took place. Mr. and Mrs. Sprouts presented their daughter Miss Limabeana Sprouts. The rooms were lit up with electric lights and here and there a chair was placed making a very tasteful setting. Wallpaper, tables, and pictures, were on all sides; and no one could have mistaken the place for a barn. The hall was profusely decorated in asparagus and mushrooms, whose harmony no one doubts who has any taste at all. Miss Sprouts came out in a gown of yellow chartreuse beautifully garnished with whipped cream and every here and there a little pretzel. About her neck was a string of Heinz pickles which set off her gown. The skirt was draped over a petticoat of blue mayonnaise, which in turn was draped over pink Porosknit. Fish net hung down from each sleeve, which trailed gracefully in her soup and ice cream. She carried an armful of fresh rhubarb and onions which added a delightful fragrance to the room. There were panniers, seams, bodices, fronts and backs to her dress, all neatly garnished. The sister of the debutante, Miss Oatmeala Sprouts, was there; she wore a brown crepe-de-cheesecloth covered with rabbit fur and dogwood. The hem-stitching on her gown was of blue horsehair. Her skirt reached the floor. Miss Oatmeala very gracefully carried a basket of eggs. In the music room was the piano upon which was a vase of wild Spinach and many scratches which were charmingly covered over with a doily. Assisting Mrs. Sprouts were: Mrs. Hamm, Mrs. Eggs, Mrs. Buttered Toast, and Mrs. H.O.T. Coffee, a very congenial group. Mrs. Sprouts showed good taste in the choice of her assistants. The favors of the dance that followed were, for the men, nickel boucoumieres; for the ladies, leather boucoumieres.

For College Senior.

Through a veritable bower of pink alfalfa and cordwood, a moon peeped, and shed its silvan glow on the gay party given by Mrs. Nutmeg for her son Horace, a college senior, at the Country Club. The large room was draped with sprigs of sweetbreads set against a background of yellow Fleur de L'Onion tapestry. The pillars were dressed up to represent golf sticks, which looked nearly lifelike. The honored son was dressed in a suit of the "House of Highbinder" around which a purple braid ran intermittently. A collar around his neck was graced in front by a necktie, below which fell his shirt in undulating folds. His full dress coat was terminated by two tails in the rear. He wore a pair of pants to match his coat; these nearly reached to his feet, by means of which he stood on the floor. He carried a bunch of purple daisies and forget-me-nots. The musicians were seated on chairs in the balcony, each carrying in his arms some musical instrument. Among the honored guests were: Miss Cheesa Limberger, Miss Sophy Cushion, Miss Lovva de Menn, Mr. O. So Simple, Mr. R. Applepie Crust and many others.

AT THE FIELD CLUB.

The fashionable set were entertained at the Field Club Friday evening by Mr. and Mrs. U.C.I. Havmoney. All about the club were silver dollars and quarters which looked well at first until most of the decorations disappeared mysteriously. It is rumored that some art lover was taken with the decorations and took them. Mrs. Coynlover looked charming in a slim yellow frock of Orange Canvas and Damaskene, covered with blue zweibach and mucilage. Two prune skins made a beautiful set of furs for her. A dainty baked apple of point lace was trimmed on her hat. Miss Iamina Highset came out in cerise crepe-de-leather with a salmon brocade of moleskins, each bearing her crest of crossed sausages (her father, the late Mr. I. Wanta B. Highset, had made his money in the hog business). Her skirt was a simple affair with seven pleats in the front and nineteen down the back, on each pleat hung little bells which tinkled prettily when the fair Iamina walked. Mrs. B. Rich wore a girdle of blue tulle flounced with black paillettes, a Faille skirt of shredded wheat completed her costume. Embroidered velours tailleurs de Grapefruit was the striking feature of the waste of Mrs. I.B. Snobbish. Many more distingué gowns were seen.

MISS CHEESE ENGAGED.

The engagement of Miss Roqueforta Cheese, daughter of Mr. and Mrs. B. Camembert Cheese of Main Street to Mr. Raisin Pie, which was announced yesterday, came as a surprise to their many friends. Mr. Pie and Miss Cheese have always gone together.

CHARMING DINNER.

A charming dinner was given by Mrs. Omelet at her home on Beauchamp Terrace. The menu comprised: Bouillon au simplon, Roast Horse a l'Indien, Snail Fritters, Pie de Lingerie, and Postum noir. After the dinner the guests withdrew to a nearby dairy lunch and partook of nourishment.

BRIDGE PARTY.

At a bridge party given for Mrs. Olive Oil of Bordentown at the home of Mrs. H. Chestnut, the house was decorated in blue and white armadillos and trailing hyenas. Nickel ante prevailed and Mrs. Suspenders won $19.45.

BIRTHDAY CELEBRATION.

Yesterday was the first birthday of Ralph Potato, son of Mr. and Mrs. Potato. Ralph's eyes are not opened as yet so he couldn't enjoy the nine rattles and the silver spoon he received from his kind friends.

9. "Our Society Column," *The Princeton Tiger*, XXVI (February 1916), p. 6. (Possible attribution.) Unsigned. Fitzgerald did not preserve a clipping in his scrapbook, but John McMaster '19, a *Tiger* editor, suggested to Matthew Bruccoli that this piece may have been by Fitzgerald. No other sources have suggested this piece might be by Fitzgerald. In the interests of being complete, we have included this piece and four others of equally questionable attribution so that readers may examine them and perhaps form their own opinions as to whether they sound like Fitzgerald.

The
April Tiger

FC '19

48

What Happened to Susie

A Tale of the Fifth Avenue Slums.

Synopsis of preceding chapters. — Susie Sniffles, a young lady of uncertain age, is engaged to Peter Q. Dustpruf, a millionaire street peddler. Susie's father, a reformed clergyman, opposes the marriage, preferring Quentin Filmstar, a moving picture hero, as a future son-in-law. Susie becomes melancholy and shoots herself. Her father is very much embarrassed and accordingly calls a doctor, who unfortunately brings her back to life. Immediately upon her recovery, Susie sits up in bed and whispers mysteriously in the doctor's ear, "Beware the Topaz Toothbrush." No sooner has she said this than the doctor faints. The next day Susie is strangely missing.

CHAPTER XVCL.

"Haha, haha, haha," Filmstar chuckled, carelessly flicking the ashes from his pipe and carefully adjusting his alabaster monocle.

"So it's you, is it?" rejoined Dustpruf, brushing his coat-tails and pompously pulling down his fur vest.

A smile of triumph passed over the star's face as he leaned over the rail and intently watched the sharks playfully fletcherizing the sailors which he tossed to them from time to time.

"Yes, it's I," was the abusive retort.

The brutal brutalness of this reply was a severe blow to Dustpruf, who submissively bowed his head and solemnly plucked a rose, as verdant as the driven snow, from a nearby plum tree.

"Come," he said, attempting to speak easily, altho his voice wavered from side to side, "Tell me where, O, where is my beloved Susie?"

"Never, never," the movie actor laughed back haughtily and heartlessly spurring his impatient charger he rode recklessly along the boulevard.

Dustpruf sank to the ground and pondered there for days in deep thought. What deception this world held in store for him! What hatred was about him on every hand! Ye Gods! Could he endure it until the end of the novel? But he must find Susie — yes, that was his job — he must find Susie.

The author would never forgive him if he did not find Susie.

Suddenly a hand was laid on his head which raised his aloft by the hair. He turned his great fathomless red eyes upward and beheld a vision draped in black which clung and clung and clung—

"What's the matter?" inquired the new arrival, her jet black hair falling down her back like a leaping torrent of gleaming cascades.

Dustpruf sprang to his feet and abruptly ringing the elevator bell, sprang in as if mad, pulling the woman in after him.

"Tell me now," he murmured hoarsely, when he had chloroformed the elevator boy after hours of silent struggle, "Have you seen her?"

"Hush!" replied the woman in black, laying her fingers on her lips as a token of warning, and brushing back her veil. "Do you not know your long lost Susie?"

Dustpruf reeled — then righted himself once more. "My own — my Susie — one fond embrace," and then — "Dear Susie, there is something about you — " He paused, and her sweet mellow tones cooed forth, "And I, Peter, I am completely wrapped up in you."

The queer old moon smiled down and whispered, "Slush."

10. "What Happened to Susie," *The Princeton Tiger*, XXVI (February 1916), p. 15. (Possible attribution.) Unsigned. Fitzgerald did not preserve a clipping in his scrapbook, but John McMaster suggested to Matthew Bruccoli that this piece may have been by Fitzgerald.

11

The Awful Optic

A Spasm in Two Fits.

Personae Non Gratae

Frank, the lighthouse keeper.

John Aquint, *alias* the Bronze Duke, our hero.

Comte Jean Pierre Mouchlein de Veuve Cliquot, salesman of intoxicating perfumes.

Merlin from Berlin, defective.

Sardiniers and Sardinieres, a mayor and a mysterious mermaid.

Premier Fit

(The curtain rises revealing to the eyes of the anxious audience — nothing; utter darkness accompanied by orchestra. When the applause has died down the chorus sings out, fearlessly secure in the fact that it is hard to hit them in the dark. By accident the scene is lit up, revealing Lingerie, a little Norman Sardinery. There is a pile of sardines on one corner, a vat of olive oil in another. Sardiniers are scattered about with here and there a Sardiniere.)

Enter Frank, C.E. (wildly waving one arm and both legs in his excitement).

Frank — Mon Dieu! *(louder)* Mon Dieu!! *(still louder)* Mon Dieu!!!

Sardiniers and Sardinieres *(looking up in surprise at his vociferous remarks)* — S'matter, Frank?

Frank — Do you know John Squint? Well, there's something crooked about him.

Sardiniers and -ieres — What?

Frank — He's cross-eyed.

Everybody — Cross-eyed!

Frank — Yep; we was a-lookin' at a barrell in front o' the lighthouse, when all of a sudden he ran down the beach and pulled out a mermaid. *(At this horrifying announcement two the Sardinieres faint and fall into a vat of olive oil. The others group themselves around the edge and sing, "We eat the fishes what we can and what we can't we can.")*

Enter John Squint, C.O.D. (a sack of potatoes over his shoulder). He glares cross-eyed at the company two at a time, throws his sack of potatoes at the door of the town liquifrectory and sings, "One-a-penny, two-a-penny, Sweet po-ta-toes!"

John Squint — How do you like it, people?

Everybody — Put him in jail.

Exit John Squint (lock-step with himself). Curtain.

Fit Two

(The curtain rises in the opposite direction to which it fell, revealing the stage.)

Enter the Mayor, M.I.K. (knock-kneed, smoking a Pittsburgh Perfecto).

Mayor — Times is hard, I wish I had a Canadian sesterce.

Enter Comte de Veuve Cliquot, S.O.S. (dressed in a suit of Louis Kaplin specials, high hat and cut-a-way to match. A green tie and a purple shirt serve to fill in the gaps. He trips lightly over the sardines to the centre of the stage.)

Comte — Ah, Monsieur, I am ravished to see your extravagant countenance so delightfully illuminated *(taking a watering can out from under his hat and putting out the mayor's cigar).* If the esteemed Monsieur will be kind enough to hold his face still a minute while I talk to it, I will tell him of a great discovery. The contents of this can are guaranteed to combine with distasteful odors in producing an atmosphere rivaled only by that of heaven itself. My dear Monsieur, if I were to pour some on yon pile of fish, you would imagine yourself in Brooklyn. In short, I ask you to purchase some of my superb perfume for your Lingerie.

Mayor — *(slightly perturbed)* — How about a rake-off?

Comte — Sure, sixty per cent.

Enter Merlin from Berlin, P.D.Q. (Song, "The Defective Detective!")

Merlin — Gentlemen, I can do everything. I wave my wand, presto, your jigger becomes a martini. Everybody — Sit right down and stay.

Mayor — Prove it by getting John Squint out of jail.

Merlin — Sure *(he waves his wand).*

Enter John Squint, D.D.

Comte — Hey, make me a milliner. (Song. "The Millionaire Milliner.")

Merlin — Sure *(he again waves his wand).*

Exit Comte, V.C.

John Squint — Get me a wife.

Merlin — Sure *(he waves his wand and in flounders the mysterious mermaid, Q.E.D. John seizes her in his arms and they sing, "What is Love Among Fish?" Everybody makes believe the play is over. When the people in the audience start to leave they go on with the play till exhaustion causes everything to drop, including the curtain.)*

The Glory of the Sun.

11. "The Awful Optic," *The Princeton Tiger*, XXVI (March 1916), p. 7. (Possible attribution.) Unsigned. Fitzgerald did not preserve a clipping in his scrapbook, but John McMaster suggested to Matthew Bruccoli that this piece may have been by Fitzgerald.

"The Awful Optic" spoofs the latest Triangle Club musical comedy, *The Evil Eye* (for which Fitzgerald had supplied the lyrics). For example, instead of the character "Harris from Paris, detective" found in *The Evil Eye*, "The Awful Optic" features one "Merlin from Ber-

lin, defective." For supporting evidence that Fitzgerald was willing to parody projects in which he was involved, compare this spoof of the 1915-16 Triangle production with "Precaution Primarily" (which ran in the February 3, 1917 *Tiger* and is definitely by Fitzgerald; see item number 33), a spoof of the following year's Triangle production, *Safety First*.

On the facing page, we see a Triangle artist's impressions of *The Evil Eye*.

12

Yais

Wouldn't it be nais
to sit on a dais
with Thais.

12. "Yais," *The Princeton Tiger*, XXVII (June 1916), p. 13. Unsigned. Fitzgerald did not preserve a clipping in his scrapbook, but John McMaster remembered this item (for which he himself supplied the title) as definitely having been written by Fitzgerald.

JUNE · · · 1916
THE · TIGER

54

13

TO MY UNUSED GREEK BOOK

(ACKNOWLEDGMENTS TO KEATS)

Thou still unravished bride of quietness,
Thou joyless harbinger of future fear,
Garrulous alien, what thou mightst express
Will never fall, please God, upon my ear.
What rhyme or reason can invest thy shape
That is not found in countless syllibi?
What trots and cribs there are, what ponies rich,
With all thou sing'st and in a clearer key.
Expose thee to a classroom's savage rape?
Nay! better far remain within thy niche.

Tasks all complete are sweet, but those untried
Are sweeter, therefore little book, with page
Uncut, stay pure, and live thy life inside,
And wait for some appreciative age.
Oh, Author, most admired and left alone,

Thou cans't not ever see the garish day.
Editor, never, never wilt thou speak,
But yellow grow and petrify to stone
Where I shall throw thee after tests next week;
Yet grieve not — ever thou'lt have much to say.

Oh happy, happy, leaves that cannot shed
Their ink, or ever bid the print adieu;
Oh happy, happy, bard who never bled
At verse of his droned out with meaning new.
No words are penciled in a barbarous tongue
Above thy dactyls oft misunderstood;
Caesuras are not marked to shame thy taste;
Thy song is as you sing it, though unsung.
If not of use at least thou'rt noble waste;
Let stand thy native accent as it should.

— F. Scott Fitzgerald

---

13. "To My Unused Greek Book (Acknowledgments to Keats)," *The Nassau Literary Magazine*, LXXII (June 1916), p. 137. Fitzgerald is credited by name in the magazine. This poem uses the ABABCDEDCE pattern of Keats' "Ode on a Grecian Urn." Fitzgerald had enormous admiration for Keats; the rhythms and imagery of Keats' poetry influenced not just Fitzgerald's own poetry but also his prose. He once remarked (in a letter in the Princeton Library, written circa the spring of 1938): "Probably the finest technical poem in English is Keats' 'Eve of St. Agnes.'"

Fitzgerald was always encouraged in his poetry-writing by his Princeton friend John Peale Bishop. Fitzgerald always looked up to Bishop, who succeeded in having poetry published in *Century* magazine while still an undergraduate. Fitzgerald was sure Bishop would have a highly glowing literary career after graduation from Princeton. Bishop did not. Although he wrote a collection of poems, *The Green Fruit*, published in 1917, and collaborated with Wilson on a book, *The Undertaker's Garland*, published in 1922, the novel Bishop subsequently tried to write on his own proved unpublishable and his literary career gradually petered out. Fitzgerald (perhaps projecting from his own situation) surmised that the woman Bishop married had spoiled Bishop's chances of realizing his full potential as a writer.

December
Chaonolitan

IN
THIS
ISSUE!

Robert W. Shameless
Harrison Christy Flagg
Dr Herbert Crane
John Phlox, Jr.
Haggard Writer
Nellie Weedles Pillbox
Mrs Wilson Van de Water-Glynn

14

OUR NEXT ISSUE

The January Chaopolitan's Tremendous Scoop.

Seventeen of America's Leading Authors caught with the ink on their fingers.

America's Greatest Enemy to Literature.

HARRISON FLAGG'S same old model appears for the first time in red hair.

JACK UNDONE. Author of *Primitive Primordial Primes*, *The Beer-Hound*, etc., etc., continues The Soul Struggle of a Passionate Duckling, a story of the North Dakota Barnyards.

ELINOR GYN, in her own inimitable and suggestive way, will portray the career of a young Count who kisses with a Viennese accent in her new novel, *Experiences of Egbert Ethelred*.

MAURICE MATTERHORN emerges from his mists of mysticism to discuss whether women have souls.

OUT JULY 15TH.

$1.50 a year $1.50 a copy (unexpurgated)

We cannot begin subscriptions with back numbers. There are no back numbers. In combination with *La Vie Parisienne* and the *Atlantic Monthly*, two dollars a term. Our agent will call every Tuesday and Friday until suppressed.

14. "Our Next Issue," *The Nassau Literary Magazine*, LXXII (December 1916), unpaged. Unsigned. Known to be by Fitzgerald because he preserved a clipping in his scrapbook. The December 1916 issue of *The Lit* (calling itself *Chaopolitan*—we've reproduced the cover on the facing page) was intended as a spoof of the popular magazine *Cosmopolitan*. Fitzgerald recalled in his 1927 article "Princeton": "We published a satirical number [of *The Nassau Lit*], a parody on the *Cosmopolitan Magazine*, which infuriated the less nimble-witted members of the English department." The next two entries, ostensibly by Robert W. Shameless and John Phlox Jr. (both of whose names you'll see listed on the *Chaoplitan* cover), come from that parody issue.

15

JEMINA

A STORY OF THE BLUE RIDGE MOUNTAINS

BY JOHN PHLOX, JR.

It was night in the mountains of Kentucky.

Wild hills rose on all sides. Swift mountain streams flowed rapidly up and down the mountains.

Jemina Tantrum was down at the stream brewing whiskey at the family still.

She was a typical mountain girl.

Her feet were bare. Her hands, large and powerful, hung down below her knees. Her face showed the ravages of work. Although but sixteen, she had for over a dozen years been supporting her aged pappy and mappy by brewing mountain whiskey.

From time to time she would pause in her task, and filling a dipper full of the pure invigorating liquid, would drain it off — then pursue her work with renewed vigor.

She would place the rye in the vat, thresh it out with her feet, and in twenty minutes the completed product would be turned out.

A sudden cry made her pause in the act of draining a dipper and look up.

"Hello," said a voice. It came form a man in hunting costume who had emerged from the wood.

"Hi, thar," she answered sullenly.

"Can you tell me the way to the Tantrums' cabin?"

"Are you uns from the settlement down thar?"

She pointed her hand down to the bottom of the hill where Louisville lay. She had never been there, but once, before she was born, her great-grandfather, old Gore Tantrum, had gone into the settlements in the company of two marshalls, and had never come back. So the Tantrums from generation to generation had learned to dread civilization.

The man was amused. He laughed a light tinkling laugh, the laugh of a Philadelphian. Something in the ring of it thrilled her. She drank off a dipper of whiskey.

"Where is Mr. Tantrum, little girl?" he asked kindly.

She raised her foot and pointed her big toe toward the woods.

"Thar in the cabing behind those thar pines. Old Tantrum air my ole man."

The man from the settlements thanked her and strode off. He was fairly vibrant with youth and personality. As he walked along he whistled and sang and turned handsprings and flapjacks, breathing in the fresh, cool air of the mountains.

The air around the still was like wine.

Jemina Tantrum watched him fascinated. No one like him had ever come into her life before.

She sat down on the grass and counted her toes. She counted eleven. She had learned arithmetic in the mountain school.

Ten years before, a lady from the settlements had opened a school on the mountain. Jemina had no money, but she had paid her way in whiskey, bringing a full pail to school every morning and leaving it on Miss Lafarge's desk. Miss Lafarge had died of delirium tremens after a year's teaching, and so Jemina's education had stopped.

Across the still stream still another still was standing. It was that of the Doldrums. The Doldrums and the Tantrums never spoke.

They hated each other.

Fifty years before old Jem Doldrum and old Jem Tantrum had quarreled in the Tantrum cabin over a game of slapjack. Jem Doldrum had thrown the king of hearts in Jem Tantrum's face, and the old Doldrum, enraged, had felled the old Tantrum with the nine of diamonds. Other Doldrums and Tantrums had joined in and The Little cabin was soon filled with flying cards. Hanstrum Doldrum lay stretched on the floor writhing in agony, the ace of hearts crammed down his throat. Jem Tantrum, standing in the doorway, ran through suit after suit, his face lit with fiendish hatred. Old Mappy Tantrum stood on the table wetting down the Doldrums with hot whiskey. Old Heck Doldrum, having finally run out of trumps, was backed out of the cabin, striking left and right with his tobacco pouch, and, gathering around him the rest of his clan, they mounted their cows and galloped furiously home.

That night old man Doldrum and his sons, vowing vengeance, had returned, put a tick-tock on the Tantrum window, stuck a pin in the doorbell and beaten a retreat.

A week later the Tantrums had put Cod Liver Oil in the Doldrum's still, and so, from year to year, the feud had continued, first one family being entirely wiped out and then the other.

Every day Jemina worked the still on her side of the stream, and Boscoe Doldrum worked the still on his side.

Sometimes, with unborn hatred, the feudists would throw whiskey at each other and Jemina would come home smelling like a Bowery saloon on election night.

But now Jemina was too thoughtful to look across. How wonderful this stranger had been and how oddly he was dressed! In her innocent way she had never believed that there were any settlements at all, and she had put it down to the credulity of the mountain people.

She turned to go up to the cabin, and as she turned something struck her in the neck. It was a sponge soaked in whiskey, and thrown by Boscoe Doldrum — a sponge soaked in whiskey from his still on the other side.

"Hi thar, Boscoe Doldrum," she shouted in her deep base voice.

"Yo', Jemina Tantrum. Gosh ding yo'!" he returned.

She continued up to the cabin.

The stranger was talking to her father. Gold had been discovered on Tantrum land, and the stranger, Edgar Edison, was trying to buy the land for a song.

She sat upon her hands and watched him.

He was wonderful. When he talked his lips moved.

She sat upon the stove and watched him.

Suddenly there came a blood-curdling scream. The Tantrums rushed to the windows.

It was the Doldrums.

They had hitched their cows to trees and concealed themselves behind the bushes and flowers and soon a perfect rattle of stones and bricks beat against the windows, bending them inward.

"Father, father," shrieked Jemina.

Her father took down his slingshot from his slingshot rack on the wall and ran his hand lovingly over the elastic band. He stepped to a loophole. Old Mappy Tantrum stepped to the coalhole.

The stranger was aroused at last. Furious to get at the Doldrums, he tried to get out of the house by crawling up the chimney. Then he thought there might be a door under the bed, but Jemina told him there was not one. He hunted for doors under the beds and sofas, but each time Jemina pulled him out and told him there were no doors there. Furious with anger, he beat upon the door and hollered at the Doldrums, but cowed, they could not answer him, but kept up their fusillade of bricks and stones against the window. Old Pappy Tantrum knew that as soon as they were able to effect an aperture they would pour in and the fight would be over.

Old Heck Doldrum, foaming at the mouth and spitting on the ground left and right, led the attack.

The terrific slingshots of old Pappy Tantrum had not been without their effect. A master shot had disabled one Doldrum, and another, shot three times through the abdomen and once through the stomach, fought feebly on.

Nearer and nearer they approached the house.

"We must fly," shouted the stranger to Jemina. "I will sacrifice myself and bear us both away."

"No," shouted Pappy Tantrum, his face begrimed with cold cream and grease paint. "You stay here and fit on. I will bar Jemina away. I will bar Mappy away. I will bar myself away."

The man from the settlements, pale and trembling with anger, turned to Ham Tantrum, who stood at the door throwing loophole after loophole at the advancing Doldrums.

"Will you cover the retreat?"

But Ham said that he too had Tantrums to bear away, but that he would leave himself here to help the stranger cover the retreat if he could think of a way of doing it.

Soon smoke began to filter through the floor and ceiling. Shem Doldrum had come up and touched a match to old Japhet Tantrum's breath as he leaned from a loophole and the alcoholic flames shot up on all sides.

The whiskey in the bathtub caught fire. The walls began to fall in.

Jemina and the man from the settlements looked at each other.

"Jemina," he whispered.

"Stranger," she answered in an answering answer.

"We will die together," he said. "If we had lived I would have taken you to the settlements and married you. With your ability to hold liquor, your social success was assured."

She caressed him idly for a moment, counting her toes softly to herself. The smoke grew thicker. Her left leg was on fire. She was a human alcohol lamp.

Their lips met in one long kiss, and then a wall fell on them and blotted them out.

When the Doldrums burst through the ring of flame ten minutes later, they found them dead where they had fallen, their arms around each other.

Old Jem Doldrum was moved.

He took off his hat.

He filled it with whiskey and drank it off.

"They air daid," he said slowly. "They hankered after each other. The fit is over now. We must not separate them."

So they threw them together into the stream and the two splashes they made were as one.

15. "Jemina, A Story of the Blue Ridge Mountains, by John Phlox Jr.," *The Nassau Literary Magazine*, LXXII (December 1916), pp. 210-215. Unsigned — but definitely Fitzgerald's; he later sold this rather trivial piece to *Vanity Fair* and also included it in *Tales of the Jazz Age*. This was intended as a parody of the work of author and *Cosmopolitan* magazine contributor John Fox Jr.

16

The Usual Thing

By Robert W. Shameless

Synopsis of Preceding Chapters

John Brabant, adopted son of Jules Brabant, the South American Peccadillo Merchant, reaches New York penniless. He has, however, six letters of introduction, one of them unsigned, unsealed, and in fact unwritten. He presents all five of them, including the sixth, to John Brabant. John Brabant, a young South American, is in love with pretty Babette Lefleur, the daughter of Jules Lefleur, a merchant from South America. Upon Jules presenting four of the six letters of introduction which Babette Brabant has written to Jules Lefleur, John begins to realize that Jules, John, and Babette are in league against Brabant and Lefleur for some sinister purpose. Upon presenting the unwritten letter, he realizes that of the five letters Jules or possibly Babette has given Brabant, the only clue to the case of Lefleur and his connection with Babette. At this point Jules and Lefleur meet in Central Park, and Jules, presenting the sixth or fifth letter, finds that Babette has given Brabant the letter that Jules presents to John. Confused by this, and in fact, not realizing the importance of the third or fourth letter, he takes tea in his boudoir one day with Brabant. Brabant believes that some sinister connection with Lefleur has driven Babette from South America, where John had been employed in Lefleur's peccadillo factory. He takes a boat to South America and, on board, sees Brabant also bound South on some secret mission. They decide to combine forces and destroy the second letter. Meanwhile, on the same ship, unknown to the other two, Brabant is disguised as a steward with the first, third and part of the fifth letters of introduction in his possession. As they pass through the Suez Canal a boat rows out from Cairo, and Brabant boards the ship. The other four notice his arrival, but fearful for the safety of the fourth and part of the sixth letter, decide among themselves not to mention peccadillo's or South America in general. Meanwhile, Babette and Lefleur, still in Newport, are falling more and more deeply in love. Lefleur hears of this, and unwilling that Babette should become involved in an affair with this man, leaves his peccadillo factory in the charge of an employee named Brabant and comes north. George meets him in Troy at the business firm of Dulong and Petit, and boarding the train, they rush to Tuxedo Park to join the others, and incidentally to seize the sixth letter, if the Countess has not already written it. Arriving in New York, they take rooms at the Ritz, and begin the search for Brabant. Babette, in her boudoir, is sorting towels when the door suddenly bursts open and Genevieve comes in.

Chapter XXXI

Tea was being served at the VanTynes. On the long lawn, the pear trees cast their shadows over the parties of three and four scattered about. Babette and Lefleur had secured a table in a secluded nook, and as the sun glimmered and danced on the burnished silver tea set, she told him the whole story. When she had finished neither spoke for a minute, while he reached into the little mother of pearl satchel that hung at his side for cigarettes.

He selected one; he lit a match.

She held it for him.

The cigarette instantly lighted.

"Well?" She smiled up at him, her eyes ringed with those long eyelashes that had evoked Rembrant's enthusiastic praise in Holland the previous summer.

"Well?" He equivocated, shifting his foot from one knee to the other; the foot that had so often booted Harvard to victory on the gridiron.

"You see I am nothing but a toy after all," she sighed, "and I've wanted to be so much more — for you." Her voice sank to a whisper.

"That night," he exclaimed impetuously. "You did, didn't you?"

She blushed.

"Perhaps."

"And that other time in the Chauncy Widdecombs limousine when you—."

"Hush," she breathed, "the servants, one is never alone. Oh! I'm tired of it all, the life I lead. I go to breakfast, what do I eat — grapefruit. I ride — where? — the same old places. Do I see life? No!"

"Poor girl," he sympathized.

"It's horrible," she went on, "Nothing to eat but food, nothing to wear but clothes, nowhere to live but here and in the city." She flung her hand in a graceful gesture towards the city.

There was a silence. An orange rolled from the table down to the grass, then up again on to a chair where it lay orange and yellow in the sun. They watched it without speaking.

"Why can't you marry me," he began.

She interrupted. "Don't, don't let's go over that again. Do you think I could ever live on your income? I — live over a stable, with the smelly horses smelling of horses. No — I'm selfish!"

"Not selfish, dear," he interrupted.

"Yes, selfish," she went on. "Do you think I could go around and bear the covert sneers of those who call themselves my friends. Yes, they would sneer at me riding around in your Saxon. No, Gordon — this morning I went down town in sections in two Pierce Arrows. I've got to have it."

"But dear," he broke in again, "I—."

"No, don't apologize. You say we do not need a box at the opera. We can sit in the stalls. But I can't sleep except in a box. I should be kept awake the whole time to bear the covert sneers of those who call themselves my friends. Yes, they would sneer at me."

He mused a moment, making the old clanging noise by snapping his lips together, that he used to make, when, as two little friends, they played together in Central Park, then his family home.

He took her hand in his, his hand that had won so many baseball games for Yale, when known as Beau Brabant, he had been the pitcher. He thought of the hot languorous days of the previous summer, when they had read Gibbon's *History of Rome* to each other, and had thrilled over the tender love passages.

Mrs. VanTyne came tripping down the lawn, tripped over the grass, and tripped over the tea table.

"What are you two dears doing here?" she asked kindly, but suspiciously. "The others are waiting." She turned to Jules, "They think you have hidden the polo balls for a joke, and they are furious at you."

He smiled wearily. What had he to do with polo balls and other gilded ornaments of the world he had renounced forever.

"They are in the kitchen," he said slowly, "in the drawer with the soap." He ran slowly toward the walk with the famous dogtrot that had made him Captain of the running team at Princeton.

Babette turned angrily to her mother.

"You have hurt him," she cried. "You are cold and cruel, mercenary and heartless, big and fat." She pushed her mother into the tea table.

The sun slowly sank out of sight, and long after the others were dressing and undressing for dinner Babette sat and watched the orange roll up and down from the lawn to the table, and wondered if, in its own dumb way, it had solved the secret of things.

As Babette left the house, followed by a deferential butler carrying her suit cases, she glanced back and saw the Countess Jenavra silhouetted in the doorway.

"Good trip," shouted the Countess.

Lefleur, his Saxon purring with energy, was waiting at the gates. She stepped in the front seat. Muffled in fur robes, blankets, overcoats, old sacking, and cotton batton, she gazed once more back at the house. The brilliant Cedric I exterior was punctuated by flashes denoting early English windows. In the Elizabethan doorway stood the Colonial figure of Babette's mother.

The butler gave the car a deferential push, and they started bowling down the long highway alone. The trees bent as if to intercept them, swooping back, however, as they burst by. Lefleur, his foot upon the cylinder, felt a wild exhilaration sweeping over him as they bobbed madly up and down, to and fro, towards the city.

"John," she began, "I know — " she paused and seemed to breathe — "that you think," her voice sank to a whisper, then lower still. Nothing could be heard but the rasping of her teeth against her jaws.

"Unghlt," she said, as they passed Bridgeport. It was not until Greenwich that she got his answering "Gthliuup."

The town was a mere speck as they sped by. He increased the speed. Leaning back against his shoulder, she felt a deep, perfect content surge through her. Surely this was living or more than living. The cold air surging by turned her senses cold and tense. Sharp as a whip, everything, all her life, stood out against the background of this ride. She wondered if all things could not be solved in this way, with the sting of the fresh night and the rat-tat of the motor.

Up to this time he had been running on two cylinders. He now threw on two more, and the car, careening up for a second on its front wheels, righted itself and continued with its speed redoubled. However, in the confusion of the change, his right arm had become disengaged and thrown around her. She did not move it.

Faster they went. He pressed harder on the steering gear, and in response to his pressure, the car sprang forward like a well-trained steed. They were late, and realizing it, he threw on the last two cylinders.

The car seemed to realize what was demanded of it. It stopped, turned around three times, and then bounded off at twice its former speed.

Along they went. Suddenly the car stopped, and with the instinct of a trained mechanic, he realized that something was the matter. After an inspection, he saw that one of the tires was punctured. He looked to see what damage had been done. They had run over a hairpin, and the rubber was torn and splintered to shreds. They looked around for another tire. They looked in the back seat, they looked under the car, they looked behind the bushes on the edge of the road. There was no tire. They must fix the old one. John put his mouth to the puncture and blew it up, sticking his handkerchief into the hole. They started off, but after several miles, the grueling strain of the road wore through the handkerchief, little by little, and the car stopped again. They tried everything, leaves and gravel, and pieces of the road. Finally Babette sacrificed her gum to stop up the gaping aperture, but after several miles this too wore out.

There was but one thing to do, to take off the tire, run into town on three wheels, and hire a man to run along beside the car and hold up the fourth side. No sooner had they had this thought than they put it into action. Three whistles, and a cry of "buckwheats," brought a crowd of Yokels in a jiffy, and the most intelligent looking one of the lot was engaged for the arduous task.

He took his place by the fender, and they again started off. They increased the speed soon, driving along at the rate of forty miles an hour. The Yokel, running beside with a long easy stride, was panting and seemed to have difficulty in keeping up the pace.

It was growing darker. Sitting up close to John's huge ratskin coat, Babette felt the old longing to see his eyes close to hers, and feel his lips brush her cheek.

"John," she murmured. He turned. Above the clatter of the motor and the harsh plebian breathing of the peasant, she heard his heart heave with emotion.

"Babette," he said.

She started, sobbing softly, her voice mingling with the roar of the fan belt.

He folded her slowly, dignifiedly, and willfully, in his arms and ki—.

The next installment of Mr. Shameless' fascinating story will appear in the July number.

16. "The Usual Thing, by Robert W. Shameless," *The Nassau Literary Magazine,* LXXII (December 1916), pp. 223-228. Unsigned, though this piece is credited to Fitzgerald in the index to volume LXXII of *The Nassau Literary Magazine.* This was intended as a parody of the work of author and *Cosmopolitan* magazine contributor Robert W. Chambers. Fitzgerald enjoyed kidding Chambers — but he also felt there were some traces of Chambers' style of writing in his own *This Side of Paradise.*

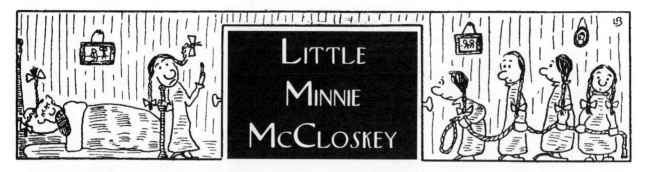

Little Minnie McCloskey

A Story for Girls

EDITOR'S NOTE — *Not since Little Women have we had so moving a picture of girlhood hopes and dreams.*

:It was midnight in Miss Pickswinger's Select Seminary for Young Ladies (country location, hot and cold water, wrestling, bull-baiting and other out-door sports; washing, ironing, and Bulgarian extra). A group of girls had gathered in a cozy room. There was going to be a midnight feast. Oh, goody! There was but little light, for, fearing to turn on the acetylene, they had built a bonfire on the table, and one girl was appointed to feed the faint flames with false hair and legs which she wrenched quietly from the chairs and tables. A saddle of venison for their little supper was turning over and over on a spit in the cooking stove in the corner, and the potatoes were boiling noiselessly in the steam radiator. Perched like a little queen on the armchair sat Louise Sangfroid the hostess, on the mantle-piece lay Mary Murgatroid in red and white striped pajamas while balancing on the molding sat Minnie McCloskey in a nightshirt of yaeger flannel. Other girls sat around the room, two on a trunk, which they had ingeniously improvised as a chair, one on an empty case of beer and three on a heap of broken glass and tin cans in the corner.

Girls will be girls! Ah, me! They would have their little frolic; a cask of Haig and Haig, stolen from Miss Pickswinger's private stock, was behind the door and the mischievous girls had almost finished it.

Minnie McCloskey was the school drudge; she was working for her education. At three every morning she rose, made the beds, washed the dishes, branded the cattle, cut the grass, and did many other tasks. She was known affectionately to her companions as "Piggy" McCloskey (all the girls had nicknames. How they got them no one knew. Amy Gulps was called "Fatty," perhaps because she was fat; Mary Munks was called "Red" conceivably because she had red hair. Phoebe Cohop was called "Boils" possibly because — (but enough, let us continue).

"Girls," said Bridget Mulcahey, a petite little French girl, whose father had been shot at Soissons (for deserting), "let's play a prank."

A chorus of ohs! And ahs! And girlish giggles greeted this suggestion.

"What shall we do?" asked Gumpsa LePage.

"Something exciting," said Bridget, "let's hang Miss Pickswinger." All assented enthusiastically except Minnie McCloskey.

" 'Fraid cat," sneered the others, " 'fraid you'll get punished."

"No," said Minnie, "but think of all she's done for me."

They struck her savagely with chairs, locked her in and rushed off. There was but one chance. Minnie quickly braided a rope out of rugs, lowered herself from the window, quickly weaved another rope out of grass, raised herself to Miss Pickswinger's window. They were not there. There was yet time to outwit them. Suddenly she gasped in horror.

* * *

A moment later the rollicking crowd of girls was confronted in front of Miss Pickswinger's door by a slender figure. It was Minnie.

"You cannot pass," she said sternly.

"Do you mean to say we cannot hang Miss Pickswinger if we wish?" cried Louise, indignantly.

Minnie shivered with emotion and sneezed with emotion. Then she spoke.

"There is no need. She had gotten one of her bedroom slippers in her mouth and choked to death."

The girls rushed off shouting "Holiday" and striking each other playfully on the head with stones, but Minnie, in the room above, threw herself down upon the heap of glass in the corner and sobbed as if her heart would break.

---

17. "Little Minnie McCloskey," *The Princeton Tiger*, XXVII (December 1, 1916), pp. 6-7. Unsigned. Known to be by Fitzgerald because he preserved a clipping in his scrapbook. The story is, of course, not to be taken seriously. But the underlying notion, that girls can be dangerous — in this case, the girls are oh-so-eager to hang their poor headmistress, whose liquor they've been stealing — would find repeated expression, albeit in subtler, more realistic forms, in Fitzgerald's later work.

18

One from Penn's Neck

Baby Ben, Baby Ben, you annoy a lot of men
With your aggravating tinkle at about eight-ten.
I'm dreaming pretty dreams about the girls who love me — when
I hear your voice a calling, Baby Ben.

18. "One from Penn's Neck," *The Princeton Tiger*, XXVII (December 18, 1916), p. 7. Unsigned. Known to be by Fitzgerald because he preserved a clipping in his scrapbook. One can easily sympathize with him groaning when the ringing of the bell reminds him that a new day of classes is about to begin.

THE GIRL I LEFT
BEHIND ME

A Litany of Slang

From "Knockouts" — Great Von Hindenburg deliver us.

From "dopeless" people — Great Von, etc.

From "sardines" — Great Von, etc.

From "trick" things — Great Von, etc.

From "trick" people — Great Von, etc.

From "I'll say" — Great Von, etc.

From lads who "have it" — Great Von, etc.

From lads who "lack it" — Great Von, etc.

From "nice fellow you are" — Great Von, etc.

From "Hotstuff" — Great Von, etc.

From "Persian Petters" — Great Von, etc.

From all last years' slang — Great Von Hindenburg do deliver us if you get time. Amen.

---

19. "A Litany of Slang," *The Princeton Tiger*, XXVII (December 18, 1916), p. 7. Unsigned. Known to be by Fitzgerald because he preserved a clipping in his scrapbook.

20

"TRIANGLE SCENERY BY BAKST."
— *Princetonian.*

We are glad to see that this scene designer has broken his fifty-thousand-dollar contract with the Russian Ballet. The Triangle Club must be prospering. Next year's score by Claude DeBussy?

---

20. "'Triangle Scenery by Bakst,'" *The Princeton Tiger*, XXVII (December 18, 1916), p. 7. Unsigned. Known to be by Fitzgerald because he preserved a clipping in his scrapbook.

21

FUTURISTIC IMPRESSIONS OF THE EDITORIAL BOARDS

The Prince — A merry-go-round game of "who read the proof?" with solid gold-filled radicalism every morning before breakfast.

The Lit — Half a dozen men who agree, at the price of appearing in print, to listen to each other's manuscript.

The Pic — The tall man with the black box who gets in front of the umpire all through May.

The Tiger — A lot of lo — yes, sir; all right, sir, a collection of artists and side-splitting humorists.

———

21. "Futuristic Impressions of the Editorial Boards," *The Princeton Tiger*, XXVII (December 18, 1916), p. 7. Unsigned.

Known to be by Fitzgerald because he preserved a clipping in his scrapbook. Naturally, in this piece, he has *The Tiger* come off best.

"A Glass of Beer Kills Him."

— New York Sun.

brought forth "Ex Princetoniensi non erat"
from the *Yale Record*.

Right again. Probably some one threw it at an Eli.

―――――

22. "'A glass of beer kills him,'" *The Princeton Tiger*, XXVII (December 18, 1916), p. 7. Unsigned. Known to be by Fitzgerald because he preserved a clipping in his scrapbook.

Oui, le Backfield Est from Paris

Oui, le backfield est from Paris
Quel les Eli studes adore,
C'est Messieurs Laroche and Neville
Messieurs Jaque et LeGore.
　　　　— Maxim of General Joffre

―――――

23. "Oui, le backfield est from Paris," *The Princeton Tiger*, XXVII (December 18, 1916), p. 7. Unsigned. Known to be by Fitzgerald because he preserved a clipping in his scrapbook.

WHEN YOU FIND A MAN...

"When you find a man doing a little more than his duty, you find that kind of patriotism not found in Blair or Campbell."

— *Oliver Wendell Holmes*

We were under the impression that Mr. Holmes went to Harvard, but he evidently roomed in North Edwards.

———

24. "When you find a man...," *The Princeton Tiger*, XXVII (December 18, 1916), p. 7. Unsigned. Known to be by Fitzgerald because he preserved a clipping in his scrapbook. To a Princetonian, Blair and Campbell were the names of dormitories first and of historic personages second; hence the gag that Oliver Wendell Holmes, in referring to Blair and Campbell, must have been a Princetonian (and a resident of another Princeton dorm, Edwards).

THINGS THAT NEVER CHANGE! NUMBER **3333**

"Oh, you fr-shm-n, where shall we go. Let's go to J-'s. I want to get a sm-ll check c-shed. We g-t g - d M-j-st-c s-ndw-tches there."

The Tiger's reward for the most complete solution will be a m-j-st-c s-ndw-tch at J-'s.

———

25. "Things That Never Change! Number 3333," *The Princeton Tiger*, XXVII (December 18, 1916), p. 7. Unsigned. Known to be by Fitzgerald because he preserved a clipping in his scrapbook. For many freshmen in Fitzgerald's day, Joe's Restaurant was a good place to get a sandwich — not to mention a check cashed. You'll find Joe's mentioned in *This Side of Paradise*, along with the Jigger Shop and Renwick's, two other popular student hangouts of the era — all now long gone. You may also have noticed that Fitzgerald worked a reference to Joe's into his *Tiger* story "The Conquest of America" (Thanksgiving 1915); he depicted the invading soldiers as finding Joe's promise of "small checks cashed" irresistible.

THE LOST LOVER

(THE SADDEST CHRISTMAS STORY EVER WRITTEN.)

Evangeline Wilhorski sat on the kitchen stove, and thought of Christmas — Christmas in the Behring Straits — Christmas in Novoskororingoski — Christmas in Siberia. So Evangeline sat and sizzled, turning herself over from time to time so that she might be well-done on all sides. Evangeline was trying to take the place of the Christmas turkey.

She reached down into the gravy tank and drew up a ladle of thin green liquid, pouring it over herself. She was determined to be juicy. She thought — thought deeply — thought the long sweet thoughts that maidens are accustomed to think while sitting on a red-hot stove. She thought of her lover, Peter Whatabearski.

Their's had been a long and poignant love. They had been taken out riding in the same baby carriage, had bitten the same nurse, had drunk the same milk and eaten the same food. Camaraderie can go no further. Evangeline had not seen Pete since her third birthday, but she had corresponded with him continually, sending long, long letters by parcel post. His replies had come by freight. She was using one of them now to heat up the stove. The stove was red-hot.

She tried herself with a fork. Yes, she was getting tender — but a little while now and she would be quite well-done. Evangeline sighed — a sigh of deep pleasure at the thought of the exercise her friends would get out of eating her. She was not so tender that she would yield without a struggle. Yet too, she was just a little sorrowful. She knew that she would never see Pete Whatabearski again. She wept softly, the tears hissing down upon the red-hot stove. She turned herself over again, and slept.

Suddenly she felt the touch of a cool hand against her epidermis. She awoke. There before her, stood Pete Whatabearski, her long-lost lover, the man she had known she would never see again (just the regular old line in here)!

Evangeline jumped from the stove and into his arms. She was so hot he dropped her. Quickly putting on his asbestos gloves, he picked her up again, and waved her in the air, trying to cool her. Slowly she went from whiteheat, to red hotness, and then to fever heat. Pete Whatabearski kissed her on the forehead. She burned his tongue.

"Fly with me, fly with me, fly with me!" Pete pleaded, throwing her up in the air and catching her, making sure she was quite cool.

"Out into the night?" she queried.

"Yes — with me, darling, with me," murmured Pete.

"And you will be mine, and I will be yours?" she asked again.

"You and me, kid, fifty-fifty," he answered.

Quickly, he swung her through the door, and out into the flying flakes of the snowy night. They were swallowed up in the hazy gloom...

And afar off, there sounded the yells of the hungry family, demanding its Christmas turkey.

26. "The Lost Lover," *The Princeton Tiger*, XXVII (December 18, 1916), p. 8. (Possible attribution.) Fitzgerald did not preserve a clipping in his scrapbook, but John McMaster '19, a *Tiger* editor suggested to Matthew Bruccoli that this piece may have been by Fitzgerald.

27

THE OLD FRONTIERSMAN

A STORY OF THE FRONTIER

It was the middle of the forest. A figure might have been noticed crawling along, sniffing at the ground. It was Old Davy Underbush, the frontiersman and b'ar hunter. He was completely invisible and inaudible. The only way you could perceive him was by the sense of smell.

He was dressed as a frontiersman (*cf.* "What the men will wear," theatre programs of 1776.) On his feet he wore moccasins made from the skin of the wood weasel. Around his legs were coonskin spats which ran into his trousers made of sheepskin; these extended to the waist. He wore a belt made of an old rattlesnake and a long bearskin coat. Around his head was wrapped a fishskin hat. At his hip hung horrible trophies of Indian warfare. One scalp of Object the Ojibway still wet with Oleaqua hung there beside the pompadour of Eardrum the Iroquois and the cowlick of Bootblack the Blackfoot. By his side walked "Tres Bien," his trusty Eskimo cheesehound.

He carried a muzzle loading shotgun, an old horse-pistol, and a set of razors. He was on the trail of Sen-Sen the Seneca and Omlette the Omega. They had come into the clearing and drunk all the fire-water from the fire-water factory. As they left they had, in the usual Indian manner, carved their initials on each tree they passed and it was by this that the astute old frontiersman had been sent out to track them.

It was now too dark to read the initials plainly and Davy often got them mixed up with those of other savages who had passed that way before. For three weeks the old b'ar hunter had followed them, living on the berries from the bushes and sometimes when no berries were to be found, snatching great handfuls of grass and dry leaves and devouring them.

As he crawled along he was thinking. If he did not find the redskins soon he would have to eat his moccasins. His scarred brow was knit with worry.

All around him were the noises of the forest; the long sad "hoo" of the Huron, the plaintive sigh of the Sioux, and the light cackle of the Apache. Suddenly a new sound broke the stillness. It was the dry harsh cawing of the Seneca. Davy ran forward noiselessly. He was careful to make no sound. He ran with his feet completely off the ground to leave no clue for the watchful redmen. Sure enough the savages were in a little clearing in the forest playing on their primitive musical instruments. Sen-Sen the Seneca sat playing "The Last Rose of Summer" on an old comb wrapped in tissue paper and Omlette the Omega accompanied him on the snare Tom-Tom. The old frontiersman burst in on them waving his gun at them and threatening their scalps with one of his tempered razors.

The fight which ensued was furious. The savages pulled his coat over his ears and hit him on the head with their bows and arrows. One would kneel behind Davy and the other would push the old frontiersman over him. Sen-Sen combed all the hair of his sheepskin trousers the wrong way and frantic with pain the old b'ar hunter fought on.

Finally Omlette the Omega withdrew to a distance and taking a station behind the old frontiersman let fly an arrow at him which passed through his sheepskin trousers and pierced his catskin underwear. The old b'ar hunter expired.

The savages fried him for dinner but found, to their disappointment that he was all dark meat owing to his lifelong exposure to the sun.

---

27. "The Old Frontiersman," *The Princeton Tiger*, XXVII (December 18, 1916), p. 11. Unsigned. Known to be by Fitzgerald because he preserved a clipping in his scrapbook.

At last I was in Bohemia, the land of the free and the home of the nutty. To the north lay Washington Square, to the east the East River and on the couch in the corner lay Flossie Flanders, the pride of Greenwich Village. Floss was recuperating from her day's work, having sold one of her paintings called "Nude Emerging from Tub." So unexpected was the blow that it had laid Flossie cold. It was the first painting that had brought any money in since her old man had lost his job as a painter and paperhanger. But artistry will out. Floss had at last come into her own.

With a neat backflip she arose from her resting place and landed on the chandelier. Swinging her besandaled foot around the room in time to "Mother Took to Washing, Cause Father Took to Drink," she cut a pretty figure. Now wearied with this byplay Floss leaped from the chandelier to the divan. Her gown, however, caught on the fixture so she barely landed on the couch. Quickly hiding her confusion in a handy robe she recited the Plutarch's Pledge to Prohibition just to show her versatility. She revealed other talents as well. After two hours or so of oratory she decided she couldn't keep pace with the Plute so she jammed on the soft petal. At length she decided to partake of her evening meal. A heaping plate of Hors d'oeuvre, a bowl of entree, a demi-tasse with crocodile dressing, a keg of "Bud" and lady-fingers satisfied her hunger. Tea over she put on her smock and sandals and set out for the Passé Club where she was to hold forth on Art for Art's Sake. After a few hours walk she arrived at the club.

Entering the sanctum she found the place crowded with fellow Bohemians. Some sat in the fireplace, some were perched on the ceiling with an indifferent air as though their little world had been turned topsy-turvy, two or three stood on their hands to get a better view, and others were scattered about the room in various attitudes of dejection. At Floss' appearance a roar of applause greeted her. News of the sale of her picture had spread rapidly and all were hunching a party. In response to the ovation Floss assumed a nonchalant air, bowed, did a Grecian dance, turned two handsprings and a somersault, kicked the hat from an interested bystander, sang "My Country 'Tis of Thee," whistled the "Marsellaise," and rolled a cigarette with one hand to show her appreciation. The assemblage looked on with a blasé air and cried bravo and Vive La Floss as that damsel recovered her breath.

Now that she was warmed up she started her speech. There was no platform from which to speak so she stood on the head of a convenient old gentleman and began, "Art, fellow Bohemians, has risen from the depths. This is due in no part" (animated applause) "to the efforts of our own circle. Many of us have succeeded" (self-satisfied look greeted these words), "and many of us have failed." (At this confession two Bohemians fell off the ceiling and bit the dust. An artist in the corner shot the girl at his side and stabbed himself). This interruption so nettled Flossie that she turned a Bakst green, jumped out of the window into a waiting taxi and was soon conveyed to her apartment. Heaving a sigh of relief she divested herself of her garments, did a couple of hours' exercise, bathed herself with aromatic spirits of ammonia, and finished the "Bud." In due time she passed out, whistling "The End of a Perfect Day."

---

28. "Bohemia," *The Princeton Tiger*, XXVII (December 18, 1916), p. 15. (Possible attribution.) Fitzgerald did not preserve a clipping in his scrapbook, but John McMaster suggested to Matthew Bruccoli that this piece, illustrated by John V. Newlin '19, may have been by Fitzgerald. In "The Spire and the Gargoyle," Fitzgerald would note that "shoddy Bohemianism had no attraction for him," an attitude that may have contributed to difficulties in his career. Fitzgerald always did love to live as well as possible. Had he chosen to live more modestly when he was making big money in the '20s, he would have been able to devote more time to writing the novels that mattered most to him and less to stories and film scripts churned out just to cover bills.

That girl
you left behind you—

is interested in Princeton and all things connected therewith—

Create that much needed drag by sending HER

The PRINCETON TIGER

My check for $2.25 is enclosed. Please send THE TIGER to:

Name..........

Pin your check for $2.25 to this ☞ and mail to *The* TIGER, P. O. Box 353

Address ....

THE DEBUTANTE

THE NASSAU LITERARY MAGAZINE
VOLUME **LXXII** JANUARY No. 6

*T*he scene is a boudoir, or whatever you call a lady's room which hasn't a bed. Smaller rooms communicate with it, one on each side. There is a window at the left and a door leading into the hall at the back. A huge pier-glass stands in the corner; it is the only object in the room which is not littered with an infinitude of tulle, hat-boxes, empty boxes, full boxes, ribbons and strings, dresses, skirts, suits, lingerie, petticoats, lace, open jewel-cases, sashes, belts, stocking, slippers, shoes — perfectly littered with more than all this. In the very middle of the confusion stands a girl. She is the only thing in the room which looks complete, or nearly complete. She needs to have her belt hooked, and has too much powder on her nose; but aside from that, looks as though she might be presented to almost anything at almost any time; which is just what is going to happen to her. She is terrifically pleased with herself and the long mirror is the focus of her activity. Her rather discontented face is consciously flexible to the several different effects. Expression number one seems to be a simple, almost childish, ingenue, upward glance, concentrated in the eyes and the exquisitely angelic eyelashes. When expression number two is assumed, one forgets the eyes and the mouth is the center of the stage. The lips seem to turn from rose to a positive unashamed crimson. They quiver slightly — where is the ingenue? Disappeared. Good evening Sapho, Venus, Madam Du

— no! ah! Eve, simply Eve! The pier-glass seems to please. Expression number three: — Now her eyes and lips combine. Can this be the last stronghold? The aesthetic refuge of womanhood; her lips are drawn down at the corners, her eyes droop and almost fill with tears. Does her face turn paler? Does — No! Expression one has dismissed tears and pallor, and again—

Helen — What time is it?

(*The sewing machine stops in the room at the left.*)

Voice — I haven't a watch, Miss Helen.

Helen — (*Assuming expression number three and singing to the mirror.*) "Poor butterfly — by the blossoms waiting — poor butter — " What time do you think it is, Narry, old lady? Where's mother, Narry?

Narry — (*Rather crossly*) I am sure I haven't the slightest idea.

Helen — Narry! (*No answer.*) Narry, I called you Old Lady, because (*She pauses. The sewing machine swings into an emphatic march*) because it's the last chance I will have.

The machine stops again and Narry comes into the room sniffing. Narry is exactly of the mould with which the collective temperaments of Helen and her family would have stamped her. She is absolutely adamant with everyone not a member of the family and absolutely putty in the hands of the least capable of them.

Narry — You might just not call me Old Lady. (*She sniffs, and handkerchiefs herself*) Goodness gracious! I feel old enough now with you going out.

Helen — Coming!

Narry — Coming—

Helen — (*Her mind wandering to her feet which carry her around the room to the sound of her voice*) "The moments pass into hours — the hours pass into years — and as she smiles through—"

Peremptory voice with the maternal rising accent ascends the stairs, and curls into the bedroom.

Voice — Hel-*en*

Helen — (*With more volume than you would imagine could go with such a deliciously useless figure*) Yes, mother.

Mother — (*Drawing near.*) Are you very nearly ready, dear?... I am coming up. I have had such a hard time with one of the waiters.

Helen — I know mother, tight as he could be. Narry and I watched him try to get up when they threw him outside into the yard.

Mother — (*Now on the stairway landing*) You and Narry should not have done any such thing, Helen dear. I am surprised at Narry. I — (*She seems to pause and pant.*)

Narry — (*Almost shouting*) I do declare, Mrs. Halycon. I—

Mrs. Halycon appears in the doorway and becomes the center of the stage. She is distinctly a factor in the family life. Neither her daughter's slang, nor her son's bills discourage her in the least. She is jeweled and rouged to the dowager point.

Mrs. Halycon — Now Narry, now Helen. (*She produces a small notebook.*) Sit down and be quiet. (*Narry sits down anxiously on a chair which emerges from the screen of dresses. Helen returns to the pier-glass and the sequence of expressions passes over her face in regular rotation.*) Now I've made some notes here — let's see. I've made notes on things you must do. Just as I have thought of them, I have put them down. (*She seats herself somewhere and becomes severely judicial.*) First, and absolutely, you must not sit out with anyone. (*Helen looks bored.*) I've stood for it at your other dances and heaven knows how many dances of other people, but I will not, understand me, I will not endure to look all over for you when some friend of mine, or of your father's wants to meet you. You must tonight, you must all season — I mean you must stay in the ballroom, or some room where I can find you when I want you. Do you understand?

Helen — (*Yawning*) Oh, yes! You would think I didn't know what to do.

Mrs. Halycon — Well, do it if you know how. I will not endure finding you in a dark corner of the conservatory, exchanging silliness with anyone, or listening to it.

Helen — (*Sarcastically*) Yes, listening to it is better.

Mrs. Halycon — And you positively cannot give more than two dances to young Cannel. I will not have everyone in town having you engaged before you have had a fair chance.

Helen — Same old line. You'd think from the way you talk that I was some horrible old man-chaser, or someone so weak and wobbly that you'd think I'd run off with someone. Mother, for heaven's sake—

Mrs. Halycon — My dear, I am doing my very best for you.

Helen — (*Wearily*) I know. (*She sits down decidedly on another invisible chair*) Mother, I happen, my dear, to have four dances with John Cannel. He called up, asked me for four of them, and what could I say? Besides, it's a cut-in-dance, and he would cut in as much as he wants anyhow. So what's the difference? (*Becoming impatient*) You can't run everything now, the way they did in the early nineties.

Mrs. Halycon — Helen, I've told you before that you can't say early nineties to me.

Helen — Don't treat me like a child then.

Mr. Halycon comes in. He is a small man with a large appearance and a board-of-directors heartiness.

Mr. Halycon — (*Feeling that the usual thing is expected of him*) Well, how is my little debutante daughter? About to flit into the wide, wide world?

Helen — No, daddy, just taking a more licensed view of it.

78

Mr. Halycon — (*Almost apologetically*) Helen, I want you to meet a particular friend of mine, a youngish man—

Helen — About forty-five?

Mrs. Halycon — Helen!

Helen — Oh, I like them forty-five. They know life, and are so adorably tired looking.

Mr. Halycon — And he is very anxious to meet you. He saw you when you came into my office one day, I believe — and let me tell you, he is a brainy man. Brought up from Providence by the—

Helen — (*Interrupting*) Yes, daddy, I'll be delighted to meet him. I'll—

Enter Cecilia, Helen's younger sister. Cecilia is sixteen, but socially precocious and outrageously wise on all matters pertaining to her sister. She has blonde hair, in contrast to her sister's dark brown; and besides, remarkable green eyes with a wistful trusting expression in them. However, there are very few people whom she trusts.

Cecilia — (*Calmly surveying the disorder around her*) Nice looking room.

Helen — Well, what do you expect? Nothing but milliners, dressmakers and clumsy maids all day (*Narry rises and leaves the room*) What's the matter with her?

Mrs. Halycon — You've hurt her feelings.

Helen — Have I? What time is it?

Mrs. Halycon — Quarter after eight. Are you ready? You've got too much powder on.

Helen — I know it.

Mr. Halycon — Well, look me up when you come down; I want to see you before the rush. I'll be in the library with your uncle.

Mrs. Halycon — And don't forget the powder.

Mr. and Mrs. Halycon go out.

Helen — Hook up my belt, will you, Cecilia?

Cecilia — Yes. (*She sets at it, Helen in the meanwhile regarding herself in the mirror*) What are you looking at yourself all the time for?

Helen — (*Calmly*) Oh, just because I like myself.

Cecilia — I am all twittered! I feel as if I were coming out myself. It is rotten of them not to let me come to the dance.

Helen — Why you've just only put your hair up. You'd look ridiculous.

Cecilia — (*Quietly*) I know where you keep your cigarettes and your little silver bottle.

Helen — (*Starting so as to unloosen several hooks which Cecilia patiently does over again*) Why, you horrible child! Do you go prying around among my things?

Cecilia — All right, tell mother.

Helen — What do you do, just go through my drawers like a common little sneak-thief?

Cecilia — No, I don't. I wanted a handkerchief, and I went to looking and I couldn't help seeing them.

Helen — That's what comes of letting you children fool around with no chaperons, read anything you want to, and dance until two every Saturday night all summer. If it comes to that, I'll tell something I saw that I didn't say anything about. Just before we came into town, that night you asked me if you could take Blaine MacDonough home in the electric, I happened to be passing at the end of the drive by the club, and I saw him kiss you.

Cecilia — (*Unmoved*) We were engaged.

Helen — (*Frantically*) Engaged! You silly little fool! If any older people heard that you two were talking like that, you wouldn't be allowed to go with the rest of your crowd.

Cecilia — That's all right, but you know why you didn't tell, because what were *you* doing down there by the drive with John Cannel?

Helen — Hush! You little devil.

Cecilia — All right We'll call it square. I just started by wanting to tell you that Narry knows where those cigarettes are too.

Helen — (*Losing her head*) You and Narry have probably been smoking them.

Cecilia — (*Amused*) Imagine Narry smoking.

Helen — Well, *you* have been anyway.

Cecilia — You had better put them somewhere else.

Helen — I'll put them where you can't find them, and if you weren't going back to school this week, I would go to mother and tell her the whole thing.

Cecilia — Oh, no you wouldn't. You wouldn't even do it for my good. You're too selfish.

Helen, still very superior, marches into the next room. Cecilia goes softly to the door, slams it without going out, and disappears behind the bureau. She emerges tip-toe, takes a cushion from an arm chair, and retires again to her refuge. Helen again reappears. Almost immediately a whistle sounds outside, twice repeated. She looks annoyed and goes to the window.

Helen — John!

John — (*From below*) Helen, can I see you a moment?

Helen — No, indeed, there are people all over the house. Mother would think I had gone mad if she saw us talking out of the window.

John — (*Hopefully*) I'll climb up.

Helen — John, don't, you'll tear your dress clothes. (*He is evidently making good, as deduced from a few muttered fragments, barely audible*) Look out for the spike by the ledge. (*A moment later he appears in the window, a young man of twenty-two, good looking, but at present not particularly cheerful.*)

Helen — (*Sitting down*) You simple boy! Do you want the family to kill me? Do you realize how conspicuous you are?

John — (*Hopefully*) I'd better come in.

Helen — No, you had better not. Mother may be up at any moment.

John — Better turn out the lights. I make a good movie standing like this on this ledge.

(*Helen hesitates and then turns out all the lights except an electric lamp on the dresser.*)

Helen — (*Assuming an effective pose in the arm chair*) What on earth do you want?

John — I want you. I want to know that you are mine when I see you dancing around with this crowd tonight.

Helen — Well, I am not. I belong to myself tonight, or rather to the crowd.

John — You have been rotten to me this week.

Helen — Have I?

John — You're tired of me.

Helen — No, not that. The family. (*They have evidently been over this ground before.*)

John — It isn't the family, and you know it.

Helen — Well, to tell the truth, it isn't exactly the family.

John — I know it isn't. It's me — and you, and I'm getting desperate. You've got to do something one way or the other. We are engaged, or—

Helen — Well, we are not engaged.

John — Then what are we? What do you think about me, or do you think about me? You never tell me any more. We're drifting apart. Please, Helen— !

Helen — It's a funny business, John, just how I do feel.

John — It isn't funny to me.

Helen — No, I don't suppose it is. You know, if you just weren't so in love with me—

John — (*Gloomily*) Well, I am.

Helen — You see, there is no novelty in that I always know just what you are going to say.

John — I wish I did. When you first met me, you used to tell me that you loved to hear me talk, because you never knew what I was going to say.

Helen — Well, I've found out. I like to run things, but it gets monotonous to always know that I am the key to the situation. If we are together, and I feel high, we enjoy ourselves. If I feel unhappy, then we don't; or anyways you don't. How you're feeling never has anything to do with it.

John — Wouldn't it be that way with most couples?

Helen — Oh, I suppose so, it would be if I were the girl.

John — Well, what do you want?

Helen — I want — Oh, I'll be frank for once. I like the feeling of going after them, I like the thrill when you meet them and notice that they've got black hair that's wavey, but awfully neat, or have dark lines under their eyes, and look charmingly dissipated, or have funny smiles, that come and go and leave you wondering whether they smiled at all. Then I like the way they begin to follow you with their eyes. They're interested. Good! Then I begin to place him. Try to get his type, find what he likes;

right then the romance begins to lessen for me and increase for him. Then come a few long talks.

John — (*Bitterly*) I remember.

Helen — Then, John here's the worst of it. There's a point where everything changes.

John — (*Mournfully interested*) What do you mean?

Helen — Well, sometimes it's a kiss and sometimes it's long before anything like that. Now if it's a kiss, it can do one of three things.

John — Three! It's done a thousand to me.

Helen — It can make him get tired of you; but a clever girl can avoid this. It's only the young ones and the heroines of magazine epigrams that are kissed and deserted. Then there's the second possibility. It can make you tired of him. This is usual. He immediately thinks of nothing but being alone with the girl, and she, rather touchy about the whole thing, gets snappy, and he's first love sick, then discouraged, and finally lost.

John — (*More grimly*) Go on.

Helen — Then the third state is where the kiss really means something, where the girl lets go of herself and the man is in deadly earnest.

John — Then they're engaged?

Helen — Exactly.

John — Weren't we?

Helen — (*Emphatically*) No, we distinctly were not. I knew what I was doing every blessed second, John Cannel.

John — Very well, don't be angry. I feel mean enough already.

Helen — (*Coldly*) Do you?

John — Where do I come in? This is all a very clever system of yours, and you've played through it, you go along your way looking for another movie hero with black hair, or light hair, or red hair, and I am left with the same pair of eyes looking at me, the same lips moving in the same words to another poor fool, the next—

Helen — For Heaven sakes don't cry!

John — Oh, I don't give a damn what I do!

Helen — (*Her eyes cast down to where her toe traces a pattern on the carpet*) You are very young. You would think from the way you talk that it was all my fault, that I tried not to like you.

John — Young! Oh, I'm in the discard, I know.

Helen — Oh, you'll find someone else.

John — I don't want anyone else.

Helen — (*Scornfully*) You're making a perfect fool of yourself.

There is a silence. She idly kicks the heel of her slipper against the rung of the chair.

John — (*Slowly*) It's this damn Charlie Wordsworth.

Helen — (*Raising her eyes quickly*) If you want to talk like that you'd better go. Please go now.

She rises. John watches her for a moment and then admits his defeat.

John — Helen, don't let's do like this. Let's be friends. Good God, I never thought I would have to ask you for just that.

She runs over and takes his hand, affecting a hopeful cheerfulness which immediately revolts him. He drops her hand and disappears from the window. She leans out and watches him.

Helen — Watch for that spike. Oh, John, I warned you. You've torn your clothes.

John — (*Drearily from below*) Yes, I've torn my clothes. I certainly play in wonderful luck. Such an effective exit.

Helen — Are you coming to the dance?

John — No, of course I am not. Do you think I'd come just to see you and Charlie—

Helen — (*Gently*) Good-night, John.

She closes the window. Outside a clock strikes nine. The clatter of a few people on the stairway comes muffled through the door. She turns on the lights and going up to glass looks long and with an intense interest at herself. At powder puff comes into use for an instant. An errant wisp of hair is tucked into position, and a necklace from somewhere slides into place.

Mrs. Halycon — (*Outside*) Oh, Helen!

Helen — Coming, mother.

She opens the top bureau drawer, takes out a silver cigarette case, a miniature silver flask, and places them in a side drawer of the writing desk.

Then she turns out all the lights and opens the door. The tuning of violins comes in nervous twangs and discords up the stairs. She turns once more and stands by the window. From below, there is a sudden burst of sound, as the orchestra swings into "Poor Butterfly." The violins and faint drums and a confused chord from a piano, the rich odor of powder, and new silk, a blend of laughters all surge together into the room. She dances toward the mirror, kisses the vague reflection of her face, and runs out the door.

Silence for a moment. Bundled figures pass along the hall, sillouhetted against the lighted door. The laughter heard from below becomes doubled and multiplied. Suddenly a moving blur takes shape behind the bureau. It resolves itself into a human figure, which arises, tip-toes over and shuts the door. It crosses the room, and the lights go on again. Cecilia looks about her, and with the light of definite purpose in her rich green eyes goes to the desk drawer, takes out the miniature flask and the cigarette case. She lights a cigarette, and puffing and coughing walks to the pierglass.

Cecilia — (*Addressing her future self*) Oh, yes! Really coming out is such a farce nowadays, y'know. We really play around so much before we are seventeen, that it's positive anticlimax. (*Shaking hands with a visionary middle-aged man of the world*) Yes, I b'lieve I've heard m' sister speak of you. Have a puff. They're very good. They're Coronas. You don't smoke? What a pity.

She crosses to the desk and picks up the flask. From downstairs the rain of clapping between encores rises. She raises the flask, uncorks it, smells it, tastes a little, and then drinks about the equivalent of two cocktails. She replaces the flask, makes a wry face and as the music starts again she foxtrots slowly around the room, waving the cigarette with intense seriousness, and watching herself in the long mirror.

CURTAIN

— F. Scott Fitzgerald

---

29. "The Debutante," *The Nassau Literary Magazine*, LXXII (January 1917), pp. 241-252. Fitzgerald is credited by name in the magazine. Reviewer H. S. Murch in *The Daily Princetonian* (January 19, 1917) found Fitzgerald's characters in "The Debutante" to be "unlikeable enough, yet we admire the skill of Helen's counterplay and the arch, if feline, naughtiness of her younger sister Cecilia. The latter's mock ennui and sophistication in the closing lines is wholly delicious."

This play, in which Fitzgerald took understandable pride, is concise and focused. Fitzgerald's depiction of the girl's rejection of the fellow who is now reduced to pathetically begging that they remain friends is wholly believable. And why not? It was drawn from his own experiences with Ginevra King. (Her rejection of him would also provide the inspiration for his story "The Pierian Springs and the Last Straw.") As he would often do in later years, Fitzgerald uses lines from a popular song — in this case the poignant "Poor Butterfly," which he noted in his journal was a hit of 1916 — to help create the atmosphere he wants.

Revised, "The Debutante" would later be published in *The Smart Set*; it would ultimately become part of *This Side of Paradise*. "The Debutante" was the first of five major pieces Fitzgerald would write in the enormously productive year of 1917 (all for *The Nassau Literary Magazine*), the others being "The Spire and the Gargoyle" (February), "Tarquin of Cheepside" (April), "Sentiment — And the Use of Rouge" (June), and "The Pierian Springs and the Last Straw" (October).

Book Talk: Penrod and Sam

Penrod and Sam by Booth Tarkington, '93, another collection of "Penrod" stories, is the typical second book of a series. At times it maintains the rather high level of humor set by its predecessor *Penrod*, but certain of the stories seem to have been turned out solely to fill a contract with the Cosmopolitan magazine.

The same set of characters figure once more. Mr. Tarkington has done what so many authors of juvenile books fail to do: he has admitted the unequaled snobbishness of boyhood and has traced the neighborhood social system which, with Penrod and Sam at the top, makes possible more than half the stories. Herman and Verman, the colored brethren, may be socially eligible, but Maurice Levy, barely a "regular fellow," is never quite admitted as an equal. Georgie Bassett, "the best boy in town," and Roddie Bitts, the hothouse plant, are clearly outside the pale; although we claim that there is still hope for Roddy, there is a certain disagreeableness about him which is too sure to be despised. It is to be regretted that Carlie Chitten, a future Machiavelli, figures in only one story. He and Penrod are truer types of success than are to be found in the intricacies of a dozen psychological novels.

The first two stories, "The Bonded Prisoner" and "Bingism," belong distinctly in the filler class, although both have Tarkington touches. The third story, "The In-or-in," the history of an ill-fated secret society, is really funny, and so is the next one, "The Story of Whitney," the horse that was rescued in spite of himself. "Conscience" and "Gypsey" are not so good, but the following tale, "Wednesday Madness," is uproarously funny. It is as good as the best parts of *Seventeen*. Penrod tries to pass off a rather sentimental letter of his sister's as his own composition, in answer to a demand made at school for a model letter to a friend. This leads to a wild Wednesday of fights, flights, and fatalities, the last of which is the spanking which awaits him as he trudges home at seven-thirty.

"Penrod's Busy Day" and "On Account of the Weather" are both amusing; the "Horn of Fame" is rather poor. The book ends with "The Party," easily the best story. From the sleek advent of Carlie Chitten to Marjorie's confession, that she loves Penrod because of his capabilities for wit, it is extremely well done, and brings back a dozen like experiences to the reader's memory. Where Mr. Tarkington gets his knowledge of child psychology, I am unable to understand. It has become a tradition to mention Tom Brown as an ideal boy's story, but as a matter of fact, the heroes of Owen Johnston, Compton McKenzie, and Booth Tarkington are far more interesting and far truer to facts.

(Penrod and Sam, *by Booth Tarkington. Doubleday Page & Co., New York. $1.35 net.*)

— F.S.F.

30. A book review of *Penrod and Sam* by Booth Tarkington, *The Nassau Literary Magazine*, LXXII (January 1917), pp. 291-292. Fitzgerald's authorship is credited by initials: F.S.F.

Best-selling author and two-time Pulitzer Prize winner Tarkington was, in his day, one of Princeton's most widely known alumni. Fitzgerald considered him a significant early influence on his own writing. In going out for *The Tiger*, *The Nassau Lit*, and The Triangle Club, Fitzgerald was also following in Tarkington's path. As an undergraduate, Tarkington made vital contributions to all three organizations; in fact, he actually wrote the Triangle Club's very first production, "The Honorable Julius Caesar," in 1893, and helped get the organization off the ground. And as a loyal alumnus, Tarkington maintained ties to the three organizations. For example, he gladly contributed a drawing to a special "all star" issue of *The Tiger* in the spring of Fitzgerald's freshman year. (Years later, he would lend his luster to *The Tiger*'s 50th anniversary volume.)

In this 1917 book review, Fitzgerald praises the way Tarkington "has admitted the unequalled snobbishness of boyhood and has traced the neighborhood social system..." — which Fitzgerald himself would later do quite masterfully in his Basil and Josephine stories.

In subsequent years, Fitzgerald would come to note quite clearly Tarkington's limitations, not just his strengths. In a review of Tarkington's *Gentle Julia* for *The St. Paul Daily News* (May 7, 1922) Fitzgerald would call Tarkington "our best humorist since Mark Twain," but observe meaningfully that Tarkington "is not a thoughtful man nor one profoundly interested in life as a whole.... It is a pity that the man who writes better prose than any other living American was brought up in a generation that considered it a crime to tell the truth." Fitzgerald was interested in the psychological makeup of his characters in a way that Tarkington never seemed to be.

In an undated letter (postmarked June 26, 1922) to a fan in St. Louis by the name of Hazel McCormack, Fitzgerald credited Compton Mackenzie and Booth Tarkington with having "together taught me all I know about the English language." (The letter is now in the Fitzgerald collection at Princeton.)

Fitzgerald wrote five book reviews (all for *The Nassau Lit*) as a Princeton undergraduate. In the early 1920s, he would write a dozen book reviews for publications ranging from *The Bookman* to *The New York Evening Post*. He stopped reviewing books altogether in 1923.

"BOY KILLS SELF RATHER THAN PET."

— New York Journal.

Nice Fellow!!

31. "Boy Kills Self Rather Than Pet," *The Princeton Tiger*, XXVII (February 3, 1917), p. 12. Unsigned. Known to be by Fitzgerald because he preserved a clipping in his scrapbook.

THINGS THAT NEVER CHANGE. NO. 3982.

Is it $\left\{ \begin{array}{c} \text{hot} \\ \text{cold} \end{array} \right\}$ enough for you?

32. "Things That Never Change. No. 3982," *The Princeton Tiger*, XXVII (February 3, 1917), p. 12. Unsigned. Fitzgerald preserved a clipping in his scrapbook.

PRECAUTION PRIMARILY

*T*he scene is a paint box. Large green and whites form the back, a blue leans against the side and many small greens edged with orange are scattered around artistically. As the curtain rises music is falling gently from the strange melancholy individuals who sit in front dressed in their blacks and whites. They all look sadly at the stage which is now filled with people dressed in purple splotched with mauve sitting on pale violets.

The chorus can be heard to remark vaguely in the old English in which all opening choruses are written.

Oh gleeumph wax wash ich
Vil na wan in bun oh
Bun-gi-wow
Il bur lee burly. Oh Gish Bush!

They accompany this by the appropriate dance. The audience lean back wearily and wait for the play to begin.

(Enter the football team disguised as chorus men and the Prom committee in pink tights.)

Cue: "Look back in your score books; look at Hank O'Day."

Song
Henry O'Day, Henry O'Day
King of the neutrals were you;
Kaisers or Kings, Hughie Jennings
All were impartially blue.
Called a ball
When you meant a strike;
Heard them call
"For the love of Mike," etc.

(Pause.)

(Enter two mere striplings, stripped, boiled in grease paint and decorated in Hawaiian straw.)

Song.
Junior, shave your mustache, you're souring all the milk.

(*At the back of the Casino the long-haired authors walk up and down feeling about as comfortable as the Kaiser's own before another offensive.*)

First Author — How do you think the thing's going?

Second Ditto — Fine! not two minutes ago I heard a laugh in the eighteenth row. It was my joke about the—

First Author — Your joke, Ha-Ha! you make me laugh — Did my line about—, etc.

First Music Writer (*aside*) — As if anyone listened to the dialogue.

Second Music Writer — How my songs do stand out.

Lyricist — Remarkable how a good lyric redeems a bad tune. (*Listens to the silent audience and wishes the senior in the front row would control his whooping-cough until the dialogue begins again.*)

(*Behind the scenes.*)

Corinne — Knockout girl in the front row.

Chlorine — No dope.

Corinne — She likes my eyes.

Chlorine — Wait till she sees your legs in the next chorus.

Fluorine (*the leading lady*) — Don't spoil my entrance.

Bromine — Grab on, freshman — one — two — pull! (*Blankety-blank! dash! dash!*)

Iodine — All right everybody — Hurry up! Get your pink silk overcoats.

The Whole Halogen Family (*simultaneously*) —

A bas with the pony ballet,
Ha-Ha to the pony ballet,
Their faces are phoney,
On places they're bony,
Scorn chases the pony ballet.

Enthusiastic Young Preceptor — Progressive! Ah! After the true Washington Square manner.

Average Student (*who doesn't know what he wants and kicks when he gets it*) — Where's the plot?

Moral of the show: You can't please all of the people all of the time.

Curtain.

F.S.F.

33. "Precaution Primarily," *The Princeton Tiger*, XXVII (February 3, 1917), pp. 13-14. Fitzgerald's authorship is credited by the printing of his initials: F.S.F. This was the first time a Fitzgerald contribution was actually credited to him in *The Tiger*. He would subsequently be credited on seven more occasions, all in 1917: once for a cover idea, twice for cartoons, twice for stories, and twice for poems.

"Precaution Primarily" parodies the Triangle Club musical comedy of 1916-17, *Safety First*, which was set in "a Futurist art community." John Biggs Jr. '18 and J. F. Bohmfalk '17 wrote the libretto of *Safety First*; Fitzgerald himself wrote the show's lyrics. Here's a sample, for comparison's sake: "Charlott Corday, Charlott Corday, / You had them all on the string; / Gee, they were mean to guillotine / A sweet, little innocent thing!" So, in "Precaution Primarily," Fitzgerald is spoofing a Triangle show that he had actually helped to create.

THE TIGER

MIDYEARS

The Spire and the Gargoyle

The Nassau Literary Magazine
Volume LXXII February No. 7

I

The night mist fell. From beyond the moon it rolled, clustered about the spires and towers, and then settled below them so that the dreaming peaks seemed still in lofty aspiration toward the stars. Figures that dotted the daytime like ants now brushed along as ghosts in and out of the night. Even the buildings seemed infinitely more mysterious as they loomed suddenly out of the darkness, outlined each by a hundred faint squares of yellow light. Indefinitely from somewhere a bell boomed the quarter hour and one of the squares of light in an east campus recitation hall was blotted out for an instant as a figure emerged. It paused and resolved itself into a boy who stretched his arms wearily, and advancing threw himself down full length on the damp grass by the sun-dial. The cool bathed his eyes and helped to force away the tiresome picture of what he had just left, a picture that, in the two strenuous weeks of examinations now just over, had become indelibly impressed upon his memory — a room with the air fairly vibrating with nervous tension, silent with the presence of twenty boys working desperately against time, searching every corner of tired brains for words and figures which seemed forever lost. The boy out on the grass opened his eyes and looked back at the three pale blurs which marked the windows of the examination room. Again he heard:

"There will be fifteen minutes more allowed for this examination." There had followed a silence broken by the snapping of verifying watches and the sharp frantic race of pencils. One by one the seats had been left vacant and the little preceptor with the tired look had piled the booklets higher. Then the boy had left the room to the music of the three last scratching pencils.

In his case it all depended on this examination. If he passed it, he would become a sophomore the following fall; if he failed, it meant that his college days faded out with the last splendors of June. Fifty cut recitations in his first wild term had made necessary the extra course of which he had just taken the examination. Winter muses, unacademic and cloistered by Forty-second Street and Broadway, had stolen hours from the dreary stretches of February and March. Later, time had crept insidiously through lazy April afternoons and seemed so intangible in the long Spring twilights. So June found him unprepared. Evening after evening the senior singing, drifting over the campus and up to his window, drew his mind for an instant to the unconscious poetry of it and he, goading on his spoiled and over-indulged faculties, bent to the revengeful books again. Through the careless shell that covered his undergraduate consciousness had broken a deep and almost reverent liking for the gray walls and gothic peaks and all they symbolized in the store of the ages of antiquity.

In view of his window a tower sprang upward, grew into a spire, yearning higher till its uppermost end was half invisible against the morning skies. The transiency and relative unimportance of the campus figures except as holders of a sort of apostolic succession had first impressed themselves on him in contrast with this spire. In a lecture or in an article or in conversation, he had learned that Gothic architecture with its upward trend was peculiarly adapted to colleges, and the symbolism of this idea had become personal to him. Once he had associated the beauty of the campus night with the parades and singing crowds that streamed through it, but in the last month the more silent stretches of sward and the quiet halls with an occasional late-burning scholastic light held his imagination with a stronger grasp — and this tower in full view of his window became the symbol of his perception. There was something terribly pure in the slope of the chaste stone, something which led and directed and called. To him the spire became an ideal. He had suddenly begun trying desperately to stay in college.

"Well, it's over," he whispered aloud to himself, wetting his hands in the damp and running them through his hair. "All over."

He felt an enormous sense of relief. The last pledge had been duly indicted in the last book, and his destiny lay no longer in his own hands, but in those of the little preceptor, whoever he was: the boy had never seen him before — and the face, — he looked like one of the gargoyles that nested in dozens of niches in some of the buildings. His glasses, his eyes, or his mouth gave a certain grotesque upward slant to his whole cast of feature, that branded him as of gargoyle origin, or at least gargoyle kinship. He was probably marking the papers. Perhaps, mused the boy, a bit of an interview, an arrangement for a re-reading in case of the ever possible failure would be — to interrupt his thought the light went out in the examination room and a moment later three figures edged along the path beside him while a fourth struck off south towards the town. The boy jumped to his feet and, shaking himself like a wet spaniel, started after the preceptor.

The man turned to him sharply as he murmured a good evening and started trudging along beside.

"Awful night," said the boy.

The gargoyle only grunted.

"Gosh, that was a terrible examination." This topic died as unfruitfully as that of the weather, so he decided to come directly to the point.

"Are you marking these papers, sir?"

The preceptor stopped and faced him. Perhaps he didn't want to be reminded of the papers, perhaps he was in the habit of being exasperated by anything of this sort, but most probably he was tired and damp and wanted to get home.

"This isn't doing you any good. I know what you're going to say — that this is the crucial examination for you and that you'd like me to go over your paper with you, and so on. I've heard the same thing a hundred times from a hundred students in the course of this last two weeks. My answer is 'No, No,' do you understand? I don't care to know your identity and I won't be followed home by a nagging boy."

Simultaneously each turned and walked quickly away, and the boy suddenly realized with an instinct as certain as divination that he was not going to pass the examination.

"Damned gargoyle," he muttered.

But he knew the gargoyle had nothing to do with it.

II

Regularly every two weeks he had been drifting out Fifth Avenue. On crisp autumn afternoons the tops of the shining auto busses were particularly alluring. From the roofs of other passing busses a face barely seen, an interested glance, a flash of color assumed the proportion of an intrigue. He had left college five years before and the busses and the art gallery and a few books were his intellectual relaxation. Freshman year Carlisle's "Heroes and Hero-Worship," in the hands of an impassioned young instructor, had interested him particularly. He had read practically nothing. He had neither the leisure to browse thoughtfully on much nor the education to cram thoughtfully on little, so his philosophy on life was molded of two elements: one the skeptical office philosophy of his associates, with a girl, a ten thousand dollar position and a Utopian flat in some transfigured Bronx at the end of it; and the other, the three or four big ideas which he found in the plain speaking Scotchman, Carlyle. But he felt, and truly, that his whole range was pitifully small. He was not naturally bookish; his taste could be stimulated as in the case of "Heroes and Hero-Worship" but he was still and now always would be in the stage where every work and every author had to be introduced and sometimes interpreted to him. "Sartor Resartus" meant nothing to him nor ever could.

So Fifth Avenue and the top of the busses had really grown to stand for a lot. They meant relief from the painted, pagan crowds of Broadway, the crowded atmosphere of the blue serge suits and grated windows that he met down town and the dingy middle class cloud that hovered on his boarding house. Fifth Avenue had a certain respectability which he would have once despised; the people on the busses looked better fed, their mouths came together in better lines. Always a symbolist, and an idealist, whether his model had been a profligate but magnetic sophomore or a Carlylized Napoleon, he sought around him in his common life for something to cling to, to stand for what religions and families and philosophies of life had stood for. He had a certain sense of fitness which convinced him that his old epicureanism, romantic as it might have been in the youth of his year at college, would have been exotic and rather disgusting in the city itself. It was much too easy; it lacked the penance of the five o'clock morning train back to college that had faced himself and his fellow student revelers, it lacked the penance of the long morning in classes, and the poverty of weeks. It had been something to have a reputation, even such a reputation as this crowd had, but dissipation from the New York standpoint seemed a matter of spats and disgustingly rich Hebrews, and shoddy Bohemeanism had no attraction for him.

Yet he was happy this afternoon. Perhaps because the bus in which he rode was resplendent in its shining new coat of green paint, and the stick-of-candy glamor of it had gone into his disposition. He lit a cigarette and made himself rather comfortable until he arrived at his destination. There were only certain sections of the museum that he visited. Statuary never attracted him, and the Italian madonnas and Dutch gentlemen with inconsequent gloves and books in the foreground rather bored him. It was only here and there in an old picture tucked away in the corner that his eye caught the glare of light on snow in a simple landscape or the bright colors and multiple figures of a battle painting, and he was drawn into long and detailed fits of contemplation and frequent revisits.

On this particular afternoon he was wandering rather aimlessly from one room to another when he suddenly noticed a small man in overshoes, his face latticed with enormous spectacles, thumbing a catalogue in front of a Flemish group. He started, and with a sense of recollection walked by him several times. Suddenly he realized that here was that one time instrument of his fate, the gargoyle, the little preceptor who had flunked him in his critical examination.

Oddly enough his first sensation was one of pleased reminiscence and a desire for conversation. Following that he had a curious feeling of shyness, untinged by any bitterness. He paused, staring heavily, and instantly the huge glasses glimmered suspiciously in his eyes.

"Pardon me sir, but do you remember me?" he asked eagerly.

The preceptor blinked feverishly.

"Ah — no."

He mentioned the college and the blinks became more optimistic. He wisely decided to let the connection rest there. The preceptor couldn't, couldn't possibly remember all the men who had passed before his two "Mirrors of Shallot" so why bring up old, accusing facts — besides — he felt a great desire to chat.

"Yes — no doubt — your face is familiar, you'll pardon my — my chilliness a moment since — a public place." He looked around depreciatingly. "You see, I've left the university myself."

"So you've gone up in the game?" He instantly

regretted this remark for the little man answered rather quickly:

"I'm teaching in a high school in Brooklyn." Rather embarrassed, the younger man tried to change the subject by looking at the painting before them, but the gargoyle grimly continued:

"I have — a — rather a large family, and much as I regretted leaving the University, the salary was unfortunately very much of a factor."

There was a pause during which both regarded the picture steadily. Then the gargoyle asked a question:

"How long since you've graduated?"

"Oh, I never graduated. I was there for only a short while." He was sure now that the gargoyle had not the slightest conception of his identity; he might rather enjoy this, however, and he had a pleasant notion that the other was not averse to his company.

"Are you staying here much longer?" The gargoyle was not, and together they moved to a restaurant two blocks down where they indulged in milk, tea and jam and discussed the university. When six o'clock pushed itself into the crowded hours it was with real regret that they shook hands, and the little man, manipulating his short legs in mad expostulation, raced after a Brooklyn car. Yes, it had been distinctly exhilarating. They had talked of academic atmospheres, of hopes that lay in the ivied walls, of little things that could only have counted after the mystic hand of separation had made them akin. The gargoyle had touched lightly upon his own story, of the work he was doing, of his own tepid, stuffy environment. It was his hope some day to get back, but now there were young appetites to satisfy (the other thought grotesquely of the young gargoyles) — if he could see his way clear in the next few years, — so it went, but through all of his hopeful talk there was a kind of inevitability that he would teach in a Brooklyn high school till the last bell called him to his last class. Yes, he went back occasionally. He had a younger brother who was an instructor there.

So they had talked, knit together by the toast and the sense of exile. That night the shrivelled spinster on his left at table asked him what college he thought would be worthy of ushering her promising nephew into the outer world. He became voluble and discoursive. He spoke of ties that bind, of old associations, and remarked carelessly as he left her, that he was running back himself for a day the next week. But afterwards he lay awake and thought until the chairs and bedposts of his room became grey ghosts in the dawn.

III

The car was hot and stuffy with most of the smells of the state's alien population. The red plush seats radiated dust in layers and stratas. The smoking car had been even more impossible with filthy floor and heavy air. So the man sat next to a partly open window in the coach and shivered against the cutting cloud of fog that streamed in over him. Lights sped by vaguely blurred and spreading, marking towns and farmhouses with the democratic indiscrimination of the mist. As the conductor heralded each station the man felt a certain thrill at the familiarity of the names. The times and conditions under which he had heard them revolved in a medley of memories of his one year. One station particularly near the university had a peculiar significance for him because of the different ways it had affected him while he had been in college. He had noted it at the time. September of his entrance year, it had been the point where he grew acutely nervous and fidgety. Returning that November from a football defeat, it had stood for all that seemed gloomy in the gloomy college he was then going back to. In February it had meant the place to wake and pull one's self together, and as he had passed it for the last time that June, he had wondered with a sudden sinking of his heart if it was to be the last time. Now as the train shook and trembled there for a moment, he stared out the window, and tried to get an impression. Oddly enough his first one came back to him; he felt rather nervous and uncertain.

He had discovered a few minutes ago that the little preceptor sat ahead of him three seats, but the younger man had not joined him or even ad-

92

dressed him. He wanted to draw to himself every impression he could from this ride.

They drew in. Grip in hand, he swung off the train, and from force of habit turned toward the broad steps that led to the campus. Then he stopped and, dropping his suit case, looked before him. The night was typical of the place. It was very like the night on which he had taken his last examination, yet somehow less full and less poignant. Inevitability became a reality and assumed an atmosphere of compelling and wearing down. Where before the spirit of spires and towers had thrilled him and had made him dreamily content and acquiescent, it now overawed him. Where before he had realized only his own inconsequence, he now realized his own impotence and insufficiency. The towers in faint outlines and the battlemented walls of vague buildings fronted him. The engine from the train he had just left wheezed and clanged and backed; a hack drove off; a few pale self-effacing town boys strode away voicelessly, swallowed up in the night. And in front of him the college dreamed on — awake. He felt a nervous excitement that might have been the very throb of its slow heart.

A figure brushed violently into him, almost knocking him off his feet. He turned and his eyes pierced the trembling darkness of the arclight to find the little preceptor blinking apprehensively at him from his gargoyle's eyes.

"Good evening."

He was hesitatingly recognized.

"Ah — how do you do? How do you do? Foggy evening, hope I didn't jar you."

"Not at all. I was just admiring the serenity." He paused and almost felt presumptuous.

"Are you — ah — pretending to be a student again?"

"I just ran out to see the place. Stay a night perhaps." Somehow this sounded far-fetched to him. He wondered if it did to the other.

"Yes? — I'm doing the same thing. My brother is an instructor here now you know. He's putting me up for a space." For an instant the other longed fiercely that he too might be invited to be "put up for a space."

"Are you walking my way?"

"No — not quite yet."

The gargoyle smiled awkwardly. "Well, goodnight." There was nothing more to say. Eyes staring, he watched the little figure walking off, propelled jerkily by his ridiculous legs.

Minutes passed. The train was silent. The several blurs on the station platform became impersonal and melted into the background. He was alone face to face with the spirit that should have dominated his life, the mother that he had renounced. It was a stream where he had once thrown a stone but the faint ripple had long since vanished. Here he had taken nothing, he had given nothing; nothing? — his eyes wandered slowly upward — up — up — until by straining them he could see where the spire began — and with his eyes went his soul. But the mist was upon both. He could not climb the spire.

A belated freshman, his slicker rasping loudly, slushed along the soft path. A voice from somewhere called the inevitable formula toward an unknown window. A hundred little sounds of the current drifting on under the fog pressed in finally on his consciousness.

"Oh God!" he cried suddenly, and started at the sound of his own voice in the stillness. He had cried out from a complete overwhelming sense of failure. He realized how outside of it all it was. The gargoyle, poor tired little hack, was bound up in the fabric of the whole system much more than he was or ever could be. Hot tears of anger and helplessness rushed to his eyes. He felt no injustice, only a deep mute longing. The very words that would have purged his soul were waiting for him in the depths of the unknown before him — waiting for him where he could never come to claim them. About him the rain dripped on. A minute longer he stood without moving, his head bent dejectedly, his hands clenched. Then he turned, and picking up his suit case walked over to the train. The engine gave a tentative pant, and the conductor, dozing in a corner, nodded sleepily at him from the end of the deserted car. Wearily he sank down onto a red plush seat, and pressed his hot forehead against the damp window pane.

— F. Scott Fitzgerald.

93

34. "The Spire and the Gargoyle," *The Nassau Literary Magazine*, LXXII (February 1917), pp. 297-307. Fitzgerald is credited by name in the magazine. With this story, it is clear that Fitzgerald has found his voice as a writer. Anyone familiar with Fitzgerald's later work would be able to recognize this piece as Fitzgerald's by the setting, the tone, and the choice of words. The student fails a crucial examination. (As Fitzgerald would comment in later years, his stories always contained "a touch of disaster.") In what may have been a bit of wish-fulfillment on Fitzgerald's part, the preceptor who gives the test also experiences failure in his career. The student eventually returns to the Princeton campus that he loved (and whose beauty Fitzgerald evokes so vividly) with a forlorn sense of being an outsider.

"The Spire and the Gargoyle" was given a mixed review in *The Daily Princetonian* (February 24, 1917) by the writer William Rose Benét, who noted that Fitzgerald "is good at the Princeton background" but alleged there was "an extravagance of figurative speech which defeats its object.... Mr. Fitzgerald has an instinct for style but very little for proportion."

Interestingly, when Fitzgerald reviewed the latest issue of *The Nassau Lit* for *The Daily Princetonian* of March 16, 1928 (calling it "a dignified but on the whole unadventurous number of the oldest college magazine in America"), his first complaint was that too many *Nassau Lit* writers were using Princeton as the setting for their tales. In his day, the 31-year-old Fitzgerald maintained, *Nassau Lit* tales had boasted much more varied and imaginative settings. Princeton undergraduates were "playing safe," he declared, by choosing to write stories with Princeton backgrounds. Of course it was the great success of Fitzgerald's own *This Side of Paradise* that inspired so many subsequent Princeton undergraduates to follow his example and write autobiographical fiction set in Princeton.

Fitzgerald never sold "The Spire and the Gargoyle" to a commercial magazine or included it in a short story collection, but he did borrow lines from it for *This Side of Paradise*, a section of which, incidentally, he decided to title "Spires and Gargoyles." Since 1922, *The Tiger*, as a way of recalling its connection with Fitzgerald, has likewise titled a section of the magazine "Spires and Gargoyles."

For modern readers, the story "The Spire and the Gargoyle" is marred slightly by Fitzgerald's gratuitous passing reference to "disgustingly rich Hebrews." There is no doubt that in his youth, like many of his social class, Fitzgerald had an anti-Jewish bias. In later years, favorably impressed by Irving Thalberg, Sheila Graham, and others he was close to who were Jewish, he outgrew his prejudice; changes in attitude can be discerned in his writings through the years. (See "Scott Fitzgerald and the Jews," *Forward,* February 12, 1993, pages 9-10.) The Princeton of Fitzgerald's era admitted very few Jewish students. V. Lansing Collins, who was the University's secretary and an admissions-committee member, wrote in 1922 (in a letter uncovered by researcher Marcia Graham Synnott): "I hope the Alumni will tip us off to any Hebrew candidate. As a matter of fact, however, our strongest barrier is our club system." (The reference was to the then-common blackballing of Jewish applicants by members of selective eating clubs.) Fitzgerald's youthful exposure to — and acceptance of — minorities in general seems to have been rather limited. In the last story he wrote before entering Princeton, "Pain and the Scientist," Fitzgerald's protagonist gets to encounter, for the first time in his life, "a real Christian Scientist," who is depicted unflatteringly; the protagonist gleefully shows up the Christian Scientist.

The Big Strong Student.

Why Boys Leave College

35. "Why Boys Leave College." This cartoon for *The Tiger*, and the following one, "Ain't it the Truth?" (both by Lawrence Boardman '18), were not written by Fitzgerald, but are included simply for the sake of context-setting. They give us a taste of Princeton college life of the period. In the first cartoon, Boardman de-picts the distractions faced by a student who must pass an exam the next day if he is to remain in Princeton—a situation with which Boardman's classmate Fitzgerald was certainly well acquainted. The next Boardman cartoon, "Ain't it the Truth?," documents the ways in which students of the era could while away the time.

Ain't it the Truth?

Rain Before Dawn

The dull, faint patter in the drooping hours
Drifts in upon my sleep and fills my hair
With damp; the burden of the heavy air
Is strewn upon me where my tired soul cowers,
Shrinking like some lone queen in empty towers
Dying. Blind with unrest I grow aware:
The pounding of broad wings drifts down the stair
And sates me like the heavy scent of flowers.

I lie upon my heart. My eyes like hands
Grip at the soggy pillow. *Now the dawn*
Tears from her wetted breast the splattered blouse
Of night; lead-eyed and moist she straggles o'er the lawn,
Between the curtains brooding stares and stands
Like some drenched swimmer — Death's within the house!

— F. Scott Fitzgerald

---

36. "Rain Before Dawn," *The Nassau Literary Magazine*, LXXII (February 1917), p. 321. Fitzgerald is credited by name in the magazine. In *The Daily Princetonian* (February 24, 1917), William Rose Benét commented that Fitzgerald's "poem, 'Rain Before Dawn' has a number of virtues but is disarticulated. The total effect is confused. There is promise, however, in his work." Benét would monitor Fitzgerald's subsequent development with care, writing with a greater understanding than many other critics, perhaps because he had known of Fitzgerald's work several years before they (or the general public) did. In *The Saturday Review of Literature* (May 9, 1925), Benét would recall that Fitzgerald had "started his literary career with enormous facility" and "a reckless confidence in himself." Benét had found *This Side of Paradise* "amazing in its excitement and gusto, amazing in phrase and epithet, amazing no less for all sorts of thoroughly bad writing pitched in with the good...." He had felt that in some of Fitzgerald's subsequent popular magazine stories "one could discern the demands of the 'market' blunting and dulling the blade" of Fitzgerald's bright sword. He had worried that the magazines might make Fitzgerald stale. "But *The Great Gatsby* comes suddenly to knock all that surmise into a cocked hat." In a judgment that has stood the test of time, Benét pronounced *The Great Gatsby* "a mature novel" with "high occasions of felicitous, almost magic phrase."

Book Talk: David Blaize

Of late years there have been really good boys' stories, with the boy treated from a subjective point of view neither cynically nor sentimentally. In the class belong *The Varmint*, *Youth's Encounter*, *Seventeen*, and perhaps a new book, *David Blaize*, by E.F. Benson, author of *Dodo*. Benson, by the way, is one of the famous Benson triology with Arthur C. Benson and the late Monsiegnuer Robert Hugh Benson. The book carries the English hero through his last year at a "private" school and through three forms at an English public school, presumably Eton under the name of Marchester.

Frank Maddox, David's first and last hero, is the strongest personality in the book, David being rather a peg on which the author hangs virtues and adventures. The book starts well and until three-quarters the way through is very interesting. Then follows a long and, to an American, dry and unintelligible account of a cricket match in which, by careful sounding, we fathom that the hero and his idol Frank Maddox, in the orthodox Ralph Henry Barbour manner, win the day for the school.

Mr. Benson's indebtedness to Compton MacKenzie and Kipling is very great. Swinburne introduces David to literature as he did Michael in *Youth's Encounter* and the disagreement of David with the prefects is very like certain chapters in Stalkey's career. The one incident which forms the background of the book is foreign to anything in our preparatory schools and although handled with an overemphasized delicacy, seems rather unnecessary and unhealthy from our point of view.

One of the great charms of the book lies in the chapters where Frank first lights upon David near the old cathedral and where David is visiting Frank at the seashore. The chapter on David's love affair is poorly written and seems a half-hearted attempt to make him seem well-rounded. The last melodramatic incident, the injury and recovery of the hero is well done, but does not go for unity. The first two-thirds of the book is immensely entertaining, the last third disappointing.

(*David Blaize, by E.F. Benson, The George Doran Company, New York. $1.35 net*).

—F.S.F.

---

37. A book review of *David Blaize* by E. F. Benson, *The Nassau Literary Magazine*, LXXII (February 1917), pp. 343-344. Fitzgerald's authorship is credited by initials: F.S.F. Of particular interest is Fitzgerald's remark: "Mr. Benson's indebtedness to Compton MacKenzie and Kipling is very great." Fitzgerald would later make a note in his copy of *This Side of Paradise* acknowledging his own indebtedness to such writers as Mackenzie, H. G. Wells, Oscar Wilde, and Booth Tarkington. (Edmund Wilson, who read *This Side of Paradise* before it was published, went so far as to call it "an exquisite burlesque of Compton MacKenzie with a pastiche of Wells thrown in at the end.") In a 1920 "self-interview," Fitzgerald proclaimed, "I want to be able to do anything with words… I want to do the wide sultry heavens of Conrad, the rolled-gold sundowns and crazy-quilt skies of Hichens and Kipling as well as the pastel dawns of Chesterton…. I am a professed literary thief, hot after the best methods of every writer in my generation." In an interview with Michael Mok of *The New York Post* (September 25, 1936), Fitzgerald called Ernest Hemingway "the greatest living writer of English. He took that place when Kipling died."

A FEW WELL-KNOWN CLUB TYPES AND THEIR FUTURES.

38. "A Few Well-Known Club Types and Their Futures," *The Princeton Tiger*, XXVII (March 17, 1917), p. 7. Fitzgerald conceived and captioned this cartoon, which was drawn by Lawrence Boardman '18 (who is credited by his initials). Fitzgerald preserved a clipping in his scrapbook. Unlike most colleges, Princeton did not have fraternities; the social life of most Princeton juniors and seniors was centered around the private Prospect Street eating clubs, where members ate and partied. Each club occupied a different position in the social hierarchy at Princeton. The individual clubs tended to retain quite consistent identities, year after year. In *This Side of Paradise*, Fitzgerald offered capsule descriptions of some of the clubs: "Ivy, detached and breathlessly aristocratic; Cottage, an impressive melange of brilliant adventurers and well-dressed philanderers; Tiger Inn, broad-shouldered and athletic, vitalized by an honest elaboration of prep-school standards; Cap and Gown, anti-alcoholic, faintly religious and politically powerful...." By the time I was at Princeton, a half-century after the publication of *This Side of Paradise*, Cap and Gown no longer had a reputation for being "anti-alcoholic, faintly religious" — but otherwise, Fitzgerald's descriptions of the clubs would no doubt have seemed fair enough to many of their members.

39

McCAULAY MISSION — WATER STREET.

SERVICE AT FIVE. DRUNKARDS ESPECIALLY INVITED.

— *N.Y. SUN.*

If we send a delegation to Northfield, we should certainly be represented here.

———

39. "McCaulay Mission—Water Street," *The Princeton Tiger*, XXVII (March 17, 1917), p. 10. Unsigned. Known to be by Fitzgerald because he preserved a clipping in his scrapbook.

40

POPULAR PARODIES — No. 1.

I'm off to the Math. School
To pass it or bust.
If Conics don't get me
Then Politics must.

Chorus.
Professor how long
Do I have to wait?
Do you debar me now
Or will you hesitate?

———

40. "Popular Parodies — No. 1," *The Princeton Tiger*, XXVII (March 17, 1917), p. 10. Unsigned. Known to be by Fitzgerald because he preserved a clipping in his scrapbook. Remembering Fitzgerald's academic difficulties, these parodies would seem inspired by real life.

The Diary of a Sophomore

Sunday — March 18th.

Felt nervous all day — temperature 99 8/10. Jim and Heck and Joe came in after dinner. We are going to stick together. Everybody says "stick to your friends" — I'm sticking like a leech — they can't shake me off. Hope I get a *Seaweed* bid.

Monday —

No mail — Jim, Heck and Joe not in rooms, college in anarchy — shall not leave room until I get a bid. Temperature 89.7.

Tuesday —

No mail — except a bill from Sinclair's. Sophomores wanted me to join commons club — Told them I'd like to but I'd promised to stick with my friends. Got Jim, Heck and Joe bids to commons club. Why don't they come to see me.

Wednesday —

Joe came over and said he and Heck were in the *Pillbox* section — Jim is going to *Star and Garter*. I have a good chance for *Pillbox* — Turned down commons again.

Thursday —

We are all going to *Star and Garter*. I'm glad I waited. We shook hands on it and Jim and Heck wept. Emotion is in the air. Temperature, 100.

Friday —

Peter Hype told me to hold off for *Lung and Coatcheck*. I told him I was going to stick with my friends. Hope he didn't think I meant it.

Saturday —

Bid for *Lung and Coatcheck*. I hate to leave Joe and Heck. Shook hands with the "Lungs." Was introduced to several fellows in my class.

Sunday —

Awful excitement. Temperature 102.

Monday —

Signed up *Seaweed*. Jim was foolish to throw away his chances. It's everyman's business to look out for himself. Heck and Joe were a drag on me. They'll be very happy in *Star and Garter*. Wrote Doris about it. Temperature, normal.

F.S.F.

———

41. "The Diary of a Sophomore," *The Princeton Tiger*, XXVII (March 17, 1917), p. 11. Unsigned. Known to be by Fitzgerald because he preserved a clipping in his scrapbook. Fitzgerald has made up the names of these clubs — there are no Princeton clubs called "Star and Garter" or "Lung and Coatcheck"; the real clubs bear such names as "Cap and Gown" and "Ivy" — but he's provided an otherwise credible portrait of the way friendships could be torn apart as students, in the spring of their sophomore year, went through Princeton's "bicker" process, seeking "bids," or invitations, to join one or another of the selective Prospect Street eating

clubs, each of which had a distinct social status. It could be psychologically damaging for a student to learn he was not judged socially acceptable by his preferred club — or, perhaps, by any of the clubs; in a given year, up to one-fourth of the sophomores might be rejected by all of the clubs. The first significant revolt against Princeton's exclusive club system by students — the clubs had been sharply criticized as undemocratic by Princeton's president, Woodrow Wilson, a decade earlier — occurred while Fitzgerald was an undergraduate. In his December 1927 *College Humor* article, "Princeton," Fitzgerald recalled "the ragged squabble of club elections with its scars of snobbishness and adolescent heartbreak."

TRUE DEMOCRACY

True Democracy.

42. "True Democracy," *The Princeton Tiger*, XXVII (March 17, 1917), p. 18. Fitzgerald conceived and captioned this cartoon, which was drawn by Alan Jackman '17, who is credited by name. Jackman confirmed that he and Fitzgerald collaborated on it. Fitzgerald preserved a clipping in his scrapbook. The cartoon appears to be set at the Nassau Inn (or "Nass," as it was known to students then). In Fitzgerald's day, Princeton was all-white. The scene depicted in this cartoon — a Princeton student getting drunk with someone who was black — was practically unimaginable to most students then. In day-to-day life, Princetonians encountered few blacks except in subservient roles, such as the white-coated waiters found at the eating clubs. Fitzgerald's racial attitudes, in his youth, were no more enlightened than most of his classmates. In *This Side of Paradise*, Fitzgerald struggles to explain why one gracious, aristocratic character, Dick Humbird, seemed so admirable to him, writing that Humbird — in presumable contrast with most of their classmates — could even "have lunched at Sherry's with a colored man, yet people would have somehow known that it was all right."

Long considered the southernmost of the northern schools in its general attitudes, Princeton was the last major college above the Mason-Dixon line to open its doors to blacks. In 1942, *The Daily Princetonian* began editorializing in favor of admitting blacks; even then, however, the majority of students polled still expressed opposition to the idea. Not until the embarrassingly late date of 1947 would Princeton finally grant a diploma to a black undergraduate (who had been admitted under a special wartime government program);

not until the 1960s, under the leadership of President Robert Goheen, would Princeton finally make a real commitment to seek black students and faculty members and truly integrate the campus. Happily, the University community has become far more diverse since the 1960s than it was in Fitzgerald's time.

Although Fitzgerald considered his own political views to be quite liberal and read H. G. Wells' and George Bernard Shaw's views on social reform with interest and respect, he was never a crusader for social justice; he believed considerable changes in society were needed but writing was always of far greater interest to him than politics. "Progressive" was how he identified his own political position in the 1917 Princeton yearbook; he took to calling himself a socialist in the 1920s. His daughter Scottie remembered him as essentially an F.D.R. Democrat. There were even times when Fitzgerald flirted with communism (which his friend Edmund Wilson, along with a number of other intellectuals, found attractive), but he wrote a cousin in 1934 that he'd given up on politics, suggesting that the American Communist Party's "treatment of the negro question finished me." Their call for self-determination for southern blacks was too radical for him.

Black characters rarely played significant, well-rounded roles in Fitzgerald's fiction. They tended to be treated sentimentally. The only one of Fitzgerald's short stories to feature black protagonists was the sympathetic and moving "Dearly Beloved," which was written in the last year of his life; however, he was unable to sell that story. "Dearly Beloved" would appear in print for the first time 29 years after Fitzgerald's death.

Undulations of an Undergraduate

I've been for North Edwards selected,
I've roomed in a cupboard in Blair
In Witherspoon dark and dejected,
I've slept without sunshine or air.
My janitress kept me from study,
And awfully long-winded she were,
Her mouth didn't shut so I overcut,
And I learned about college from her.

A senior who came from our city
And practically lived for the glass,
Would tell me in epigrams witty
The way to be big in my class.
He took me to hatters and tailors
And coached me on how to look slim;
He taught me to drink but forbade me to think,
And I learned about college from him.

A girl that I met at the seashore
And took for a summer-day sail
Told stories of brothers at Princeton
Of friends and fiancees at Yale.
She knew all the men who played hockey,
She knew when the promenades were,
She thought me a bore till I asked her to four,
And I learned about college from her.

The dean, since my marks were pathetic,
Had sent me a summons to call,
He greeted me, apologetic,
And smiled, "This is social, that's all."
He said if I chanced to the city
I might be remembering him
To Babbie Larove at the Cocoanut Grove,
And I learned about college from him.

---

43. "Undulations of an Undergraduate," *The Princeton Tiger*, XXVII (March 17, 1917), p. 20. Unsigned. Known to be by Fitzgerald because he preserved a clipping in his scrapbook.

This cartoon by Lawrence Boardman '18 is included for the sake of context-setting. (Fitzgerald was not involved in its creation.) It shows members of Princeton's Class of 1919 — depicted as goody-goody's with halos over their heads — thumbing their noses at the Prospect Street clubs.

KENILWORTH SOCIALISM

Kenilworth Socialism.
An eighth member measuring the mashed potatoes.

44. "Kenilworth Socialism," *The Princeton Tiger*, XXVII (March 17, 1917), p. 22. This is the first time that this piece has been reproduced in a book with the complete caption. Fitzgerald wrote this cartoon, which was drawn by Alan Jackman '17; their collaboration is credited by name: Fitzgerald '18 and Jackman '17. Jackman confirmed that this was written by Fitzgerald and that Jackman had illustrated it.

The anti-club movement was the talk of the campus in the spring of 1917. A number of respected sophomores (such as Richard Cleveland, son of former President Grover Cleveland, and Carl Mickey) refused to join clubs, and a number of juniors and seniors resigned from their clubs, opting to dine elsewhere — as the students in this cartoon are doing — rather than be part of the snobbery they felt the clubs fostered. Although Fitzgerald was a friend of two leading members of the anti-club movement, Henry Strater and David K. E. Bruce (the son of a U.S. senator and later a distinguished diplomat himself), he was quite happy remaining a member of the highly selective Cottage Club, which, incidentally, boasted a strong southern contingent. Fitzgerald is mocking some of the anti-club idealists here, his reference to the black waiter as being a member of their group intended as a put-down.

I trust that this cartoon will be viewed as a historic artifact, included in the interest of being complete and in the hope of gaining a fuller understanding of Fitzgerald's era. I briefly pondered whether this cartoon should be reprinted at all. I come from a large and diverse extended family, including members who are black as well as white, and am aware that some people may feel offended by the reprinting of a cartoon such as this one. However, to delete this cartoon — or to omit the bothersome second line of the caption, as was done when this cartoon was reproduced in *F. Scott Fitzgerald in his Own Time*, edited by Matthew Bruccoli and Jackson Bryer — would be to rewrite history. We're better off examining the past, embarrassments and all, with our eyes wide open.

Tarquin of Cheepside

Running footsteps. — Light, soft-soled shoes, made of queer leather cloth brought from Ceylon, setting the pace; thick flowing boots, two pairs, dark blue and gilt, reflecting the moonlight in blunt gleams and flashes, following, a hundred yards behind. Soft Shoes cleaves the moonlight for a haggard second, then darts into a blind labyrinth of alleys and becomes merely an unsteady scuffle in the darkness ahead. In go Flowing Boots with swords lurching and with clumsy stumbling, cursing the black lanes of London. Soft Shoes leaps a gate and straggles through a hedge-row. Flowing Boots leaps the gate and straggles through the hedge-row; — and there is the watch ahead — two murderous pikemen with ferocious expressions acquired in Calais and the Spanish marshes. But there is no cry for help. The pursued does not fall panting and clutching his purse at their feet nor do the pursuers raise a hue and cry — Soft Shoes goes by like a rush of air. The watch curse and hesitate, look behind and then spread their pikes grimly across the road and wait. A cloud scurries across the sky and blackens the narrow street.

Again the pale sheen skims the eaves and roofs; the chase is on once more, but one of Flowing Boots leaves a little black trail until he binds himself clumsily as he runs, with fine lace caught from his throat.

It was no case for the watch tonight. There had been devil's work and the devil seemed to be he who appeared faintly in front, heel over gate, knee over fence. Moreover, the adversary was evidently travelling near home, or in any rate, in that part of London consecrated to him, for the streets were narrowing and the houses hung over more and more, furnishing natural ambushes often utilized for battle, murder and sudden death. So they twisted, down long sinuous lanes where the moonlight was shut away, except for tiny patches and glints. Ahead the quarry was running blindly, minus his leather jerkin, dripping with sweat and scanning his ground carefully on both sides. Suddenly he slowed down and, retracing his steps, darted down an alley darker and narrower and longer than any he had yet explored. Two hundred yards down he stopped short and crammed himself into a nitch in the wall where he huddled and panted silently like a grotesque god, very faintly outlined in the gloom.

Twenty yards beyond him the others stopped and he heard a whispered colloquy.

"Within thirty yards now."

"Yes, I was atune to that scuffle; it stopped!"

"He's hid."

"Stay together and, by the Virgin, we'll split him!"

Their voices lowered and Soft Shoes could hear no more, nor did he wait to, for at a stealthy step in his direction, he sprang in three paces across the alley where he bounded up, flapped for a moment on the edge of the wall like a huge bird, and disappeared, gulped down by the hungry night at a mouthful.

* * *

Peter Caxter read late, too late, he had recently discovered. His eyes were getting particularly dim for his young time of life, his stomach was swelling to portliness. Tall and misbuilt, lazy too, he was spurred on in his studies by conscience got in heartfuls at Cambridge, and ambition carefully distilled though her subjects by Elizabeth, by the grace of Luther, Queen of England. Peter having completed a rather painful sea-voyage, and stored up great hunks of Elizabethan anecdote for his future grandchildren, was now flitting cumberously back to his neglected books — and what a book he had this night! The *Faery Queene,* by one Edmund Spencer, lay before him under the wavering candle light.

"The Legend of Britomartis of Chastity
It palls* me here to write of Chastity
The fayrest vertue, far above the rest" —

A sudden rush of feet on the stairs, and a man darted into the room, a man panting and gasping and on the verge of a collapse.

"Peter," he blurted out, "I must be hidden — I'm in a scrape — it's death if the two men who will come here after me find me!"

Peter showed little surprise. His guest had been in various difficulties before and had entrusted him with his extrication. And the visitor, when his gasps gave way to quick precise breathing, lost his culprit's air and looked very much at his ease. Indeed a casual observer might have said that he was proud of some recent exploit.

"Two fools with long swords and short wits harrying me over half of London like a terrified rabbit!"

"There were three fools in the chase then," said Peter ironicly, as he took a pole from a corner and dislodged a trap door which led to a sort of garret above. He pointed upward. The other crouched, jumped, caught the edge of the aperture and, struggling for a moment, swung himself up and was lost in the darkness above. The hatch was replaced, there was a scurry like the exodus of rats, an oath muffled by the floor, then silence. Peter picked up the "Legend of Britomartis of Chastity" and settling himself — waited.

Five minutes later a scramble on the stairs was followed by a prolonged hammering on the door. He sighed, put down the book, and picking up the candle, rose.

---

*I.e., falls.

"Who is there?"

"Open — Or we will burst in the door!"

Peter opened it a bare eight inches and held the candle high. He pitched his voice so that it sounded timorous and querulous.

"May not a peaceable citizen of London rest undisturbed from marauders for one small hour of the night?"

"Open gossip, and quick, or we'll pitch a yard of steel through the crack there!"

The shadows of the two gallants fell in huge wavering outlines over the moonlit stairs, and by the light Peter characterized his opponents in a quick glance. They were gentlemen, hastily but richly attired. One was a man of thirty, greatly distraught and nervous from intense excitement and anxiety. The other, the one with the bloody hand, was younger, and though he was quiet and restrained, his lips were set with grim purpose. Peter let them in.

"Is there a man hidden here?" said the elder fiercely.

"No."

"Has there been anyone on the stairs?"

Peter replied that ten minutes ago there had been someone on the landing below trying to get into a room, but that whoever he had been, he had failed and gone away. Would they be so kind as to inform him for whom they were searching and why.

"There has been violence done — to a woman," said the younger man slowly. "My sister — and his wife. Who we are does not matter. If you are hiding this man it may cost you your life."

"Do you know who he — this man — is?" asked Peter quickly.

The elder man sank onto a chair and dropped his face in his hands.

"God's Word — We do not know even that."

Peter rather winced. This was more tragedy than he had bargained for.

The younger man had been searching about Peter's two rooms, poking his sword into anything that looked at all suspicious. He noticed the trap door.

"What's that?"

"It is not used," said Peter. "It is an attic — the trap is nailed down." Suddenly he thought of the pole and drew in his breath sharply, but the other turned away with an air of finality.

"It would take ten minutes to get up there without a ladder unless the man were a tumbler."

"A tumbler," repeated the elder dully.

"Let us go."

They went silently, sad and impotent, and Peter closed and barred the door after them. After a safe ten minutes he took the pole and poked the trap door open. When the other stood before him he began:

"There has been deviltry in your life, and much of it — there have been drinking and women and blood, but when I face two men with a tale even half told like this— "

His guest stopped him.

"Peter—you'd never understand. You've helped me before. You've got to, got to help me now. Do you hear? I shall not argue. I want pen and paper and your bedroom, Peter." He grew angry. "Peter are you trying to interfere — what right have you? I am responsible only to myself for what I do."

He took a pen and ink and a sheaf of paper from the table and without another word walked into the other room and shut the door. Peter grunted, started after him and then reconsidering, went back and picking up *The Faery Queene* sank into his chair.

Three o'clock went into four. The room paled and the dark outside became damp and chill — and Peter bent low over his table, tracing through the pattern of *The Faery Queene*. Dragons chortled along the narrow streets outside; when the sleepy armourer's boy began his work at five, the heavy clink and clank of plate and linked mail swelled to the significance of marching cavalcades.

The fog shut down the first streak of dawn and the room was a greyish yellow at six when Peter tiptoed to his cupboard bedroom and opened the door. His guest turned to him red-eyed, death pale, unseeing. He had been writing hard and the Priedieu on which he wrote was piled with a stack of paper, while around on the floor were littered scraps of almost virgin pages. Peter softly closed the door and returned to his syren. Outside, the clump of boots, the croaking of old beldames from attic to attic, the dull murmur of morning, unnerved him, and, half dozing, he slumped in his chair and his dreaming brain worked chaoticaly on the im-

108

agery that stacked it. He was on a cloud and the way to heaven lay over groaning bodies crushed near the sun. He shuddered and tread the way. He was in a wood where he killed a bird of paradise for its plumage. Some one was trying to barter his soul for the world, and the soul was bartered. When a hot hand touched his shoulder he awoke with a start. The fog was thick in the room and his guest seemed a grey ghost, made of some like misty stuff, where he stood beside him, the sheaf of paper in his hand.

"Read this, Peter, and lock it away and let me sleep until tomorrow."

Peter took the pile and looked at it cautiously. The other threw himself down full length on the couch and sank almost immediately into a deep slumber, with breathing regular, but brow wrinkled in queer corners.

Peter yawned sleepily and glanced at the scrawled first page — then he began reading aloud softly:

The Rape of Lucrece
"From the besieged Ardea all in post,
Borne by the trustless wings of false desire,
Lust-breathing Tarquin leaves the Roman
host,— "

---

45. "Tarquin of Cheepside," *The Nassau Literary Magazine*, LXXIII (April 1917), pp. 13-18. Fitzgerald is credited by name in the magazine. In a review in *The Daily Princetonian* (April 24, 1917), Katherine Fullerton Gerould expressed enthusiasm for the way "Tarquin of Cheepside" was written, while making it clear she could not accept the story's basic premise — that William Shakespeare had raped the real-life model of Lucrece. Fitzgerald, she felt, had likely libeled Shakespeare — but he had done so with grand style. She pronounced the story "strikingly well-written. If one does not believe the plot, that is because most of us made up our minds long ago as to what manner of man Shakespeare was and was not. We may have made up our minds wrongly; Mr. Fitzgerald's little hypothetical adventure may be plausible. But I think most people will laugh and say 'Fie!' Personally, I am very glad Mr. Fitzgerald wrote it. I got a new thrill out of it. I think it is as delightful as it is funny, to show Shakespeare up, at this stage of the game, as that sort of hero. Mr. Fitzgerald's story has the noble element of surprise.... " This was as glowing a review of his writing as Fitzgerald got for any of his undergraduate stories—which may have something to do with why Fitzgerald retained, ever afterwards, an inordinate fondness for this story. It was really just a surprise-ending story, hardly the sort of thing we usually associate with Fitzgerald. (Several of the lively stories

Fitzgerald wrote while in prep school — "Pain and the Scientist," "A Luckless Santa Claus," and "The Trail of the Duke" — also featured surprise endings, as if he were, perhaps, under the influence of O. Henry. As Fitzgerald matured, his interest in expressing subtleties of character replaced an attraction to plot twists.) In addition, the point of "Tarquin of Cheepside" would likely be obscure to plenty of ordinary readers who hadn't recently been studying Shakespeare, as Fitzgerald and many of his Princeton friends had been doing. But Fitzgerald insisted, over the objections of editor Max Perkins, who didn't think the story paid off, that "Tarquin" be included in *Tales of the Jazz Age*.

Incidentally, Gerould also noted in her review that Fitzgerald had made a spelling error in writing "Cheepside" (the spelling would be corrected to "Cheapside" when the story was reworked for *The Smart Set* and eventually reprinted in *Tales of the Jazz Age*). Fitzgerald was a natural story teller. He was never, however, much of a speller. His letters, in the Princeton Library, contain frequent misspellings ("etc." is invariably rendered as "ect.," "criticism" as "critisism," and so on). The first edition of *This Side of Paradise* contained many words that were either misspelled (beginning with the name of the book's dedicatee) or misused. Scribners did not do a very conscientious job of proofreading the book. In all, 42 corrections eventually had to be made in the printed text.

A Story of the War

:It was a night in July, 1914. A man and his board of directors sat around a table in a palace at Berlin. The man was tall, with a moustache and a short arm. Who was he? — oh, reader, can you guess? He wore a military uniform, green with grey facings; his pants were blue with red facings.

"Your Highness," Von Boodlewaden was saying, "everything is ready."

The Kaiser shook his head sadly and folded his arms, at least he tucked the short one in with the other. Then he took his short leg and crossed it over his long one, and having scratched his long ear come to business.

"Nietzsche," he said, and waited for his words to have effect. Von Nicklebottom immediately sprang upon the table and led the customary cheer for Nietzsche — three locomotives with three sidels of beer on the end.

"Neitzsche," continued the Kaiser, "has said it. We will conquer by the sword." As he said this he ran his hand lovingly along his sword, then trying its edge on a bit of celery which he munched tentatively.

"Your Highness," cried Von Munchennoodle, "Belgium must be sacrificed."

The Kaiser bit his lip until the blood ran slowly down to the table where it spread into little livid pools of red and yellow liquid. His councillors dipped their fingers in it and reverently crossed themselves. Deeply affected, the Kaiser pledged them.

"And what of America?" asked Pistachio, Chancellor of the Domino Club.

"America?" said the Kaiser, rising to his full height. "Charles II had his Cromwell, Caesar had his Brutus, and Wilson—"

There were cries of "plagiarism" and the Kaiser paused.

"Daniel Webster was a German," he continued, rather abashed. Turning to the man in his center, Baron Badenuf, Chancellor of the Shakespearegoetheteutonic League, he commanded him.

"Look him up, Baddy."

There was an hour while Badenuf looked up Webster, during which an absolute silence was maintained, broken only by the Kaiser as he ran his sword rapidly up and down his neck, where he had caught prickly heat the summer before playing leap-frog in the beach at Ostend with Czar Nicholas. Badenuf finally returned.

"I find in the life of Webster," he announced, "the relevant news that he once stopped at the Sauerkraut Inn while passing through Pennsylvania. This proved the case, for no one but a German would stop at a German Inn unless he has to, and Daniel didn't."

There were three wild cheers at this and according to the ancient German custom they prepared to pledge each other in royal blood. The Kaiser tried his lip again, but all the blood had gone out long ago. So he opened an artery in his leg with an olive fork.

They all gulped it down heartily while a German band played "Ach du lieber Augustine" and the Kaiser's valet strapped his paralyzed arm to his sword so he could have his picture taken.

———

46. "The Prince of Pests," *The Princeton Tiger*, XXVII (April 28, 1917), p. 7. Fitzgerald's authorship is credited by initials: F.S.F.

THESE RIFLES...

"These rifles*** will probably not be used for shooting, although they are of a powerful type capable of before commencing actual firing reaching a distance of two miles"
— *The Daily Princetonian.*

Some rifles! Lord help Germany!

———

47. "These rifles," *The Princeton Tiger*, XXVII (April 28, 1917), p. 8. Unsigned. Known to be by Fitzgerald because he preserved a clipping in his scrapbook.

It Is Assumed...

"It is assumed that the absence of submarines from the Pacific will not necessitate American naval activities in that ocean."

— *New York Evening Post.*

Will it not not?

———

48. "It is assumed... ," *The Princeton Tiger*, XXVII (April 28, 1917), p. 8. Unsigned. Known to be by Fitzgerald because he preserved a clipping in his scrapbook.

Ethel Had Her Shot of Brandy . . .

Ethel had her shot of brandy while she powdered for the ball,
If a quart of wine was handy she was sure to drink it all;
People thought she was a dandy — called her Ethyl Alcohol.

———

49. "Ethel had her shot of brandy... ," *The Princeton Tiger*, XXVII (April 28, 1917), p. 8. Unsigned. Known to be by Fitzgerald because he preserved a clipping in his scrapbook.

Yale's Swimming Team...

Yale's swimming team will take its maiden plunge to-night.
— *New York Sun.*

How perfectly darling!

———

50. "Yale's swimming team... ," *The Princeton Tiger*, XXVII (April 28, 1917), p. 8. Unsigned. Known to be by Fitzgerald because he preserved a clipping in his scrapbook.

Babes in the Woods

I.

At the top of the stairs she paused. The emotions of divers on spring-boards, leading ladies on opening nights, and lumpy, bestriped young men on the day of the Big Game, crowded through her. She felt as if she should have descended to a burst of drums or to a discordant blend of gems from Thaïs and Carmen. She had never been so worried about her appearance, she had never been so satisfied with it. She had been sixteen years old for two months.

"Isabelle!" called Elaine from her doorway.

"I'm ready," she caught a slight lump or nervousness in her throat.

"I've got on the wrong slippers and stockings — you'll have to wait a minute."

Isabelle started toward Elaine's door for a last peak at a mirror, but something decided her to stand there and gaze down the stairs. They curved tantalizingly and she could just catch a glimpse of two pairs of masculine feet in the hall below. Pump-shod in uniform black they gave no hint of identity, but eagerly she wondered if one pair were attached to Kenneth Powers. This young man, as yet unmet, had taken up a considerable part of her day — the first day of her arrival. Going up in the machine from the station Elaine had volunteered, amid a rain of questions and comment, revelation and exaggeration —

"Kenneth Powers is simply *mad* to meet you. He's stayed over a day from college and he's coming to-night. He's heard so much about you—"

It had pleased her to know this. It put them on more equal terms, although she was accustomed to stage her own romances with or without a send-off. But following her delighted tremble of anticipation came a sinking sensation which made her ask:

"How do you mean he's heard about me? What sort of things?"

Elaine smiled — she felt more or less in the capacity of a showman with her more exotic guest.

"He knows you're good looking and all that." She paused — "I guess he knows you've been kissed."

Isabelle shuddered a bit under the fur robe. She was accustomed to be followed by this, but it never failed to arouse in her the same feeling of resentment; yet — in a strange town it was an advantage. She was a speed, was she? Well? Let them find out. She wasn't quite old enough to be sorry nor nearly old enough to be glad.

"Anne (this was another schoolmate) told him, I didn't — I knew you wouldn't like it." Elaine had gone on naively. "She's coming over to-night to the dinner."

Out the window Isabelle watched the high-piled snow glide by in the frosty morning. It was ever so much colder here than in Pittsburg; the glass of the side door was iced and the windows were shirred with snow at the corners. Her mind played still with the one subject. Did he dress like that boy there who walked calmly down what was evidently a bustling business street, in moccasins and winter-carnival costume? How very *western*! Of course he wasn't that way: he went to college, was a freshman or something. Really she had no distinct idea of him. A two year back picture had not impressed her except by the big eyes, which he had probably grown up to by now. However in the last two weeks at school, when her Christmas visit to Elaine had been decided on, he had assumed the proportions of a worthy adversary. Children, the most astute of matchmakers, plot and plan quickly and Elaine had cleverly played a word sonata to Isabelle's excitable temperament. Isabelle was and had been for some time capable of very strong, if not very transient emotions.

They drew up at a spreading red stone building, set back from the snowy street. Mrs. Terrell greeted her rather impersonally and Elaine's various younger brothers were produced from the corners where they skulked politely. Isabelle shook hands most tactfully. At her best she allied all with whom she came in contact, except older girls and some women. All the impressions that she made were conscious. The half dozen girls she met that morning were all rather impressed — and as much by her direct personality as by her reputation. Kenneth Powers seemed an unembarrassed subject of conversation. Evidently he was a bit light of love. He was neither popular nor unpopular. Every girl there seemed to have had an affair with him at some time or other, but no one volunteered any really useful information. He was going to fall for her.... Elaine had issued that statement to her young set and they were retailing it back to Elaine as fast as they set eyes on Isabelle. Isabelle resolved mentally, that if necessary, she would force herself to like him — she owed it to Elaine. What if she were terribly disappointed. Elaine had painted him in such glowing colors — he was good looking, had a "line" and was properly inconstant. In fact he summed up all the romance that her age and environment led her to desire. Were those his dancing shoes that fox-trotted tentatively around the soft rug below?

All impressions and in fact all ideas were terribly kaleidoscopic to Isabelle. She had that curious mixture of the social and artistic temperaments, found often in two classes, society women and actors. Her education, or rather her sophistication, had been absorbed from the boys who had dangled upon her favor, her tact was instinctive and her capacity for love affairs was limited only by the number of boys she met. Flirt smiled from her large, black-brown eyes and figured in her intense physical magnetism.

So she waited at the head of the stairs that evening while slippers and stockings were changed. Just as she was getting impatient Elaine came out beaming with her accustomed good nature and high spirits. Together they descended the broad stairs while the nervous searchlight of Isabelle's mind flashed on two ideas. She was glad she had high color to-night and she wondered if he danced well.

Downstairs the girls she had met in the afternoon surrounded her for a moment, looking unbelievably changed by the soft yellow light; then she heard Elaine's voice repeating a cycle of names and she found herself bowing to a sextette of black and white and terribly stiff figures. The name Powers figured somewhere, but she did not place him at first. A confused and very juvenile moment of awkward backings and bumpings, and everyone found themselves arranged talking to the very persons they least desired to. Isabelle manouvered herself and Peter Carroll, a sixth-former from Hotchkiss whom she had met that afternoon, to a seat at the piano. A reference, supposedly humorous, to the afternoon, was all she needed. What Isabelle could do socially with one idea was remarkable. First she repeated it rapturously in an enthusiastic contralto; then she held it off at a distance and smiled at it — her wonderful smile; then she delivered it in variations and played a sort of mental catch with it, all this in the nominal form of dialogue. Peter was fascinated and totally conscious that this was being done not for him but for the black eyes that glistened under the shining, carefully watered hair a little to her left. As an actor even in the fullest flush of his own conscious magnetism gets a lasting impression of most of the people in the front row, so Isabelle sized up Kenneth Powers. First, he was of middle height, and from her feeling of disappointment, she knew that she had expected him to be tall and of Vernon Castle-ish slenderness. His hair and eyes were his most noticeable possessions — they were black and they fairly glittered. For the rest, he had rather dark skin with a faint flush, and a straight romantic profile, the effect set off by a closefitting dress suit and a silk ruffled shirt of the kind that women still delight in on men, but men were just beginning to get tired of.

Kenneth was just quietly smiling.

"Don't *you* think so?" she said suddenly, turning to him innocent eyed.

There was a stir near the door and Elaine led the way to dinner. Kenneth struggled to her side and whispered:

"You're my dinner partner — Isabelle."

Isabelle gasped — this was rather quick work. Of course it made it more interesting, but really she felt as if a good line had been taken from the star and given to a minor character. She mustn't lose the leadership a bit. The dinner table glittered with laughter at the confusion of getting places and then curious eyes were turned on her, sitting near the head. She was enjoying this immensely, and Peter Carroll was so engrossed with the added sparkle of her rising color that he forgot to pull out Elaine's chair and fell into a dim confusion. Kenneth was on the other side, full of confidence and vanity, looking at her most consciously. He started directly and so did Peter.

"I've heard a lot about you—"

"Wasn't it funny this afternoon—"

Both stopped. Isabelle turned to Kenneth shyly. Her face was always enough answer for anyone, but she decided to speak.

"How — who from?"

"From everybody — for years." She blushed appropriately. On her right Peter was hors-de-combat already, although he hadn't quite realized it.

"I'll tell you what I thought about you when I first saw you," Kenneth continued. She leaned slightly toward him and looked modestly at the celery before her. Peter sighed — he knew Kenneth and the situations that Kenneth was born to handle. He turned to Elaine and asked her when she was going back to school.

II.

Isabelle and Kenneth were distinctly not innocent, nor were they particularly hardened. Moreover, amateur standing had very little value in the game they were beginning to play. They were simply very sophisticated, very calculating and finished, young actors, each playing a part that they had played for years. They had both started with good looks and excitable temperaments and the rest was the result of certain accesable popular novels, and dressing-room conversation culled from a slightly older set. When Isabelle's eyes, wide and innocent, proclaimed the ingenue most, Kenneth was proportionally less deceived. He waited for the mask to drop off, but at the same time he did not question her right to wear it. She, on her part, was not impressed by his studied air of blasé sophistication. She came from a larger city and had slightly an advantage in range. But she accepted his pose. It was one of the dozen little conventions of this kind of affair. He was aware that he was getting this particular favor now because she had been coached. He knew that he stood for merely the best thing in sight, and that he would have to improve his opportunity before he lost his advantage. So they proceeded, with an infinite guile that would have horrified the parents of both.

After dinner the party swelled to forty and there was dancing in a large ex-play-room downstairs. Everything went smoothly — boys cut in on Isabelle every few feet and then squabbled in the corners with: "You might let me get more than an *inch*," and "She didn't like it either — she told me, so next time I cut in." It was true — she told everyone so, and she gave every hand a parting pressure that said "You know that your dances are *making* my evening."

But time passed, two hours of it, and the less subtle beaux had better learned to focus their pseudo-passionate glances elsewhere, for eleven o'clock found Isabelle and Kenneth on a leather lounge in a little den off the music-room. She was conscious that they were a handsome pair and seemed to belong so distinctively on this leather lounge while lesser lights fluttered and chattered down stairs. Boys who passed the door looked in enviously — girls who passed only laughed and frowned, and grew wise within themselves.

They had now reached a very definite stage. They had traded ages, eighteen and sixteen. She had listened to much that she had heard before. He was a freshman at college, sang in the glee club and expected to make the freshman hockey-team. He had learned that some of the boys she went with in Pittsburg were "terrible speeds" and came to parties intoxicated — most of them were nineteen or so, and drove alluring Stutzes. A good half of them seemed to have already flunked out of various boarding schools and colleges, but some of them bore good collegiate names that made him feel rather young. As a matter of fact Isabelle's acquaintance with college boys was mostly through older cousins. She had bowing acquaintance with a lot of young men who thought she was "a pretty kid" and "worth keeping an eye on." But Isabelle strung the names into a fabrication of gaiety that would have dazzled a Viennese nobleman. Such is the power of young contralto voices on leather sofas.

I have said that they had reached a very definite stage — nay more — a very critical stage. Kenneth had stayed over a day to meet her and his train left at twelve-eighteen that night. His trunk and suitcase awaited him at the station and his watch was already beginning to worry him and hang heavy in his pocket.

"Isabelle," he said suddenly. "I want to tell you something." They had been talking lightly about "that funny look in her eyes," and on the relative merits of dancing and sitting out, and Isabelle knew from the change in his manner exactly what was coming — indeed she had been wondering how soon it would come. Kenneth reached above their heads and turned out the electric light so that they were in the dark except for the glow from the red lamps that fell through the door from the music room. Then he began:

"I don't know — I don't know whether or not you know what you — what I'm going to say. Lordy Isabelle — this sounds like a line but it isn't."

"I know," said Isabelle softly.

"I may never see you again — I have darned hard luck sometimes." He was leaning away from her on the other arm of the lounge, but she could see his black eyes plainly in the dark.

"You'll see me again — silly." There was just the slightest emphasis on the last word — so that it became almost a term of endearment. He continued a bit huskily:

"I've fallen for a lot of people — girls — and I guess you have too — boys, I mean but honestly you—" he broke off suddenly and leaned forward, chin on his hands, a favorite and studied gesture. "Oh, what's the use, you'll go your way and I suppose I'll go mine."

Silence for a moment. Isabelle was quite stirred — she wound her handkerchief into a tight ball and by the faint light that streamed over her, dropped it deliberately on the floor. Their hands touched for an instant but neither spoke. Silences were becoming more frequent and more delicious. Outside another stray couple had come up and were experimenting on the piano. After the usual preliminary of "chopsticks," one of them started "Babes in the Woods" and a light tenor carried the words into the den—

Give me your hand
I'll understand
We're off to slumberland.

Isabelle hummed it softly and trembled as she felt Kenneth's hand close over hers.

"Isabelle," he whispered. "You know I'm mad about you. You *do* give a darn about me."

"Yes."

"How much do you care — do you like anyone better?"

"No." He could scarcely hear her, although he bent so near that he felt her breath against his cheek.

"Isabelle, we're going back to school for six long months and why shouldn't we — if I could only just have one thing to remember you by —."

"Close the door." Her voice had just stirred so that he half wondered whether she had spoken at all. As he swung the door softly shut, the music seemed quivering just outside.

117

Moonlight is bright
Kiss me goodnight.

What a wonderful song she thought — everything was wonderful to-night, most of all this romantic scene in the den with their hands clinging and the inevitable looming charmingly close. The future vista of her life seemed an unended succession of scenes like this, under moonlight and pale starlight, and in the backs of warm limousines and in low cosy roadsters stopped under sheltering trees — only the boy might change, and this one was so nice.

"Isabelle!" His whisper blended in the music and they seemed to float nearer together. Her breath came faster. "Can't I kiss you Isabelle — Isabelle?" Lips half parted, she turned her head to him in the dark. Suddenly the ring of voices, the sound of running footsteps surged toward them. Like a flash Kenneth reached up and turned on the light and when the door opened and three boys, the wrathy and dance-craving Peter among them, rushed in, he was turning over the magazines on the table, while she sat, without moving, serene and unembarrassed, and even greeted them with a welcoming smile. But her heart was beating wildly and she felt somehow as if she had been deprived.

It was evidently over. There was a clamour for a dance, there was a glance that passed between them, on his side, despair, on hers, regret, and then the evening went on, with the reassured beaux and the eternal cutting in.

At quarter to twelve Kenneth shook hands with her gravely, in a crowd assembled to wish him good-speed. For an instant he lost his poise and she felt slightly foolish, when a satirical voice from a concealed wit on the edge of the company cried:

"Take her outside, Kenneth." As he took her hand he pressed it a little and she returned the pressure as she had done to twenty hands that evening — that was all.

At two o'clock upstairs Elaine asked her if she and Kenneth had had a "time" in the den. Isabelle turned to her quietly. In her eyes was the light of the idealist, the inviolate dreamer of Joan-like dreams.

"No!" she answered. "I don't do that sort of thing any more — he asked me to, but I said 'No.' "

As she crept into bed she wondered what he'd say in his special delivery to-morrow. He had such a good looking mouth — would she ever?

"Fourteen angels were watching over them" sang Elaine sleepily from the next room.

"Damn!" muttered Isabelle and punched the pillow into a lucurious lump — "Damn!"

— F. Scott Fitzgerald.

---

51. "Babes in the Woods," *The Nassau Literary Magazine*, LXXIII (May 1917), pp. 55-64. Fitzgerald is credited by name in the magazine. Revised, this deftly crafted short story — one of the best pieces in this collection — would later be published in *The Smart Set*; it was the first story Fitzgerald ever sold to a commercial magazine, and would ultimately wind up as part of *This Side of Paradise*.

In his 1927 article "Princeton," Fitzgerald recalled *The Nassau Lit* thusly: "I wrote stories about current prom girls, stories that were later incorporated into a novel; John Biggs imagined the war with sufficient virtuosity to deceive veterans; and John Bishop made a last metrical effort to link up the current crusade with the revolution — while we all, waiting to go to training camps, found time heartily to despise the bombast and rhetoric of the day."

PRINCETON —THE LAST DAY

The last light wanes and drifts across the land,
The low, long hand, the sunny land of spires.
The ghosts of evening tune again their lyres
And wander singing, in a plaintive band
Down the long corridors of trees. Pale fires
Echo the night from tower top to tower.
Oh sleep that dreams and dream that never tires,
Press from the petals of the lotus-flower
Something of this to keep, the essence of an hour!

No more to wait the twilight of the moon
In this sequestrated vale of star and spire;
For one, eternal morning of desire
Passes to time and earthly afternoon.
Here, Heracletus, did you build of fire
And changing stuffs your prophecy far hurled
Down the dead years; this midnight I aspire
To see, mirrored among the embers, curled
In flame, the splendor and the sadness of the world.

— F. Scott Fitzgerald

52. "Princeton — The Last Day," *The Nassau Literary Magazine*, LXXIII (May 1917), p. 95. Fitzgerald is credited by name in the magazine. In a letter to Fitzgerald, Edmund Wilson offered some back-handed praise for this poem, noting that it had a "depth and dignity of which I didn't suppose you capable."

Fitzgerald's love of Princeton, clearly voiced in this poem, was deep and enduring; it did not however, always seem to be requited. In 1934, for example, Fitzgerald proposed to Princeton's Dean Christian Gauss that he give a series of lectures on writing at Princeton, under the sponsorship of the University's English department (he even promised he would stay sober); he was deeply hurt when his proposal was quickly dismissed by Gauss, who suggested that Fitzgerald see if one of the eating clubs might be willing to have him as a speaker instead.

Book Talk: The Celt and the World

After his most entertaining *End of a Chapter*, Mr. Leslie has written what I think will be a more lasting book. *The Celt and the World* is a sort of bible of Irish patriotism. Mr. Leslie has endeavored to trace a race, the Bretton, Scotch, Welsh, and Irish Celt, through its spiritual crises and he emphasizes most strongly the trait that Synge, Yeats and Lady Gregory have made so much of in their plays, the Celt's inveterate mysticism. The theme is worked out in an era-long contrast between Celt and Teuton, and the book becomes ever ironical when it deals of the ethical values of the latter race. "Great is the Teuton indeed," it says, "Luther in religion, Bessemer in steel, Neitzche in philosophy, Rockefeller in oil — Cromwell and Bismarck in war." What a wonderful list of names! Could anyone but an Irishman have linked them in such damning significance?

In the chapter on the conversion of the Celt to christianity, is traced the great missionary achievements of the Celtic priests and philosophers, Dungal, Fergal, Abelard, Duns Scotus and Ereugena. At the end of the book that no less passionate and mystical, although unfortunate, incident of Pearse, Plunkett and the Irish Republic, is given sympathetic but just treatment.

To an Irishman the whole book is fascinating. It gives one an intense desire to see Ireland free at last to work out her own destiny under Home Rule. It gives one the idea that she would do it directly under the eyes of God and with so much purity and so many mistakes. It arouses a fascination with the mystical lore and legend of the island which "can save others, but herself she cannot save." The whole book is colored with an unworldliness, and an atmosphere of the futility of man's ambitions. As Mr. Leslie says in the foreword to *The End of a Chapter* (I quote inexactly) we have seen the suicide of the Aryan race, "the end of one era and the beginning of another to which no Gods have as yet been rash enough to give their names."

The Celt and the World is a rather pessimistic book: not with the dreary pessimism of Strinberg and Sudermann, but with the pessimism which might have inspired "What doth it profit a man if he gaineth the whole world and loseth his own soul." It is worth remarking that it ends with a foreboding prophecy of a Japanese-American war in the future. The book should be especially interesting to anyone who has enjoyed *Riders to the Sea*, or *The Hour-Glass*. He will read an engrossing view of a much discussed race and decide that the Irishman has used heaven as a continued referendum for his ideals, as he has used earth as a perennial recall for his ambitions.

(*The Celt and the World*, *by Shane Leslie*, New York; *Charles Scribner's Sons*.)

— F.S.F.

53. A book review of *The Celt and the World* by Shane Leslie, *The Nassau Literary Magazine*, LXXIII (May 1917), pp. 104-105. Fitzgerald's authorship is credited by initials: F.S.F. Writer and lecturer Shane Leslie (1885-1971) was an important mentor and friend to Fitzgerald. Of Anglo-Irish descent, Leslie seemed to know everyone, from leaders of the Roman Catholic Church (to which he vainly urged Fitzgerald to remain anchored) to poets W. B. Yeats and Rupert Brooke (it pleased Fitzgerald that Leslie called him "an American Rupert Brooke") to Winston Churchill (who happened to be Leslie's first cousin). Leslie volunteered for ambulance corps service in World War One.

Sentiment — And the Use of Rouge

The Nassau Literary Magazine
Volume LXXIII June 1917 No. 3

I.

This story has no moral value. It is about a man who had fought for two years and how he came back to England for two days, and then how he went away again. It is unfortunately one of those stories which must start at the beginning, and the beginning consists merely of a few details. There were two brothers (two sons of Lord Paxton) who sailed to Europe with the first hundred thousand. Lieutenant Richard Harrington Syneforth, the elder, was killed in some forgotten raid; the younger, Lieutenant Clay Harrington Syneforth is the hero of this story. He was now a Captain in the Seventeenth Sussex and the immoral thing in the story happens to him. The important part to remember is that when his father met him at Paddington station and drove him up town in his motor, he hadn't been in England for two years — and this was in the early spring of nineteen-seventeen. Various circumstances had brought this about, wounds, advancement, meeting his family in Paris, and mostly being twenty-two and anxious to show his company an example of indefatigable energy. Besides, most of his friends were dead and he had rather a horror of seeing the gaps they'd leave in his England. And here is the story.

He sat at dinner and thought himself rather stupid and unnecessarily moody as his sister's light chatter amused the table, Lord and Lady Blachford, himself and two unsullied aunts. In the first place he was rather doubtful about his sister's new manner. She seemed, well, perhaps a bit loud and theatrical, and she was certainly pretty enough not to need so much paint. She couldn't be more than eighteen, and paint — it seemed so useless. Of course, he was used to it in his mother, would have been shocked had she appeared in her unrouged furrowedness, but on Clara it merely accentuated her youth. Although he had never seen such obvious paint, and, as they had always been a shockingly frank family, he told her so.

"You've got too much stuff on your face." He tried to speak casually and his sister nothing wroth, jumped up and ran to a mirror.

"No, I haven't," she said, calmly returning.

"I thought," he continued rather annoyed, "that the criterion of how much paint to put on, was whether men were sure you'd used any or not."

His sister and mother exchanged glances and both spoke at once.

"Not now, Clay, you know — " began Clara.

"Really, Clay," interrupted his mother, "you don't know exactly what the standards are, so you can't quite criticize. It happens to be a fad to paint a little more."

Clayton was now rather angry.

"Will all the women at Mrs. Severance's dance tonight be striped like this?"

Clara's eyes flashed.

"Yes!"

"Then I don't believe I care to go."

Clara, about to flare up, caught her mother's eye and was silent.

"Clay, I want you to go," said Lady Blachford hastily. "People want to see you before they forget what you look like. And for tonight let's not talk about war or paint."

In the end Clay went. A navy subaltran called for his sister at ten and he followed in lonesome state at half-past. After half an hour he had had all he wanted. Frankly, the dance seemed all wrong. He remembered Mrs. Severance's antebellum affairs — staid, correct occasions they were, with only a mere scattering from the faster set, just those people who couldn't possibly be left out. Now it all was blent, some how, in one set. His sister had not exaggerated, practically every girl there was painted, over-painted; girls whom he remembered as curate-hunters, holders of long conversations with earnest young men on incence and the validity of orders, girls who had been terrifyingly masculine and had talked about dances as if they were the amusement of the feebleminded — all were there, trotting through the most extreme steps from over the water. He danced stiffly with many who had delighted his youth, and he found that he wasn't enjoying himself at all. He found that he had come to picture England as a land of sorrow and acetisism and while there was little extravagance displayed tonight, he thought that the atmosphere had fallen to that artificial gayety rather than risen to a stern calmness. Even under the carved, gilt ceiling of the Severances' there was strangely an impression of dance-hall rather than dance, people arrived and departed most informally and, oddly enough, there was a dearth of older people rather than of younger. But there was something in the very faces of the girls, something which was half enthusiasm and half recklessness, that depressed him more than any concrete thing.

When he had decided this and had about made up his mind to go, Eleanor Marbrooke came in. He looked at her keenly. She had not lost, not a bit. He fancied that she had not quite so much paint on as the others, and when he and she talked he felt a social refuge in her cool beauty. Even then he felt that the difference between she and the others was in degree rather than in kind. He stayed, of course, and one o'clock found them sitting apart, watching. There had been a drifting away and now there seemed to be nothing but officers and girls; the Severances themselves seemed out of place as they chattered volubly in a corner to a young couple who looked as if they would rather be left alone.

"Eleanor," he demanded, "why is it that everyone looks so — well, so loose — so socially slovenly?"

"It's terribly obvious, isn't it?" she agreed, following his eyes around the room.

"And no one seems to care" he continued.

"No one does," she responded, "but my dear man, we can't sit here and criticize our hosts. What about me? How do I look?"

He regarded her critically.

"I'd say on the whole, that you've kept your looks."

"Well, I like that," she raised her brows at him in reproof. "You talk as if I were some shelved, old play-about, just over some domestic catastrophy."

"How about Dick?"

She grew serious at once.

"Poor Dick — I suppose we were engaged."

"Suppose," he said astonished, "why it was understood by everyone, both our families knew. I know I used to lie awake and envy my lucky brother."

She laughed.

"Well, we certainly thought ourselves engaged. If the war hadn't come we'd be comfortably married now, but if he were still alive under these circumstances, I doubt if we'd be even engaged."

"You weren't in love with him?"

"Well, you see, perhaps that wouldn't be the question, perhaps he wouldn't marry me and perhaps I *wouldn't* marry him."

123

He jumped to his feet astounded and her warning hush just prevented him from exclaiming aloud. Before he could control his voice enough to speak she had whisked off with a staff officer. What could she mean? — except that in some moment of emotional excitement she had — but he couldn't bear to think of Eleanor in that light. He must have misunderstood — he must talk more with her. No, surely — if it had been true she wouldn't have said it so casually. He watched her — how close she danced. Her bright brown hair lay against the staff officer's shoulder and her vivacious face was only two or three inches from his when she talked. All things considered Clay was becoming more angry every minute with things in general.

Next time he danced with her she seized his arm, and before he knew her intention, they had said goodbyes to the Severances' and were speeding away in Eleanor's limousine.

"It's a nineteen-thirteen car — imagine having a four year old limousine before the war."

"Terrific privation," he said ironically. "Eleanor, I want to speak to you—"

"And I to you. That's why I took you away. Where are you living?"

"At home."

"Well then we'll go to your old rooms in Grove Street. You've still got them haven't you?"

Before he could answer she had spoken to the chauffer and was leaning back in the corner smiling at him.

"Why Eleanor, we can't do that — talk there."

"Are the rooms cleaned?" she interrupted.

"About once a month I think, but—"

"That's all that's necessary. In fact it'll be wonderfully proper, won't be clothes lying around the room as there usually are at bachelor teas. At Colonel Hotesane's farewell party, Gertrude Evarts and I saw — in the middle of the floor, well, my dear, a series of garments and — as we were the first to arrive we—"

"Eleanor," said Clay firmly, "I don't like this."

"I know you don't, and that's why we're going to your rooms to talk it over. Good heavens, do you think people worry these days about where conversations take place, unless they're in wireless towers, or shoreways in coast towns?"

The machine had stopped and before he could bring argument to bear she had stepped out and scurried up the steps, where she announced that she would wait until he came and opened the door. He had no alternative. He followed, and as they mounted the stairs inside he could hear her laughing softly at him in the darkness.

He threw open the door and groped for the electric light, and in the glow that followed both stood without moving. There on the table sat a picture of Dick, Dick almost as they had last seen him, worldly wise and sophisticated, in his civilian clothes. Eleanor was the first to move. She crossed swiftly over, the dust rising with the swish of her silk, and elbows on the table said softly:

"Poor old handsome, with all your beautiful self all smashed." She turned to Clay. "Dick didn't have much of a soul, such a small soul. He never bothered about eternity and I doubt if he knows any — but he had a way with him, and oh, that magnificent body of his, red gold hair, brown eyes—" her voice trailed off and she sank lazily onto the sofa in front of the hearth.

"Build a fire and then come and put your arm around me and we'll talk." Obediently he searched for wood while she sat and chatted. "I won't pretend to busybody around and try to help — I'm far too tired. I'm sure I can give the impression of home much better by just sitting here and talking, can't I?"

He looked up from where he knelt at her feet manipulating the kerosene, and realized that his voice was husky as he spoke.

"Just talk about England — about the country a little and about Scotland and tell me things that have happened, amusing provincial things and things with women in them — put yourself in" he finished rather abruptly.

Eleanor smiled and kneeling down beside him lit the match and ran it along the edge of the paper that undermined the logs. She twisted her head to read it as it curled up in black at the corners, "August 14, 1915. Zeppelin raid in — there it goes" as it disappeared in little, licking flames. "My little sister — you remember

124

Katherine; Kitty, the one with the yellow hair and the little lisp — she was killed by one of those things — she and a governess, that summer."

"Little Kitty," he said sadly, "a lot of children were killed I know, a lot, I didn't know she was gone," he was far away now and a set look had come into his eyes. She hastened to change the subject.

"Lots — but we're not on death tonight. We're going to pretend we're happy. Do you see?" She patted his knee reprovingly, "we *are* happy. We *are*! Why you were almost whimsical awhile ago. I believe you're a sentimentalist. Are you?"

He was still gazing absently at the fire but he looked up at this.

"Tonight, I am — almost — for the first time in my life. Are you, Eleanor?"

"No, I'm a romantic. There a huge difference; a sentimental person thinks things will last, a romantic person hopes they wont."

He was in a reverie again and she knew that he had hardly heard her.

"Excuse please," she pleaded, slipping close to him. "Do be a nice boy and put your arm around me." He put his arm gingerly about until she began to laugh quietly. When he hastily withdrew it, and bending forward, talked quickly at the fire.

"Will you tell me why in the name of this mad world we're here tonight? Do you realize that this is — was — a bachelor apartment before the bachelors all married the red widow over the channel — and you'll be compromised?"

She seized the straps of his shoulder belt and tugged at him until his grey eyes looked into hers.

"Clay, Clay, don't — you mustn't use small petty words like that at this time. Compromise! What's that to words like Life and Love and Death and England. Compromise! Clay I don't believe anyone uses that word except servants." She laughed. "Clay, you and our butler are the only men in England who use the word compromise. My maid and I have been warned within a week — How odd — Clay, look at me."

He looked at her and saw what she intended, beauty heightened by enthusiasm. Her lips were half parted in a smile, her hair just so slightly disarranged.

"Damned witch," he muttered. "You used to read Tolstoy, and believe him."

"Did I?" her gaze wandered to the fire. "So I did, so I did." Then her eyes came back to him and the present. "Really, Clay, we must stop gazing at the fire. It puts our minds on the past and tonight there's got to be no past or future, no time, just tonight, you and I sitting here and I most tired for a military shoulder to rest my head upon." But he was off on a old tack thinking of Dick and he spoke his thoughts aloud.

"You used to talk Tolstoy to Dick and I thought it was scandalous for such a good-looking girl to be intellectual."

"I wasn't, really," she admitted. "It was to impress Dick."

"I was shocked, too, when I read something of Tolstoy's, I struck the something Sonata."

"Kreutzer Sonata," she suggested.

"That's it. I thought it was immoral for young girls to read Tolstoy and told Dick so. He used to nag me about that. I was nineteen."

"Yes, we thought you quite the young prig. We considered ourselves advanced."

"You're only twenty, aren't you?" asked Clay suddenly. She nodded.

"Don't you believe in Tolstoy any more?" he asked, almost fiercely.

She shook her head and then looked up at him almost wistfully.

"Won't you let me lean against your shoulder just the smallest bit?" He put his arm around her, never once taking his eyes from her face, and suddenly the whole strength of her appeal burst upon him. Clay was no saint, but he had always been rather decent about women. Perhaps that's why he felt so helpless now. His emotions were not complex. He knew what was wrong, but he knew also that he wanted this woman, this warm creature of silk and life who crept so close to him. There were reasons why he oughtn't to have her, but he had suddenly seen how love was a big word like Life and Death, and she knew that he realized and was glad. Still they sat without moving for a long while and watched the fire.

125

II.

At two-twenty next day Clay shook hands gravely with his father and stepped into the train for Dover. Eleanor, comfortable with a novel, was nestled into a corner of his compartment, and as he entered she smiled a welcome and closed the book.

"Well," she began. "I felt like a minion of the almighty secret service as I slid by your inspiring and impecable father, swathed in yards and yards of veiling."

"He wouldn't have noticed you without your veil," answered Clayton, sitting down. "He was really most emotional under all that brusqueness. Really, you know he's quite a nice chap. Wish I knew him better."

The train was in motion; the last uniforms had drifted in like brown, blown leaves, and now it seemed as if one tremendous wind was carrying them shoreward.

"How far are you going with me?" asked Clayton.

"Just to Rochester, an hour and a half. I absolutely had to see you before you left, which isn't very Spartan of me. But really, you see, I feel that you don't quite understand about last night, and look at me, as—" she paused "well — as rather exceptional."

"Wouldn't I be rather an awful cad if I thought about it in those terms at all?"

"No," she said cheerily, "I, for instance, am both a romanticist and a psychologist. It does take the romance out of anything to analyze it, but I'm going to do it if only to clear myself in your eyes."

"You don't have to — " he began.

"I know I don't," she interrupted, "but I'm going to, and when I've finished you'll see where weakness and inevitability shade off. No, I don't believe in Zola."

"I don't know him."

"Well, my dear, Zola said that environment is environment, but he referred to families and races, and this is the story of a class."

"What class?"

"Our class."

"Please," he said, "I've been wanting to hear."

She settled herself against his shoulder, and gazing out at the vanishing country, began to talk very deliberately.

"It was said, before the war, that England was the only country in the world where women weren't safe from men of their own class."

"One particular fast set," he broke in.

"A set, my dear man, who were fast but who kept every bit of their standing and position. You see even that was reaction. The idea of physical fitness came in with the end of the Victorians. Drinking died down in the Universities. Why you yourself once told me that the really bad men never drank, rather kept themselves fit for moral or intellectual crimes."

"It was rather Victorian to drink much," he agreed. "Chaps who drank were usually young fellows about to become curates, sowing the conventional wild oats by the most orthodox tippling."

"Well," she continued, "there had to be an outlet — and there was, and you know the form it took in what you called the fast set. Next enter Mr. Mars. You see as long as there was moral pressure exerted, the rotten side of society was localized. I won't say it wasn't spreading, but it was spreading slowly, some people even thought, rather normally, but when men began to go away and not come back, when marriage became a hurried thing and widows filled London, and all traditions seemed broken, why then things were different."

"How did it start?"

"It started in cases where men were called away hurriedly and girls lost their nerve. Then the men didn't come back — and there were the girls—"

He gasped.

"That was going on at the beginning? — I didn't know at all."

"Oh it was very quiet at first. Very little leaked out into daylight, but the thing spread in the dark. The next thing, you see, was to weave a sentimental mantle to throw over it. It was there and it had to be excused. Most girls either put on trousers and drove cars all day or painted their faces and danced with officers all night."

"And what mighty principle had the honor of being a cloak for all that?" he asked sarcastically.

"Now, here, you see, is the paradox. I can talk like this and pretend to analyze and even sneer at the principle. Yet I'm as much under the spell as the most wishy-washy typist who spends a week end at Brighton with her young man before he sails with the conscripts."

"I'm waiting to hear what the spell is."

"It's this — self sacrifice with a capitol S. Young men are going to get killed for us. — We would have been their wives — we can't be — therefore we'll be as much as we can. And that's the story."

"Good God!"

"Young officer comes back," she went on; "Must amuse him, must amuse him; must give him the impression that people here are with him, that it's a big home he's coming to, that he's appreciated. Now you know, of course, in the lower classes that sort of thing means children. Whether that will ever spread to us will depend on the duration of the war."

"How about old ideas, and standards of woman and that sort of thing?" he asked, rather sheepishly.

"Sky-high, my dear — dead and gone. It might be said for utility that it's better and safer for the race that officers stay with women of their own class. Think of the next generation in France."

To Clay the whole compartment had suddenly become smothering. Bubbles of conventional ethics seemed to have burst and the long stagnant gas was reaching him. He was forced to seize his mind and make it cling to whatever shred of the old still floated on the moral air. Eleanor's voice came to him like the grey creed of a new materialistic world, the contrast was the more vivid because of the remains of errotic honor and sentimental religiosity that she flung out with the rest.

"So you see, my dear, utility, heroism and sentiment all combine and *levoice*. And we're pulling into Rochester," she turned to him pathetically. "I see that in trying to clear myself I've

only indicted my whole sex," and with tears in their eyes they kissed.

On the platform they talked for half a minute more. There was no emotion. She was trying to analyze again and her smooth brow was wrinkled in the effort. He was endeavoring to digest what she had said, but his brain was in a whirl.

"Do you remember," he asked, "what you said last night about love being a big word like Life and Death?"

"A regular phrase; part of the technique of — of the game; a catch word." The train moved off and as Clay swung himself on the last car she raised her voice so that he could hear her to the last — "*Love* is a big word, but I was flattering us. Real Love's as big as Life and Death, but not that love — not that—" Her voice failed and mingled with the sound of the rails, and to Clay she seemed to fade out like a grey ghost on the platform.

III.

When the charge broke and the remnants lapped back like spent waves, Sergeant O'Flaherty, a bullet through the left side, dropped beside him, and as weary castaways fight half listlessly for shore, they crawled and pushed and edged themselves into a shell crater. Clay's shoulder and back were bleeding profusely and he searched heavily and clumsily for his first aid package.

"That'll be the Seventeenth Sussex gets reorganized," remarked O'Flaherty, sagely. "Two weeks in the rear and two weeks home."

"Damn good regiment, it was, O'Flaherty," said Clay. They would have seemed like two philosophic majors commenting from safe behind the lines had it not been that Clay was flat on his back, his face in a drawn ecstasy of pain, and that the Irishman was most evidently bleeding to death. The latter was twining an improvised tourniquet on his thigh, watching it with the careless casual interest a bashful suitor bestows upon his hat.

"I can't get up no good emotion over a regiment these nights," he commented disgustedly. "This'll be the fifth I was in that I seen smashed to hell. I joined these Sussex Byes so I needn't see more o'me own go."

"I think you know every one in Ireland, Sergeant."

"All Ireland's me friend, Captain, though I niver knew it 'till I left. So I left the Irish, what was left of them. You see when an English bye dies he does play some actin' before. Blood on an Englishman always calls rouge to me mind. It's a game with him. The Irish take death damn serious."

Clayton rolled painfully over and watched the night come softly down and blend with the drifting smoke. They were certainly between the devil and deep sea and the slang of the next generation will use "no man's land" for that. O'Flaherty was still talking.

"You see you has to do somethin'. You haven't any God worth remarkin' on. So you pass from life in the names of your holy principles, and hope to meet in Westminster."

"We're not mystics, O'Flaherty," muttered Clay, "but we've got a firm grip on God and reality."

"Mystics, my eye, beggin' your pardon, lieutenant," cried the Irishman, "a mystic ain't no race, it's a saint. You got the most airy way o'thinkin' in the wurruld an yit you talk about plain faith as if it was cloud gazin'. There was a lecture last week behind Vimy Y.M.C.A., an' I stuck my head in the door; 'Tan-gi-ble,' the fellow was sayin' 'we must be Tan-gi-ble in our religion, we must be practicle' an' he starts off on Christian brotherhood an' honorable death — so I stuck me head out again. An' you got lots a good men dyin' for that every day — tryin' to be tan-gi-ble, dyin' because their father's a Duke or because he ain't. But that ain't what I got to think of. An' right here let's light a pipe before it gets dark enough for the damn burgomasters to see the match and practice on it."

Pipes, as indispensable as the hard ration, were going in no time, and the sergeant continued as he blew a huge lung full of smoke towards the earth with incongruous supercaution.

"I fight because I like it, an' God ain't to blame for that, but when it's death you're talkin' about

I'll tell you what I get an' you don't. Pere Dupont gets in front of the Frenchies an' he says: 'Allon mes enfants!' fine! an' Father O'Brien, he says: 'Go on in byes and bate the Luther out o' them' — great stuff! But can you see the reverent Updike — Updike just out o' Oxford, yellin' 'mix it up, chappies,' or 'soak 'em blokes?' — No, Captain, the best leader you ever get is a six foot rowin' man that thinks God's got a seat in the House o' Commons. All sportin' men have to have a bunch o' cheerin' when they die. Give an Englishman four inches in the sportin' page this side of the whistle an' he'll die happy — but not O'Flaherty."

But Clay's thoughts were far away. Half delirious, his mind wandered to Eleanor. He had thought of nothing else for a week, ever since their parting at Rochester, and so many new sides of what he had learned were opening up. He had suddenly realized about Dick and Eleanor, they must have been married to all intents and purposes. Of course Clay had written to Eleanor from Paris, asking her to marry him on his return, and just yesterday he had gotten a very short, very kind, but definite refusal. And he couldn't understand at all.

Then there was his sister — Eleanor's words still rang in his ear. "They either put on trousers and act as chauffers all day or put on paint and dance with officers all night." He felt perfectly sure that Clara was still well — virtuous. Virtuous — what a ridiculous word it seemed, and how odd to be using it about his sister. Clara had always been so painfully good. At fourteen she had sent to Boston for a souvenir picture of Louisa M. Alcott to hang over her bed. His favorite amusement had been to replace it by some startling soubrette in tights, culled from the pages of the *Pink Un*. Well Clara, Eleanor, Dick, he himself, were all in the same boat, no matter what the actuality of their innocence or guilt. If he ever got back—

The Irishman, evidently sinking fast, was talking rapidly.

"Put your wishy-washy pretty clothes on everythin' but it ain't no disguise. If I get drunk it's the flesh and the devil, if you get drunk it's your wild oats. But you ain't disguisin' death, not to me you ain't. It's a damn serious affair. I may get killed for me flag, but I'm going to die for meself. 'I die for England' he says. 'Settle up with God, you're through with England' I says."

He raised himself on his elbow and shook his fist toward the German trenches.

"It's you an' your damn Luther," he shouted. "You been protestin' and analyzin' until you're makin' my body ache and burn like hell; you been evolvin' like mister Darwin, an' you stretched yourself so far that you've split. Everythin's in-tan-gi-ble except your God. Honor an' Fatherland an' Westminster Abbey, they're all in-tan-gi-ble except God an' sure you got him tan-gi-ble. You got him on the flag an' in the constitution. Next you'll be writin' your bibles with Christ sowin' wild oats to make him human. You say he's on your side. Onc't, just onc't, he had a favorite nation and they hung Him up by the hands and feet and his body hurt him and burn't him," his voice grew fainter. "Hail Mary, full of grace, the Lord is wit' thee—" His voice trailed off, he shuddered and was dead.

The hours went on. Clayton lit another pipe, heedless of what German sharpshooters might see. A heavy March mist had come down and the damp was eating into him. His whole left side was paralyzed and he felt chill creep slowly over him. He spoke aloud.

"Damned old mist — damned lucky old Irishman — Damnation." He felt a dim wonder that he was to know death but his thoughts turned as ever to England, and three faces came in sequence before him. Clara's, Dick's and Eleanor's. It was all such a mess. He'd like to have gone back and finished that conversation. It had stopped at Rochester — he had stopped living in the station at Rochester. How queer to have stopped there — Rochester had no significance. Wasn't there a play where a man was born in a station, or a handbag in a station, and he'd stopped living at — what did the Irishman say about cloaks, Eleanor said something about cloaks, too, he couldn't see any cloaks, didn't feel sentimental — only cold and dim and mixed up. He didn't know about God — God was a good thing for curates — then there was the Y.M.C.A. God — and he always wore short sleeves, and bumpy Oxfords — but that wasn't God — that was just the man who talked about God to soldiers. And then there was O'Flaherty's God. He felt as if he knew him, but then he'd never called him God — he was fear and love, and it wasn't dignified to fear God — or even to love him except in a calm respectable way. There were so many Gods it seemed — he had thought that Christianity was monotheistic, and it seemed pagan to have so many Gods.

Well, he'd find out the whole muddled business in about three minutes, and a lot of good it'd do anybody else left in the muddle. Damned muddle — everything a muddle, everybody offside, and the referee gotten rid of — everybody trying to say that if the referee were there he'd have been on their side. He was going to go and find that old referee — find him — get hold of him, get a good hold — cling to him — cling to him — ask him —

— F. Scott Fitzgerald.

———

54. "Sentiment—And the Use of Rouge," *The Nassau Literary Magazine,* LXXIII (June 1917), pp. 107-123. Fitzgerald is credited by name in the magazine. Overall, the tale has an admirable frankness. (And note the brief allusion—rare in Fitzgerald's fiction — to lesbianism.) Fitzgerald makes us feel the male protagonist's discomfort and bewilderment at the breakdown of traditional sexual standards. Although this story was never sold by Fitzgerald to a commercial magazine or reprinted in one of his short-story collections, it has greater impact than a number of stories that were.

In this story, the leading male character is weakened when, succumbing to the temptations of a female, he goes against his principles. In Fitzgerald's later works, as well, females will often be depicted as posing threats of one kind or another to the well-being of men.

Take note of the rather well-turned line the female lead utters when asked if she's a sentimentalist: "No, I'm romantic. There's a huge difference; a sentimental person thinks things will last, a romantic person hopes they won't." Fitzgerald, who called himself a romantic, was forever chronicling in his prose the ways in which things do not last.

Fitzgerald knew he'd crafted his prose well when he expressed the confusion and despair felt by a World War participant thusly: "Damned muddle — everything a muddle, everybody offside, and the referee gotten rid of — everybody trying to say that if the referee were there he'd have been on their side." Fitzgerald would subsequently reuse those lines in *This Side of Paradise*.

Throughout his career, Fitzgerald would go back through short stories that he had written for magazines and strip them of their best lines, transferring those lines to his notebooks for possible future use in novels. Material from the short stories "Love in the Night," "Jacob's Ladder," and "A Short Trip Home," for example, would eventually reappear in the novel *Tender is the Night*. Some stories he marked "Stripped and Permanently Buried" — meaning that because he had borrowed so many lines from them for use in novels, he did not want those stories to ever be reprinted. When he decided to include "A Short Trip Home" in his collection *Taps at Reveille*, he apologized to any readers who might feel he was serving "warmed-over fare" because the story included one paragraph that also appeared in *Tender is the Night*; in that particular case, he felt he had erred in transferring to a novel lines which more properly belonged to the original story.

ON A PLAY TWICE SEEN

Here in the figured dark I watch once more;
There with the curtain rolls a year away,
A year of years — There was an idle day
Of ours, when happy endings didn't bore
Our unfermented souls, and rocks held ore:
Your little face beside me, wide-eyed, gay,
Smiled its own repertoire, while the poor play
Reached me as a faint ripple reaches shore.

Yawning and wondering an evening through
I watch alone — and chatterings of course
Spoil the one scene which somehow *did* have charms;
You wept a bit, and I grew sad for you
Right there, where Mr. X defends divorce
And What's-Her-Name falls fainting in his arms.

— F. Scott Fitzgerald

55. "On a Play Twice Seen," *The Nassau Literary Magazine*, LXXIII (June 1917), p. 149. Fitzgerald is credited by name in the magazine. Fitzgerald, who had been dumped by Ginevra King not long before, writes how a play seems to have lost its appeal, when going to see it by himself rather than with the girl with whom he had previously seen it.

Fitzgerald recalled in a *Saturday Evening Post* article (September 18, 1920), by 1917 he had come to feel "that poetry was the only thing worthwhile, so with the meters of Swinburne and the matters of Rupert Brooke I spent the spring doing sonnets, ballads, and rondels into the small hours." For a while, he was even unsure whether he wanted to concentrate more on poetry or on prose after finishing his Princeton education. He felt encouraged when *Poet Lore* magazine, in September of 1917, accepted one of his poems ("The Way of Purgation," later incorporated into *This Side of Paradise*), but they never published it. Although a lifelong poetry lover, Fitzgerald was never as gifted a writer of poetry as of prose.

Book Talk: Verses in Peace and War

Mr. Leslie, after starting out as a sort of Irish Chesterton, now produces a diminutive volume of poetry under the title of *Verses In Peace and War.* In this poetical era of titles like "Men Women and Ghosts," and "Sword Blades and Poppy Seeds," Mr. Leslie is liable to be out-advertised by that dashing soubrette of American rhyming, Miss Amy Lowell, but if one desires poetry instead of the more popular antics of the School of Boston Bards and Hearst Reviewers, let him sit down for an hour with Mr. Leslie's little book. At first, one gets the impression of rather light verse, but soon finds that it is the touch rather than the verse which is light. The same undercurrent of sadness which runs through Mr. Leslie's prose is evident in his poetry, and gives it a most rare and haunting depth. In the series, "Epitaphs for Aviators," two are particularly apt. The one on Lieutenant Hamel:

Nor rugged earth, nor untamed sky,
Gave him his death to die,
But gentlest of the Holy Three;
The long grey liquid sea.
And the one on Lieutenant Chavez:
One flying past the Alps to see
What lay behind their crest —
Behind the snows found Italy;
Beyond the mountains — rest.

There is a savor of the Greek in his poem "The Hurdlers," dedicated to two of England's representatives in the last Olympian games, since killed in Flanders. The lines:

Oh, how are the beautiful broken
And how are the swiftest made slow —

sound as if they'd scan as well in Greek as in English. The lighter poems, such as "Nightmare" and "Rubies," are immensely well done as are the Irish poems "The Two Mothers" and "A Ballad of China Tea," but the brightest gem of the coffer is the poem "The Dead Friend," beginning:

I drew him then unto my knees
My friend who was dead,
And set my live lips over his,
And my heart to his head.

Mr. Leslie has a most distinct gift, and the only pity is that his book is so small. Poets are really so very rare that it seems almost unfair for them to become essayists. Despite Mr. Taine, in the whole range from Homer's Oddysey to Master's idiocy, there has been but one Shakespeare, and every lost name leaves a gap that it, and it only, could have filled.

(Verses in Peace and War *by Shane Leslie; Scribner's.*)

— F.S.F.

---

56. A book review of *Verses in Peace and War* by Shane Leslie, *The Nassau Literary Magazine*, LXXIII (June 1917), pp. 152-153. Fitzgerald's authorship is credited by initials: F.S.F. Shane Leslie was as enthusiastic about young Fitzgerald's writing as Fitzgerald was about his. In 1919, Leslie would strongly urge Scribners to publish Fitzgerald's first novel. In a review of Leslie's 1922 novel, *The Oppidan*, in *The New York Tribune*, Fitzgerald would call him "the most romantic figure I had ever known." Leslie would eventually be knighted.

BOOK TALK: GOD, THE INVISIBLE KING

The fad of rediscovering God has reached Mr. Wells. Started by Tolstoi (who has since backed his case by fathering a brand new revolution) it has reached most of the Clever People, including Bernard Shaw, who tried to startle us last year with his preface to *Androcles and the Lion*. But Mr. Wells has added very little. Like Victor Hugo, he has nothing but genius and is not of the slightest practical help. Neither a pacifist nor a crusader, he has been wise enough to keep God out of the war, which is only what the sanest people have been doing all along; if any war was ever made on earth it is this one.

If there is anything older than the old story it is the new twist. Mr. Wells supplies this by neatly dividing God into a creator and a Redeemer. On the whole we should welcome *God, the Invisible King*, as an entertaining addition to our supply of fiction for light summer reading.

(God the Invisible King *by H.G. Wells; MacMillian Co.*)

— F.S.F.

57. A book review of *God, the Invisible King* by H. G. Wells, *The Nassau Literary Magazine*, LXXIII (June 1917), p. 153. In an undated letter from the fall of 1917, Fitzgerald wrote Edmund Wilson, who was then serving in France, that he was rather bored at Princeton "but I see Shane Leslie occasionally and read Wells and Rousseau. I read Mrs. Gerould's *British Novelists Limited* and think she underestimates Wells but is right in putting Mackenzie at the head of his school…. Do you realize that Shaw is 61, Wells 51, Chesterton 41, Leslie 31, and I 21. (Too bad I haven't a better man for 31. I can hear your addition to this remark)."

In a September 26, 1917 letter to Wilson, Fitzgerald raved that Wells' *The New Machiavelli* was "the greatest English novel of the century."

In an April 1920 "self-interview," in which he listed writers he admired, Fitzgerald expressed a desire to be able to "handle slashing, flaming descriptions like Wells."

Within the pages of *This Side of Paradise*, Fitzgerald expressed his admiration for what he termed "quest" books, naming as examples *None Other Gods* by Robert Hugh Benson, *Sinister Street* by Compton Mackenzie, and *The Research Magnificent* by H. G. Wells.

THE CALL

58. "The Call." This drawing from *The Tiger* by John M. Foster '17 is not connected with Fitzgerald, but is included for the sake of context-setting. Drawings such as this one, intended to generate patriotism, were common during the war. "Buy a Liberty Bond!" *The Tiger* encourages readers (in a drawing by F. A. Comstock '19) on the next page. Youths were encouraged to feel a sense of pride when asked to leave college and report to military camp; their nation was calling them to serve.

Buy A Liberty Bond

135

ENNUI
The Typical Princeton Loafer in the Trenches

The Caws of War.

59. "Ennui. A Typical Princeton Loafer in the Trenches." This cartoon for *The Tiger* by Lawrence Boardman '18 is not connected with Fitzgerald, but is included for the sake of context-setting. The next cartoon, by an unidentified *Tiger* artist, "The Caws of War," offers a realistic depiction of aerial combat. In the spring of 1917, it was still possible for students at Princeton to make some jokes about the war. But as each passing month brought news of more casualties, a light tone became harder to maintain.

60. "Somewhere in France," *The Princeton Tiger*, XXVII (June 15, 1917), front cover. This is the first time that this cover has been reproduced in a book, aside from the limited-distribution *Roaring at One Hundred*, published by *The Princeton Tiger*.

Fitzgerald conceived and captioned this cover of *The Tiger*'s "war number" (originally printed in color, at a size of eight-and-one-half by eleven inches), which was drawn by John V. Newlin '19; their collaboration is credited on the cover itself: J. V. Newlin and F.S.F. Newlin, who also contributed Aubrey Beardsley-style drawings to *The Nassau Literary Magazine*, would die in the war himself about a month after this cover appeared; Fitzgerald would write Edmund Wilson, then in the service: "Yes — Jack Newlin is dead — killed in ambulance service. He was, potentially, a great artist...." (from an undated letter of 1917). The war, which the United States officially entered on April 6, 1917, would claim the lives of one man out of twenty in Fitzgerald's Princeton class.

The Tiger. WAR NUMBER

JUNE 15, 1917
VOL. 28   No. 1

SOMEWHERE IN FRANCE
The Girl With Whom He Strolled Along Lake Carnegie

The Dream and the Awakening.

61. "The Dream and the Awakening," *The Princeton Tiger*, XXVII (June 15, 1917), p. 16. This is the first time that this piece has been reproduced in a book, aside from the limited-distribution *Roaring at One Hundred*.

Fitzgerald wrote this comic strip, which was drawn by Alan Jackman '17; their collaboration is credited by initials: F.S.S. '18 and A.J. '17. Jackman confirmed that this was in fact written by Fitzgerald and that Jackman had printed the initials F.S.S. (instead of F.S.F.) by accident. A check of *Tiger* records provides additional confirmation, since there was no *Tiger* contributor in that period who had the initials F.S.S. After Fitzgerald was forced to repeat his junior year, he was officially a member of Princeton's class of 1918, although he still thought of himself as a member of the class of 1917.

Concerning Fitzgerald, Jackman noted in a letter to Andrew Turnball (which Jackman kindly shared with members of the *Tiger* graduate board): "Genius appears so seldom, we are never ready for it. We human beings deceive ourselves in wanting to become part of the brilliance of our fellows. Brilliance has an uphill fight to win its rightful recognition. Would that I could recall the 'bull sessions' of these freshman, sophomore, and senior years with Scott Fitzgerald, when the droll remarks, the piercing truths and revolutionary outbursts shocked even the sensibilities of us who were now a part of the world — or thought we were."

"The Dream and the Awakening" is quintessential Fitzgerald. In later years he would remark that the two key disappointments of his life were that he was never able to become a football hero or go overseas to fight in World War One (in 1936, he even wrote a story on the latter theme, "I Didn't Get Over"); he said he still had dreams in which he achieved those goals.

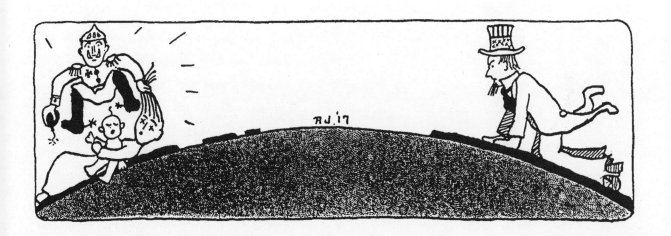

THE CAMEO FRAME

I

Golden, golden is the air,
Golden is the air,
Golden frets of golden mandolins,
Golden notes of golden violins,
Fair...Oh wearily fair;
Skeins from woven basket
Mortal may not hold,
Oh what young extravagant god,

Who would know or ask it...
Who could give such gold...

Oh the proud page
In the gold gloaming,
When the light whispers
And the souls roaming,
Ports the grey train,
Sees the gold hair
In the gay
The golden air

She posed that day by the marble pool
At half after five, so her fancy led;
Her slim grey pages, her lord her fool
Clacked various clacks as they watched the head
Acomba was doing...his own request...
Her head — just from swirling hair to throat,

With clinging silk for a shoulder sheath
And half the curve of a breast beneath.
"Head to the left...so... Can you stand
A little more sun on hair and face?"
Then as lightly he touched her hand
She whispered to him a time, a place
Then he aloud "Here's the very light,
My Lord, for the gold and rose effect...
Such a light over pool and sky
As cameo was graven by."

Over her grey and velvet dress
Under her molten, beaten hair
Color of rose in mock distress
Flushes and fades and makes her fair
Fills the air from her to him
With light and languor and little sighs
Just so subtly he scarcely knows
Laughing lightening, color of rose.

And grey to rose, and rose to gold
The color of day is twain, is one;
And he blinds his eyes that his heart may hold
This cameo on the setting sun,
And lip and fingers as lip and lip
Burn together and chill apart
And he turns his head as he sees her go,
Beautiful, pitiful, cameo.

Oh the proud page
In the green gloaming,
When the grass whispers
And the souls roaming,
Ports the grey train,
Sees the gold hair
In the gay
The golden air.

II

The night was another fragile frame
Tall and quiet and fair to fill;
It made for Acomba when he came
A silver setting...He watched until
She fluttered down from the guarded hall
A weary leaf from a dreary tree,
Fluttered to him where the breezes cool
Made pale love to the marble pool.

Then the moon and his heart sank low...
All that he knew of a sudden there
Was just that light on the cameo
Was not the light that had made it fair...
Not the grey and not the rose,
Not the gold of the afternoon,
So he kissed it sadly and spoke a name
And he pressed it back in its silver frame.

And youth in anger, and time in tears
Sat at his feet and bade him take...
"Once a day for a thousand years
Think of the gold her hair will make...
Shaper of lips you may not kiss
Scorn you the soul where colors touch
Kept for you in a golden sleep!..."
But he could never say why...or weep.

So ice by day and ghost by night
The cameo lay till its moment came
And blushed for the sunset bold and bright
Gold and rose in its velvet frame,
And he who made it would stand and smile,
Pause and pity and count the years,
Watch and watch till the frame turned blue
Knower of things was he...he knew...

Golden, golden is the air,
Golden is the air,
Golden frets of golden mandolins,
Golden notes of golden violins,
Fair, oh wearily fair;
Skeins from woven basket
Mortal may not hold,
Oh what young extravagant god
Who would know or ask it
Who could give such gold!

— F. Scott Fitzgerald

---

62. "The Cameo Frame," *The Nassau Literary Magazine*, LXXIII (October 1917), p. 169-172. Fitzgerald is credited by name in the magazine.

In an undated letter Fitzgerald sent to Edmund Wilson in the fall of 1917, Fitzgerald suggested he found John Peale Bishop's poetry a bit too precious to have a broad audience appeal, adding, "John really is an anachronism in this country at this time — people want ideas and not fabrics." Fitzgerald's criticism of Bishop's poetry would seem to apply quite nicely to this poem of Fitzgerald's.

The Pierian Springs and the Last Straw

My Uncle George assumed, during my childhood, almost legendary proportions. His name was never mentioned except in verbal italics. His published works lay in bright, interesting binding on the library table — forbidden to my whetted curiosity until I should reach the age of corruption. When one day I broke the orange lamp into a hundred shivers and glints of glass, it was in search of closer information concerning a late arrival among the books. I spent the afternoon in bed and for weeks could not play under the table because of maternal horror of severed arteries in hands and knees. But I had gotten my first idea of Uncle George — he was a tall angular man with crooked arms. His opinion was founded upon the shape of the handwriting in which he had written "To you, my brother, with the heartiest of futile hopes that you will enjoy and approve of this: George Rombert." After this unintelligible beginning whatever interest I had in the matter waned, as would have all my ideas of the author, had he not been a constant family topic.

When I was eleven I unwillingly listened to the first comprehensible discussion of him. I was figeting on a chair in the barbarous punishment when a letter arrived and I noticed my father growing stern and formidable as he read it. Instinctively I knew it concerned Uncle George — and I was right.

"What's the matter Tom? — Some one sick?" asked my mother rather anxiously.

For answer father rose and handed her the letter and some newspaper clippings it had enclosed. When she had read it twice (for her naive curiosity she could never resist a preliminary skim) she plunged—

"Why should she write to you and not to me?"

Father threw himself wearily on the sofa and arranged his long limbs decoratively.

"It's getting tiresome, isn't it? This is the third time he's become — involved." I started for I distinctly hear him add under his breath "Poor damn fool!"

"It's much more than tiresome," began my mother. "It's disgusting; a great strong man with money and talent and every reason to behave and get married (she implied that these words were synonymous) playing around with serious women like a silly, conceited college boy. You'd think it was a harmless game!"

Here I put in my word. I thought perhaps my being *de trop* in the conversation might lead to an early release.

"I'm here," I volunteered.

"So I see," said father in the tones he used to intimidate other young lawyers downtown; so I sat there and listened respectfully while they plumbed the iniquitous depths.

"It is a game to him," said my father; "That's all part of his theory."

My mother sighed. "Mr. Sedgewick told me yesterday that his books had done inestimable harm to the spirit in which love is held in this country."

"Mr. Sedgewick wrote him a letter," remarked my father rather dryly, "and George sent him the book of Solomon by return post—"

"Don't joke, Thomas," said mother crowding her face with eyes, "George is treacherous, his mind is unhealthy—"

"And so would be mine, had you not snatched me passionately from his clutches — and your son here will be George the second, if he feeds on this sort of conversation at his age." So the curtain fell upon my Uncle George for the first time.

Scrappy and rough-pieced information on this increasingly engrossing topic fitted gradually into my consciousness in the next five years like the parts of a picture puzzle. Here is the finished portrait from the angle of seventeen years — Uncle George was a Romeo and a mesogamist, a combination of Byron, Don Juan, and Bernard Shaw, with a touch of Havelock Ellis for good measure. He was about thirty, he had been engaged seven times and drank ever so much more than was good for him. His attitude toward women was the *piece-de-resistance* of his character. To put it mildly he was not an idealist. He had written a series of novels, all of them bitter, each of them with some woman as the principal character. Some of the women were bad. None of them were quite good. He picked a rather weird selection of Lauras to play muse to his whimsical Petrarch; for he could write, write well.

He was the type of author that gets dozens of letters a week from solicitors, aged men and enthusiastic young women who tell him that he is "prostituting his art" and "wasting golden literary opportunities." As a matter of fact he wasn't. It was very conceivable that he might have written better despite his unpleasant range of subject, but what he had written had a huge vogue that strangely enough, consisted not of the usual devotees of prostitute art, the eager shopgirls and sentimental salesmen to whom he was accused of pandering, but of the academic and literary circles of the country. His shrewd tenderness with nature (that is, everything but the white race), his well drawn men and the particularly cynical sting to his wit gave him many adherents. He was ranked in the most staid and severe of reviews as a coming man. Long psychopathic stories and dull germanized novels were predicted of him by optimistic critics. At one time he was the Thomas Hardy of America and he was several times heralded as the Balzac of his century. He was accused of having the great American novel in his coat pocket trying to peddle it from publisher to publisher. But somehow neither matter nor style had improved, people accused him of not "living." His unmarried sister and he had an apartment where she sat greying year after year with one furtive hand on the bromo-seltzer and the other on the telephone receiver of frantic feminine telephone calls. For George Rombert grew violently involved at least once a year. He filled columns in the journals of society gossip. Oddly enough most of his affairs were with debutantes — a fact which was considered particularly annoying by sheltering mothers. It seemed as though he had the most serious way of talking the most outrageous nonsense and as he was most desirable from an economic point of view, many essayed the perilous quest.

Though we had lived in the East since I had been a baby, it was always understood that home meant the prosperous Western city that still supported the roots of our family tree. When I was twenty I went back for the first time and made my only acquaintance with Uncle George.

I had dinner in the apartment with my aunt, a very brave, gentle old lady who told me, rather proudly, I thought, that I looked like George. I was shown his pictures from babyhood, in every attitude; George at Andover, on the Y.M.C.A. committee, strange anatomy; George at Williams in the center of *The Literary Magazine* Picture, George as the head of his fraternity. Then she handed me a scrap-book containing accounts of his exploits and all favorable criticism of his work.

"He cares nothing at all about all this," she explained. I admired and questioned, and remember thinking as I left the apartment to seek Uncle George at his club, that between my family's depressed opinion of him and my aunt's elated one my idea of him was muddled to say the least. At the Iroquois Club I was directed to the grill, and there standing in the doorway, I picked one out of the crowd, who, I was immediately sure, was he. Here is the way he looked at the time. He was tall with magnificent iron grey hair and the pale soft skin of a boy, most remarkable in a man of his mode of life. Drooping green eyes and a sneering mouth complete my picture of his physical self. He was rather drunk, for he had been at the club all afternoon and for dinner, but he was perfectly conscious of himself and the dulling of faculties was only perceivable in a very cautious walk and a crack in his voice that sank it occasionally to a hoarse whisper. He was talking to the table of men all in various stages of inebriation, and holding them by a most peculiar and magnetic series of gestures. Right here I want to remark that this influence was not dependent so much upon a vivid physical personality but on a series of perfectly artificial mental tricks, his gestures, the peculiar range of his speaking voice, the suddenness and terseness of his remarks.

I watched him intently while my hall boy whispered to him and he walked slowly and consciously over to me to shake hands gravely and escort me to a small table. For an hour we talked of family things, of healths and deaths and births. I could not take my eyes off him. The blood-shot streakedness of his green eyes made me think of weird color combinations in a child's paint-box. He had been looking bored for about ten minutes and my talk had been dwindling despondently down when suddenly he waved his hand as if to brush away a veil, and began to question me.

"Is that damn father of yours still defending me against your mother's tongue?"

I started, but, strangely, felt no resentment.

"Because," he went on, "It's the only thing he ever did for me all his life. He's a terrible prig. I'd think it would drive you wild to have him in the house."

"Father feels very kindly toward you, sir," I said rather stiffly.

"Don't," he protested smiling. "Stick to veracity in your own family and don't bother to lie to me. I'm a totally black figure in your mind, I'm well aware. Am I not?"

Well — you've — you've had a twenty years' history."

"Twenty years — hell—," said Uncle George. "Three years history and fifteen years aftermath."

"But your books — and all."

"Just aftermath, nothing but aftermath, my life stopped at twenty-one one night in October at six-teen minutes after ten. Do you want to hear about it? First I'll show you the heifer and then I'll take you upstairs and present you to the altar."

"I, you — if you—," I demurred feebly, for I was on fire to hear the story.

"Oh, — no trouble. I've done the story several times in books and life and around many a litered table. I have no delicacy any more — I lost that in the first smoke. This is the totally blackened heifer whom you're talking to now."

So he told me the story.

"You see it began Sophomore year — began most directly and most vividly in Christmas vacation of Sophomore year. Before that she'd always gone with a younger crowd — set, you young people call it now," — he paused and clutched with mental fingers for tangible figures to express himself. "Her dancing, I guess, and beauty and the most direct, unprincipled personality I've ever come in contact with. When she wanted a boy there was no preliminary scouting among other girls for information, no sending out of tentative approaches meant to be retailed to him. There was the most direct attack by every faculty and gift that she possessed. She had no divergence of method — she just made you conscious to the highest degree that she was a girl" — he turned his eyes on me suddenly and asked:

"Is that enough — do you want a description of her eyes and hair and what she said?"

"No," I answered, "go on."

"Well, I went back to college an idealist, I built up a system of psychology in which dark ladies with alto voices and infinite possibilities floated through my days and nights. Of course we had the most frantic correspondence — each wrote ridiculous letters and sent ridiculous telegrams, told all our acquaintances about our flaming affair and — well you've been to college. All this is banal, I know. Here's an odd thing. All the time I was idealizing her to the last possibility, I was perfectly conscious that she was about the faultiest girl I'd ever met. She was selfish, conceited and uncontrolled and since these were my own faults I was doubly aware of them. Yet I never wanted to change her. Each fault was knit up with a sort of passionate energy that transcended it.

Her selfishness made her play the game harder, her lack of control put me rather in awe of her and her conceit was punctuated by such delicious moments of remorse and self-denunciation that it was almost — almost dear to me— Isn't this getting ridiculous? She had the strongest effect on me. She made me want to do something for her, to get something to show her. Every honor in college took on the semblance of a presentable trophy."

He beckoned to a waiter to my infinite misgiving, for though he seemed rather more sober than when I had arrived, he had been drinking steadily and I knew my own position would be embarrasing if he became altogether drunk.

"Then" — between sips — "we saw each other at sporadic intervals, quarreled, kissed and quarreled again. We were equals, neither was the leader. She was as interested in me as I was fascinated by her. We were both terrifically jealous but there was little occasion to show it. Each of us had small affairs on the side but merely as relaxations when the other was away. I didn't realize it but my idealism was slowly waning — or increasing into love — and rather a gentle sort of love." His face tightened. "This isn't cup sentiment." I nodded and he went on; "Well, we broke off in two hours and I was the weak one."

"Senior year I went to her school dance in New York, and there was a man there from another college of whom I became very jealous and not without cause. She and I had a few words about it and half an hour later I walked out on the street in my coat and hat, leaving behind the melancholy statement that I was through for good. So far so good. If I'd gone back to college that night or if I'd gone and gotten drunk or done almost anything wild or resentful the break would never have occurred — she'd have written next day. Here's what did happen. I walked along Fifth Avenue letting my imagination play on my sorrow, really luxuriating in it. She'd never looked better than she had that night, never; and I had never been so much in love. I worked myself up to the highest pitch of emotional imagination and moods grow real on me and then — Oh poor damn fool that I was — am — will always be — I went

back. Went back! Couldn't I have known or seen — I knew her and myself — I could have plotted out for anyone else or in a cool mood, for myself just what I should have done, but my imagination made me go back, drove me. Half a thought in my brain would have sent me to Williamstown or the Manhattan bar. Another half thought sent me back to her school. When I crossed the threshold it was sixteen minutes after ten. At that minute I stopped living."

"You can imagine the rest. She was angry at me for leaving, hadn't had time to brood and when she saw me come in she resolved to punish me. I swallowed it hook and bait and temporarily lost confidence, temper, poise, every single jot of individuality or attractiveness I had. I wandered around that ballroom like a wild man trying to get a word with her and when I did I finished the job. I begged, pled, almost wept. She had no use for me from that hour. At two o'clock I walked out of that school a beaten man."

"Why the rest — it's a long nightmare — letters with all the nerve gone out of them, wild imploring letters; long silences hoping she'd care; rumors of her other affairs. At first I used to be sad when people still linked me up with her, asked me for news of her but finally when it got around that she'd thrown me over people didn't ask me about her anymore, they told me of her — crumbs to a dog. I wasn't the authority any more on my own work, for that's what she was — just what I'd read into her and brought out in her. That's the story — " He broke off suddenly and rose; tottering to his feet, his voice rose and rang through the deserted grill.

"I read history with a new viewpoint since I had known Cleopatra and Messaline and Montespan," — he started toward the door.

"Where are you going?" I asked in alarm.

"We're going upstairs to meet the lady. She's a widow now for awhile so you must say Mrs. — see — Mrs."

We went upstairs, I carefully behind with hands ready to be outstretched should he fall. I felt particularly unhappy. The hardest man in the world to handle is one who is too sober to be vacillating and too drunk to be persuaded; and I had,

145

strange to say, an idea that my Uncle was eminently a person to be followed.

We entered a large room. I couldn't describe it if my life depended on it. Uncle George nodded and beckoned to a woman at a bridge four across the room. She nodded and rising from the table walked slowly over. I started — naturally—

Here is my impression — a woman of thirty or a little under, dark, with intense physical magnetism and a most expressive mouth capable, as I soon found out, of the most remarkable change of expression by the slightest variance in facial geography. It was a mouth to be written to, but, though it could never have been called large, it could never have been crowded into a sonnet — I confess I have tried. Sonnet indeed! It contained the emotions of a drama and the history, I presume, of an epic. It was, as near as I can fathom, the eternal mouth. There were eyes also, brown, and a high warm coloring; but oh the mouth....

I felt like a character in a Victorian romance. The little living groups scattered around seemed to move in small spotlights around us who were acting out a comedy "down stage." I was self-conscious about myself but purely physically so; I was merely a property; but I was very self-conscious for my Uncle. I dreaded the moment when he should lift his voice or overturn the table or kiss Mrs. Fulham bent dramatically back over his arm while the groups would start and stare. It was enormously unreal. I was introduced in a mumble and then forgotten.

"Tight again," remarked Mrs. Fulham.

My uncle made no answer.

"Well, I'm having a heavy bridge game and we're ever so much behind. You can just have my dummy time. Aren't you flattered?" She turned to me. "Your Uncle probably told you all about himself and me. He's been behaving so badly this year. He used to be such a pathetic innocent little boy and such a devil with the debutantes."

My Uncle broke in quickly with a rather grandiose air: "That's sufficient, I think, Myra, for you."

"You're going to blame me again?" she asked in feigned astonishment. "As if I—"

"Don't — Don't," said my Uncle thickly. "Let one poor damn fool alone."

Here I found myself suddenly appreciating a sudden contrast. My Uncle's personality had dropped off him like a cloak. He was not the romantic figure of the grill, but a less sure, less attractive and somewhat contemptible individual. I had never seen personalities act like that before. Usually you either had one or you didn't. I wonder if I mean personality or temperament or perhaps that brunette alto tenor mood that lies on the borderland.... At any rate my Uncle's mood was now that of a naughty boy to a stern aunt, almost that of a dog to his master.

"You know," said Mrs. Fulham, "your Uncle is the only interesting thing in town. He's such a perfect fool."

Uncle George bowed his head and regarded the floor in a speculative manner. He smiled politely, if unhappily.

"That's your idea."

"He takes all his spite out on me."

My Uncle nodded, Mrs. Fulham's partners called over to her that they had lost again and that the game was breaking up. She got rather angry.

"You know," she said coldly to Uncle George, "you stand there like a trained spaniel letting me say anything I want to you — Do you know what a pitiful thing you are?

My Uncle had gone a dark red. Mrs. Fulham turned again to me.

"I've been talking to him like this for ten years — like this or not at all. He's my little lap dog. Here George, bring me my tea, write a book about me; you're snippy Georgie but interesting." Mrs. Fulham was rather carried away by the dramatic intensity of her own words and angered by George's unmovable acceptance. So she lost her head.

"You know," she said tensely, "My husband often wanted to horsewhip you but I've begged you off. He was very handy in the kennels and always said he could handle any kind of dog!"

Something had snapped. My Uncle rose, his eyes blazing. The shift of burden from her to her husband had lifted a weight from his shoulders.

His eyes flashed but the words stored up for ten years came slow and measured.

"Your husband— Do you mean that crooked broker who kept you for five years. Horsewhip me! That was the prattle he may have used around the fireside to keep you under his dirty thumb. By God, I'll horsewhip your next husband myself." His voice had risen and the people were beginning to look up. A hush had fallen on the room and his words echoed from fireplace to fireplace.

"He's the damn thief that robbed me of everything in this hellish world."

He was shouting now. A few men drew near. Women shrank to the corner. Mrs. Fulham stood perfectly still. Her face had gone white but she was still sneering openly at him.

"What's this?" he picked up her hand. She tried to snatch it away but he tightened his grip and twisting the wedding ring off her finger he threw it on the floor and stamped it into a beaten button of gold.

In a minute I had his arms held. She screamed and held up her broken finger. The crowd closed around us.

In five minutes Uncle George and I were speeding homeward in a taxi. Neither of us spoke; he sat staring straight before him, his green eyes glittering in the dark. I left next morning after breakfast.

* * *

The story ought to end here. My Uncle George should remain with Mark Anthony and DeMusset as a rather tragic semigenius, ruined by a woman. Unfortunately the play continues into an inartistic sixth act where it topples over and descends like Uncle George himself in one of his more inebriated states, contrary to all the rules of dramatic literature. One month afterward, Uncle George and Mrs. Fulham eloped in the most childish and romantic manner the night before her marriage to the Honorable Howard Bixby was to have taken place. Uncle George never drank again, nor did he ever write or in fact do anything except play a middling amount of golf and get comfortably bored with his wife.

Mother still doubts and predicts gruesome fates for his wife, Father is frankly astonished and not too pleased. In fact I rather believe he enjoyed having an author in the family, even if his books did look a bit decadent on the library table. From time to time I receive subscription lists and invitations from Uncle George. I keep them for use in my new book on *Theories of Genius.* You see, I claim that if Dante had ever won — but a hypothetical sixth act is just as untechnical as a real one.

— F. Scott Fitzgerald

---

63. "The Pierian Springs and the Last Straw," *The Nassau Literary Magazine*, LXXIII (October 1917), p. 173-185. Fitzgerald is credited by name in the magazine. In a tongue-in-cheek review of "The Pierian Springs and the Last Straw" in the *Williams Literary Magazine*, November 1917, one John Bakeless proclaimed that Fitzgerald has "gone and went and done it. Williams College has been shown up, and there is nothing to do but close down the college and sit in sackcloth and ashes, a-repenting of our sins. The dreadful *expose* occurs in... 'The Pierian Springs and the Last Straw.' Though what the Pierian Springs have to do with the last straw, or whether the straw is intended for convenience in drinking out of the springs, or not, goodness knows, and Mr. Fitzgerald doesn't say. The story is about a talented author, who is also a Regular Devil, and who used to be a member of the board of this staid and respectable Williams journal. Mr. Fitzgerald says so....But why does he wish Uncle George on to the *Williams Literary Monthly?*... Mr. Fitzgerald is a very clever young man, and he has written some extraordinarily good verse, which Mr. Alfred Noyes printed in his recent *Book of Princeton Verse.* But why does Mr. Fitzgerald dismount from Pegasus to attack the short story? Not to mention the *Williams Lit.*"

"The Pierian Springs and the Last Straw" is, along with "Babes in the Wood" and "The Debutante," the most fully realized and memorable of Fitzgerald's undergraduate writings. Although it was never sold by Fitzgerald to a commercial magazine or collected by him in one of his books, this little-known story is finer than many of his other stories that were. It is far more substantive and engaging than, say, "Jemina," which he chose to include in *Tales of the Jazz Age*, or "The Four Fists," which he chose to include in *Flappers and Philosophers*. We want to know more about Uncle George, who feels his "life stopped at twenty-one one night in October at sixteen minutes after ten." Uncle George is a writer who has been damaged by his involvement with a woman. In later years, a number of Fitzgerald's friends would come to feel that he had been damaged by his involvement with the demanding and unstable Zelda.

64

THE STAYING UP ALL NIGHT

THE WARM FIRE.

THE COMFORTABLE CHAIRS.

THE MERRY COMPANIONS.

THE STROKE OF TWELVE.

THE WILD SUGGESTION.

THE GOOD SPORTS.

THE MAN WHO HASN'T SLEPT FOR WEEKS.

THE PEOPLE WHO HAVE DONE IT BEFORE.

THE LONG ANECDOTES.

THE BEST LOOKING GIRL YAWNS.

THE FORCED RAILLERY.

THE STROKE OF ONE.

THE BEST LOOKING GIRL GOES TO BED.

THE STROKE OF TWO.

THE EMPTY PANTRY.

THE LACK OF FIREWOOD.

THE SECOND BEST LOOKING GIRL GOES TO BED.

THE WEATHER-BEATEN ONES WHO DON'T.

THE STROKE OF FOUR.

THE DOZING OFF.

THE AMATEUR "LIFE OF THE PARTY."

THE BURGLAR SCARE.

THE SCORNFUL CAT.

THE TRYING TO IMPRESS THE MILKMAN.

THE SCORN OF THE MILKMAN.

THE LUNATIC FEELING.

THE CHILLY SUN.

THE STROKE OF SIX.

THE WALK IN THE GARDEN.

THE SNEEZING.

THE EARLY RISERS.

THE VOLLEY OF WIT AT YOU.

THE FEEBLE COME BACK.

THE TASTELESS BREAKFAST.

THE MISERABLE DAY.

8 P.M. — BETWEEN THE SHEETS.

F.S.F.

---

64. "The Staying Up All Night," *The Princeton Tiger*, XXVIII (November 10, 1917), p. 6. Fitzgerald's authorship is credited by initials: F.S.F. Written with a sure, deft touch, this evocative piece is one of Fitzgerald's most successful *Tiger* creations.

Intercollegiate Petting—Cues.

2. "You really don't look comfortable there."

65. "Intercollegiate Petting-Cues," *The Princeton Tiger*, XXVIII (November 10, 1917), p. 8. Unsigned. Known to be by Fitzgerald because he preserved a clipping in his scrapbook.

"You really don't look comfortable there" is a line Fitzgerald overheard a fellow student use to coax a girl into getting cozy with him. Guys with good "lines" were known as "parlor snakes" in the Princeton of Fitzgerald's day. (Incidentally, Cottage Club, to which Fitzgerald belonged, had a reputation as "the parlor snake's delight," as Fitzgerald recorded.) Fitzgerald wrote memorably about the subject of "petting" in *This Side of Paradise*. In a favorable review of that book that appeared in *The Dartmouth* (April 24, 1920), a Dartmouth undergraduate by the name of R. F. McPartin informed his fellow students: "The book abounds in slang, much of it wholly individual to Princeton, but every word has its Dartmouth synonym. 'Petting,' promising title of one episode, is locally known by the less euphemistic 'mugging.'"

66. "The Petting Party." This cartoon for *The Tiger* by Lawrence Boardman '18 is not connected with Fitzgerald, but is included simply for the sake of context-setting. It gives us a feel for life of that time—another look at the topic of "petting," courtesy of Fitzgerald's classmate Boardman.

66

THE PETTING PARTY

151

OUR AMERICAN POETS

I
ROBERT SERVICE

The red blood throbs
And forms in gobs
On the nose of Hank McPhee.
With a wild "Ha-Ha!" he shoots his pa
Through the frozen artic lea.

II
ROBERT FROST

A rugged young rhymer named Frost,
Once tried to be strong at all cost
The mote in his eye
May be barley or rye,
But his right in that beauty is lost.

Though the meek shall inherit the land,
He prefers a tough bird in the hand,
He puts him in inns,
And feeds him on gins,
And the high brows say, "Isn't he grand?"

F.S.F.

67. "Our American Poets," *The Princeton Tiger*, XXVIII (November 10, 1917), p. 11. Fitzgerald's authorship of these parodies of Robert Service and Robert Frost is credited by initials: F.S.F.

Aviators Going to Breakfast—As It Sounds from Campbell Hall.

68. "Aviators Going to Breakfast — As It Sounds from Campbell Hall." This unsigned cartoon, which is not known to have any connection to Fitzgerald (he did not save a copy in his scrapbook), is included for the sake of context-setting. It is supposed to show the noise created by members of Princeton's wartime aviator-training program, who would march through the archway of Campbell Hall on their way to and from breakfast in Commons. At the time this cartoon appeared in *The Tiger* (November 10, 1917), Fitzgerald and John Biggs Jr. were living in Campbell Hall (quite accurately depicted in this cartoon) — and undoubtedly being awakened some mornings by the aviators' noise.

CEDRIC THE STOKER

(THE TRUE STORY OF THE BATTLE OF THE BALTIC)

The grimy coal-hole of the battle ship of the line was hot, and Cedric felt the loss of his parasol keenly. It was his duty to feed the huge furnace that sent the ship rolling over and over in the sea, heated the sailors' bedrooms, and ran the washing machine. Cedric was hard at work. He would fill his hat with a heap of black coals, carry them to the huge furnace, and throw them in. His hat was now soiled beyond recognition, and try as he might he could not keep his hands clean.

He was interrupted in his work by the jingle of the telephone bell. "Captain wishes to speak to you, Mr. Cedric," said the girl at the exchange. Cedric rushed to the phone.

"How's your mother," asked the Captain.

"Very well, thank you, sir," answered Cedric.

"Is it hot enough for you, down there?" said the Captain.

"Quite," replied Cedric, courteously.

The Captain's voice changed. He would change it every now and then. "Come to my office at once," he said, "we are about to go into action and I wish your advice."

Cedric rushed to the elevator, and getting off at the fourth floor, ran to the office. He found the Captain rubbing his face with cold cream to remove sunburn.

"Cedric," said the Captain, sticking a lump of the greasy stuff in his mouth and chewing it while he talked, "You are a bright child, rattle off the binomial theorem."

Cedric repeated it forwards, backwards, and from the middle to both ends.

"Now name all the salts of phosphoric acid!"

Cedric named them all, and four or five extra.

"Now the Iliad!"

Here Cedric did his most difficult task. He repeated the Iliad backwards leaving out alternately every seventh and fourth word.

"You *are* efficient," said the Captain smilingly. He took from his mouth the cold cream, which he had chewed into a hard porous lump, and dropped it back into the jar. "I shall trust you with all our lives." He drew Cedric closer to him.

"Listen," he whispered; "the enemy are attacking in force. They are far stronger than we. We outnumber them only five to one: nevertheless we shall fight with the utmost bravery. As commander of the fleet, I have ordered the crews of all my ships to struggle to the last shell and powder roll, and then to flee for their lives. This ship is not so fast as the others so I guess it had better begin fleeing now!"

"Sir—" began Cedric, but he was interrupted by the stacatto noise of the huge forward turret pop-guns as the two fleets joined in battle. They could hear the sharp raps of the paddles as the bosuns spanked their crews to make them work faster. Their ears were deafened by the cursing of the pilots as the ships fouled one another. All the hideous sounds of battle rose and assailed them. Cedric rushed to the window and threw it open. He shrank back, aghast. Bearing down upon them, and only ten miles away, was the huge *Hoboken*, the biggest of all ferry boats, captured by the enemy from the Erie Railroad in the fall of '92. So close she was that Cedric could read her route sign "Bronx West to Toid Avenoo." The very words struck him numb. On she came, and on, throwing mountains of spray a mile in front of her and several miles to her rear.

"Is she coming fast, boy?" asked the Captain.

"Sir, she's making every bit of a knot an hour," answered Cedric, trembling.

The Captain seized him roughly by the shoulders. "We'll fight to the end," he said: "even though she is faster than we are. Quick! To the cellars and stoke, stoke, STOKE!"

Cedric, unable to take his eyes from the terrible sight, ran backwards down the passageway, fell down the elevator shaft, and rushed to the furnace. Madly he carried coal back and forth, from the bin to the furnace door, and then back to the bin. Already the speed of the ship had increased. It tore through the water in twenty-foot jumps. But it was not enough. Cedric worked more madly, and still more madly. At last he had thrown the last lump of coal into the furnace. There was nothing more to be done. He rested his tired body against the glowing side of the furnace.

Again the telephone rang. Cedric answered it himself, not wishing to take the exchange girl away from her knitting. It was the Captain.

"We must have more speed," he shouted: "We must have more speed. Throw on more coal — more coal!"

For a moment Cedric was wrapped in thought, his face twitching with horror. Then he realized his duty, and rushed forward.

***

Late that evening, when they were safe in port, the Captain, smoking his after-dinner cigar, came down to the stoke-hole. He called for Cedric. There was not a sound. Again he called. Still there was silence. Suddenly the horror of the truth rushed upon him. He tore open the furnace door, and convulsed with sobs, drew forth a Brooks-Livingstone Collar, a half-melted piece of Spearmint gum, and a suit of Yerger asbestos underwear. For a moment he held them in his arms, and then fell howling upon the floor. The truth had turned out to be the truth.

Cedric had turned himself into calories.

F.S.F. / J.B.

---

69. "Cedric the Stoker," *The Princeton Tiger*, XXVIII (November 10, 1917), p. 12. Fitzgerald and John Biggs Jr. co-authored this; their authorship is credited by initials: F.S.F., J.B.

This would be Fitzgerald's last contribution to *The Tiger*. On October 20, 1917, he received his commission as an infantry second lieutenant. On November 20, 1917, he reported to Fort Leavenworth, Kansas. There, he used whatever spare time he could find to work on a novel, writing Shane Leslie on December 22, 1917: "The reason I've abandoned my idea of a book of poems is that I've only about twenty poems and can't write any more in this atmosphere—while I can write prose so I'm sandwiching the poems between reams of autobiography and fiction."

Fitzgerald wrote Edmund Wilson presciently on January 10, 1918 that if Scribners were to accept the novel he was working on, "I know I'll wake some morning and find that the debutantes have made me famous over night. I really believe that no one else could have written so searchingly the story of the youth of our generation."

Fitzgerald also informed Wilson that another of their Princeton friends, Stuart Wolcott, had been killed in service; the war, Fitzgerald noted, was "really beginning to irritate me — but the maudlin sentiment of most people is still the spear in my side."

Wilson, who was then serving in France, had written Fitzgerald that he found solace in thinking about his Princeton literary circle; he had also mailed Fitzgerald two new poems he'd written for *The Nassau Lit.* (Fitzgerald forwarded them to *The Lit* and encouraged Wilson to write more.) Fitzgerald noted that now that he, Bishop, and another member of their circle had all departed Princeton for military life, only Biggs was left behind to try and carry on.

CITY DUSK

Come out . . . out
To this inevitable night of mine
Oh you drinker of new wine,
Here's pageantry.... Here's carnival,
Rich dusk, dim streets and all
The whisperings of city night.…

I have closed my book of fading harmonies,
(The shadows fell across me in the park)
And my soul was sad with violins and trees,
And I was sick for dark,
When suddenly it hastened by me, bringing
Thousands of lights, a haunting breeze,
And a night of streets and singing....

I shall know you by your eager feet
And by your pale, pale hair;

I'll whisper happy incoherent things
While I'm waiting for you there....

All the faces unforgettable in dusk
Will blend to yours,
And the footsteps like a thousand overtures
Will blend to yours,
And there will be more drunkenness than wine
In the softness of your eyes on mine....

Faint violins where lovely ladies dine,
The brushing of skirts, the voices of the night
And all the lure of friendly eyes.... Ah there
We'll drift like summer sounds upon the summer
   air....
— F. Scott Fitzgerald, Lieutenant 45th Infantry

———

70. "City Dusk," *The Nassau Literary Magazine*, LXXIII (April 1918), p. 315. Fitzgerald is credited by name in the magazine: F. Scott Fitzgerald, Lieutenant 45th Infantry. He probably submitted this poem to *The Lit* during that period in March and April of 1918 when, on leave, he was living in Princeton and working on the novel that would ultimately become *This Side of Paradise*.

In July of 1918, Fitzgerald met Zelda Sayre (whom he'd wed in April of 1920) at a country club dance in Montgomery, Alabama. Although late in his life he would conclude that their turbulent marriage had been a mistake from the start, in their early years together they seemed to many onlookers to be wonderfully matched — the definitive Jazz Age couple. Edmund Wilson was not alone in remarking favorably upon their joint ability to carry "people away by their spontaneity, charm, and good looks."

My First Love

All my ways she wove of light
Wove them half alive,
Made them warm and beauty-bright…
So the shining, ambient air
Clothes the golden waters where
The pearl fishers dive.

When she wept and begged a kiss
Very close I'd hold her,
Oh I know so well in this

Fine, fierce joy of memory
She was very young like me
Tho half an aeon older.

Once she kissed me very long,
Tip-toed out the door,
Left me, took her light along,
Faded as a music fades...
Then I saw the changing shades,
Color-blind no more.

— F. Scott Fitzgerald, '18

71. "My First Love," *The Nassau Literary Magazine*, LXXIV (February 1919), p. 102. Fitzgerald is credited by name in the magazine.

In February of 1919, Fitzgerald was discharged from the army. He moved to New York City, seeking work as a writer. He was disappointed to see how little interest prospective employers showed in his *Tiger* and *Nassau Lit* clippings. He finally found a job with an advertising agency. He quit it a few months later, determined to support himself by his fiction.

In the Spring of 1919, Fitzgerald sold "Babes in the Woods" for $30 to *The Smart Set*, which was edited by George Jean Nathan and H. L. Mencken — his first short-story sale to a commercial magazine. Others soon followed. On September 16, 1919, Scribners accepted Fitzgerald's manuscript of *This Side of Paradise*.

MARCHING STREETS

Death slays the moon and the long dark deepens,
Hastens to the city, to the drear stone-heaps,
Films all eyes and whispers on the corners,
Whispers to the corners that the last soul sleeps.

Gay grow the streets now torched by yellow lamplight,
March all directions with a long sure tread.
East, west they wander through the blinded city,
Rattle on the windows like the wan-faced dead.

Ears full of throbbing, a babe awakens startled,
Sends a tiny whimper to the still gaunt room.
Arms of the mother tighten round it gently,
Deaf to the patter in the far-flung gloom.

Old streets hoary with dear, dead foot-steps
Loud with the tumbrils of a gold old age
Young streets sand-white still unheeled and soulless,
Virgin with the pallor of the fresh-cut page.

Black streets and alleys, evil girl and tearless,
Creeping leaden footed each in thin, torn coat,
Wine-stained and miry, mire choked and winding,
Wind like choking fingers on a white, full throat.

White lanes and pink lanes, strung with purpled roses,
Dance along the distance weaving o'er the hills,
Beckoning the dull streets with stray smiles wanton,
Strung with purpled roses that the stray dawn chills.

Here now they meet tiptoe on the corner,
Kiss behind the silence of the curtained dark;
Then half unwilling run between the houses,
Tracing through the pattern that the dim lamps mark.

Steps break steps and murmur into running,
Death upon the corner spills the edge of dawn
Dull torches waver and the streets stand breathless;
Silent fades the marching and the night-noon's gone.

— F. Scott Fitzgerald, '18

72. "Marching Streets," *The Nassau Literary Magazine*, LXXIV (February 1919), pp. 103-104. Fitzgerald is credited by name in the magazine.

THE POPE AT CONFESSION

The gorgeous vatican was steeped in night,
The organs trembled to my heart no more,
But with the blend of colors on my sight
I loitered through a sombre corridor
And suddenly I heard behind a screen
The faintest whisper, as from one in prayer,
I glanced around, then passed, for I had seen
A hushed and lonely room...and two were there—

A ragged friar, half in a dream's embrace
Leaned sideways, soul intent, as if to seize
The last grey ice of sin that ached to melt
And faltered from the lips of him who knelt —
A little bent old man upon his knees
With pain and sorrow in his holy face.

— F. Scott Fitzgerald, '18

73. "The Pope at Confession," *The Nassau Literary Magazine,* LXXIV (February 1919), p. 105. Fitzgerald is credited by name in the magazine.

"My First Love," "Marching Streets," and "The Pope at Confession" are reproduced here as they appeared in *The Nassau Lit* in February of 1919. Fitzgerald made subsequent revisions to all three poems. Fitzgerald scholars may want to compare these original versions with the slightly revised versions of "My First Love" (re-titled "First Love") and "The Pope at Confession" and a much more extensively revised version of "Marching Streets" which Fitzgerald preserved in his notebook (now at Princeton) and which editor Edmund Wilson included in *The Crack-Up.*

Sleep of a University

Watching through the long, dim hours
Like statued Mithras, stand ironic towers;
Their haughty lines severe by light
Are softened and gain tragedy at night.
Self-conscious, cynics of their charge,
Proudly they challenge the dreamless world at large.

From pseudo-ancient Nassau Hall, the bell
Crashes the hour, as if to pretend "All's well!"
Over the campus then the listless breeze

Floats along drowsily, filtering through the trees,
Whose twisted branches seem to lie
Like *point d'Alencon* lace against a sky
Of soft gray-black — a gorgeous robe
Buttoned with stars, hung over a tiny globe.

With life far off, peace sits supreme:
The college slumbers in a fatuous dream,
While, watching through the moonless hours
Like statued Mithras, stand the ironic towers.

---

74. "Sleep of a University," *The Nassau Literary Magazine*, LXXVI (November 1920), p. 161. This was a revision by Fitzgerald of a poem by Aiken Reichner.

It seems fitting that the last entry in this collection of Fitzgerald's early writings, like the very first one, deals with Princeton. By the time this poem appeared in *The Nassau Lit*, in November of 1920, Fitzgerald had made it big as a professional writer. In the previous year, he'd placed a half-dozen of his stories with *The Smart Set* (for fees ranging from $30 to $200), another half-dozen with *The Saturday Evening Post* (for fees ranging from $360 to $450), and a couple of others with *Metropolitan* (for $810 each).

Scribners published *This Side of Paradise* in March of 1920. The book was a success nationwide, selling 49,000 copies by the end of 1921. (You'll note that the vintage Scribners ad for *This Side of Paradise* which we've reproduced on the next page proudly proclaims, "Twelfth Printing.") Though Fitzgerald would write

finer books in years to come, none would sell as many copies as quickly upon initial publication as *This Side of Paradise*. The novel was particularly well-received at Princeton, where its release actually caused a run on the University Store. To many students, Fitzgerald seemed very much a hero and role model; he was one of them who had made good. (Richard Halliburton, then a Princeton undergraduate, asked rhetorically in a letter who wouldn't want to be another Scott Fitzgerald?) In the spring of 1920, Fitzgerald returned to the campus a couple of times — once for a *Nassau Lit* banquet — to bask in his success. But he drank too much and got rowdy. Cottage Club — expressing outrage over his supposedly disgraceful behavior — even suspended his membership for a while. That rebuke smarted.

Scribners followed up *This Side of Paradise* with *Flappers and Philosophers* — Fitzgerald's first short story collection — in September of 1920. It was warmly embraced by reviewers and public alike. Movie studios were optioning Fitzgerald's stories. His magazine fees (which would reach as high as $3,600 per story by decade's end — he knew of no one getting more money) were continuing to escalate. His name on a magazine cover, editors realized, sold copies.

By this point it was quite clear that — much as he may have loved them — Fitzgerald had outgrown the Princeton student publications. He would make one final (and unsigned) contribution to *The Nassau Literary Magazine* in June of 1934, "Anonymous '17" — an appreciative remembrance of *The Lit* of his youth.

By F. Scott Fitzgerald

THIS
SIDE OF PARADISE

"A Novel about Flappers Written for Philosophers"

"It is probably one of the few really American novels extant."—HARRY HANSEN in the *Chicago Daily News*.

"A very enlivening book, indeed; a book really brilliant and glamorous, making as agreeable reading as could be asked."—*New York Evening Post*.

"The glorious spirit of abounding youth glows throughout this fascinating tale. . . . It could have been written only by an artist who knows how to balance his values, plus a delightful literary style."—*New York Times*.

"It is abundantly worth while; it is delightful, consciously and unconsciously, amusing, keenly and diversely interesting; cracking good stuff to read, in short."—*New York Sun*.

Twelfth Printing

CHARLES SCRIBNER'S SONS

THE END.

ACKNOWLEDGMENTS

My thanks to editors John Fremont and Cynthia Frank and their associates at Cypress House for their conscientious help, ideas, and good cheer.

My thanks, too, to Frank Reuter, the first reader of this book — as he has been for all of my other books — whose comments have strengthened the text. I'm indebted also to Gary Westby-Gibson and Frank Jolliffe for vetting the manuscript and certainly saving me from an embarrassment or two. I'm fortunate to be able to work on a ongoing basis with such caring and knowledgeable people. I greatly appreciate Fitz Gitler's proofreading assistance.

This book makes use of public-domain material not just by F. Scott Fitzgerald but also some by a number of his fellow *Tiger* contributors: artists Alan Jackman (who was kind enough to share with *Tiger* trustees, shortly before his death in 1981, some of his recollections of working with Fitzgerald), Lawrence Boardman, I. E. Swart, F. A. Comstock, E. A. Georgi, A. C. M. Azoy Jr., Walter Boadway, G. B. Steriker, J. M. Foster, and John V. Newlin and writer/editors John Biggs Jr. and John McMaster. Because *The Tiger* did not always credit contributors, it has not been possible to identify all of the artists whose vintage drawings have been reprinted in this book. But I'm indebted to all whose work has been used. And of course I'm indebted to the late Scottie Fitzgerald Smith, not just for her personal encouragement to me but for the many informative writings about her father that she left (particularly relevant for this book was one of her earliest articles, "Princeton and F. Scott Fitzgerald," originally published in *The Nassau Literary Magazine* in 1942 and reprinted in *The Princeton Alumni Weekly*, March 9, 1956).

This book evolved, in part, out of one I helped work on which celebrated the centennial of *The Tiger, Roaring at One Hundred*. (Eleven of us assisted in the creation of that book.) It certainly would not have come into existence had I not worked on *The Tiger* myself as an undergraduate or served as a trustee of it for the past 15 or so years. It has been published by Cypress House with the cooperation of the Princeton Tiger, Inc. (although I take full and sole responsibility for any opinions expressed herein). So I'd like to express my appreciation to *Tiger* alumni who either helped work on the *Roaring at One Hundred* project or have served with me since then as trustees of *The Tiger*: José W. Pincay-Delgado, W. Allen Scheuch, Henry R. Martin, Truman M. Talley, William F. Brown, Edward M. Strauss, Michael C. Witte, Vasil J. Pappas, Bret T. Watson, Derick D. Schermerhorn, Katherine R. R. Carpenter, Donald W. Arbour, Edward H. Tenner, Frank T. Buchner, Mark V. Dowden, Charles R. Fry, Jonathan M. Bumas, John Farr II, Andrew C. Rose, Keith Blanchard, Jim Kirchman, Kenneth Miller, Peter O. Price, Eric Mulheim, J.

Carlo Cannell, Rob Middleton, and David A. Iams (whose essay in *Roaring at One Hundred* was particularly informative about the magazine's early history). My hat is off to Jonathan Bumas, who (with some input from fellow *Tiger* alumnus Allen Scheuch) designed this book's cover. I might add that Bumas and Scheuch, who also were responsible for the cover of *Roaring at One Hundred*, were generous in suggestions concerning this book, not just the cover.

I'm grateful that as an undergraduate I was given a chance to work at Princeton reunions where I got to meet various contemporaries of Fitzgerald's (nearly all of whom are now deceased), who helped make the world of *This Side of Paradise* seem less distant to me. I'm fortunate to have shared some of their time. (And I was amazed to find that in his 80s, Alan Jackman was still drawing in the very same style he'd used when he'd drawn for *The Tiger* as a teenager.) More recently, Don Oberdorfer's splendid book *Princeton University, The First 250 Years*, published by the University in 1995, has been a valuable source of Princeton-related background information for me.

I'd like to express gratitude to Earle Coleman, Alexander Clark, Charles Greene, Mardel Pacheco, Mary Ann Jensen, Carl Esche, Ben Primer, Nancy Young, Chris Mills, William L. Joyce, Alice V. Clark, and their dedicated associates, past and present, on the staff of the Princeton University Library, who've aided my research, whether supplying xeroxes, photos, or useful suggestions. And to other warmly appreciated members of the larger Princeton community who've helped in one way or another through the years: Chris Burchfield, Billy and Julie Heinz, Mark Anderson, Randy Block, Katie Maratta, Jeff Bryan, Rick Cagan, Henry Baird, and the Huehnergarths. The guidance and kindness of Irving Dilliard and Lanny Jones, early on, has been greatly appreciated. A. Scott Berg, author of *Max Perkins*, has been more helpful than I suspect he realizes, as has Jess Sanders of Austin, Texas. Special thanks go to *Princeton Alumni Weekly* editors Chuck Creesy, Jim Merritt, and Andrew Mytelka for not running what I enthusiastically wrote about Fitzgerald for them years ago — had they done so, I probably would have felt I'd satisfied my interest in writing about Fitzgerald and would *not* have done this book.

I owe thanks to Peter Tomlinson and Tim Feleppa of Culver Pictures, for helping find photos and artwork. I don't want to forget Geoffrey Vasile's spirited assistance in assorted ways; he's been an important part of this project. Howard Cruse's thoughtful comments are always valued. I thank, too, my ever-supportive *New York Post* editors, Matt Diebel and V. A. Musetto, for giving me an unusually flexible, enjoyable work-schedule, which permits me to tackle projects like this one. Matthew Broderick and Sarah Jessica Parker shared some food, energy, and inspiration at just the right time.

John Kuehl, editor of *The Apprentice Fiction of F. Scott Fitzgerald, 1909–1917*, deserves particular acknowledgment. His writing about Fitzgerald has helped shape my thinking since I first discovered that book almost 30 years ago; I've benefited heavily from his work. I've also benefited from the groundbreaking research of Henry Dan Piper, who dealt with the early writings of Fitzgerald in *The Princeton University Library Chronicle*, XII (Summer of 1951). Arthur Mizener's *The Far Side of Paradise* was the first of many books about Fitzgerald that I read; reliable and concise, it still provides an excellent entry-point for anyone studying Fitzgerald. Jeffrey Meyers' *Scott Fitzgerald, A Biography* may be the most colorful and vivid — if not necessarily judicious — book about Fitzgerald. Matthew J. Bruccoli is the pre-eminent Fitzgerald scholar of our time — the author or editor of well over 20 valuable, recommended Fitzgerald-related volumes — and like so many Fitzgerald enthusiasts I've long savored his writings. Though I've never met Bruccoli, Kuehl, Piper, Meyers, or Mizener, their work has enabled my own, and I'm profoundly in their debt.

Finally — as ever — deep thanks are extended to my family.

———

About the Editor

ASCAP-Deems Taylor Award-winning critic Chip Deffaa has been covering jazz and other forms of popular entertainment for *The New York Post* since 1986. He is the author of such books as *Jazz Veterans: A Portrait Gallery* (in collaboration with photographers Nancy Miller Elliott and John and Andreas Johnsen) (Cypress House, 1996), *Blue Rhythms: Six Lives in Rhythm-and Blues* (University of Illinois Press, 1996), *C'Mon Get Happy* (in collaboration with David Cassidy) (Warner Books, 1994), *Traditionalists and Revivalists in Jazz* (Scarecrow Press, 1993), *In the Mainstream: 18 Portraits in Jazz* (Scarecrow Press, 1991), *Voices of the Jazz Age* (University of Illinois Press, 1990), and *Swing Legacy* (Scarecrow Press, 1989). Deffaa has been an enthusiast of Fitzgerald since his own student days at Princeton, where he was an art director of *The Tiger*; he continues his association as a trustee of *The Tiger* today. He previously included some of Fitzgerald's early work in *Roaring at One Hundred* (The Princeton Tiger, Inc., 1983), which he helped co-edit. Deffaa is a member of the National Academy of Recording Arts and Sciences, the Sonneck Society, the Jazz Journalists Association, and the American Theatre Critics Association. Further details about Deffaa may be found in *Who's Who in the World*, 13th Edition (Marquis).

CREDITS

Page 4: A photograph of F. Scott Fitzgerald at age 15, courtesy of the Papers of F. Scott Fitzgerald, Manuscripts Division, Department of Rare Books and Special Collections, Princeton University Libraries.

Page 5: A photograph of F. Scott Fitzgerald as a Triangle "showgirl," courtesy of the Papers of F. Scott Fitzgerald, Manuscripts Division, Department of Rare Books and Special Collections, Princeton University Libraries.

Page 7, upper left-hand column: A photograph of Edmund Wilson from the 1916 *Nassau Herald* (a Princeton yearbook), courtesy of the University Archives, Seeley G. Mudd Manuscript Library, Princeton University Libraries.

Page 7, lower right-hand column: A photograph of John Peale Bishop from the 1917 *Nassau Herald,* courtesy of the University Archives, Seeley G. Mudd Manuscript Library, Princeton University Libraries.

Page 11: A photograph of 1917-18 Tiger board members from the 1919 *Bric-a-Brac* (a Princeton yearbook), courtesy of the University Archives, Seeley G. Mudd Manuscript Library, Princeton University Libraries. The photograph shows, from left to right (in the back row): Associate Editor L. L. Wylie '20, F. Scott Fitzgerald '18, and Cyril Sloane '19, and (in the front row): Business Manager Joseph C. Buchanan '18, Managing Editor John Biggs Jr. '18, and Art Editor Francis A. Comstock '19.

Page 12: The front of the dust jacket of *This Side of Paradise* (1920), courtesy of the Papers of F. Scott Fitzgerald, Manuscripts Division, Department of Rare Books and Special Collections, Princeton University Libraries.

Page 13: A photograph of Ginevra King, courtesy of the Papers of F. Scott Fitzgerald, Manuscripts Division, Department of Rare Books and Special Collections, Princeton University Libraries.

Page 15, lower right-hand column: A photograph of F. Scott Fitzgerald from the 1917 *Nassau Herald,* courtesy of the University Archives, Seeley G. Mudd Manuscript Library, Princeton University Libraries.

Page 16: The front cover of *The Smart Set* (June 1922), featuring Fitzgerald's "The Diamond as Big as the Ritz," courtesy of Culver Pictures.

Page 20: The front cover of *Roaring at One Hundred,* designed by Jonathan Bumas, courtesy of The Princeton Tiger, Inc.

Page 21: A photograph of F. Scott and Zelda Fitzgerald, and their daughter, Scottie, courtesy of Culver Pictures.

Page 23: A drawing of F. Scott Fitzgerald by Gordon Bryant, courtesy of Culver Pictures.

Page 36: An advertisement for *Flappers and Philosophers,* courtesy of Culver Pictures.

Page 157: A photograph of F. Scott and Zelda Fitzgerald, courtesy of Culver Pictures.

Page 162: An advertisement for *This Side of Paradise,* courtesy of Culver Pictures.

A portion of the front page of *The Daily Princetonian* (October 28, 1915) has been reproduced on page 39. The drawings reproduced on pages 108, 121, and 133, together with the magazine covers and pages reproduced on pages 8, 26, and 56, originally appeared in *The Nassau Literary Magazine* between 1915 and and 1917. With the exception of a few pieces of artwork culled from earlier issues of *The Tiger* (on pages i, viii, 2, and 25), the remaining artwork reproduced in this book originally appeared in *The Tiger* between 1914 and 1917. The above items have been reproduced courtesy of the University Archives, Seeley G. Mudd Manuscript Library, Princeton University Libraries, and (in the case of selected *Tiger* materials) the archives of *The Tiger* itself.